Gettysburg 1963

CIVIL WAR AMERICA

Peter S. Carmichael, Caroline E. Janney, and Aaron Sheehan-Dean, editors

This landmark series interprets broadly the history and culture of the Civil War era through the long nineteenth century and beyond. Drawing on diverse approaches and methods, the series publishes historical works that explore all aspects of the war, biographies of leading commanders, and tactical and campaign studies, along with select editions of primary sources. Together, these books shed new light on an era that remains central to our understanding of American and world history.

Gettysburg 1963

Civil Rights, Cold War Politics, and Historical Memory in America's Most Famous Small Town

Jill Ogline Titus

The University of North Carolina Press CHAPEL HILL

The University of North Carolina Press has been a member of the
Green Press Initiative since 2003.

Library of Congress Cataloging-in-Publication Data
Names: Titus, Jill Ogline, author.
Title: Gettysburg 1963 : civil rights, Cold War politics, and historical memory
 in America's most famous small town / Jill Ogline Titus.
Other titles: Civil War America (Series)
Description: Chapel Hill : University of North Carolina Press, 2021. |
 Series: Civil War America | Includes bibliographical references and index.
Identifiers: LCCN 2021030563 | ISBN 9781469665337 (cloth ; alk. paper) |
 ISBN 9781469665344 (paperback ; alk. paper) | ISBN 9781469665351 (ebook)
Subjects: LCSH: Gettysburg, Battle of, Gettysburg, Pa., 1863—Centennial
 celebrations, etc. | Collective memory—United States. | United States—
 Race relations—History—20th century. | United States—Politics and
 government—20th century. | Gettysburg (Pa.)—History.
Classification: LCC E475.582 .T58 2021 | DDC 973.7/349—dc23
LC record available at https://lccn.loc.gov/2021030563

Cover illustration: U.S. Marine Band playing for the 1963 centennial of the Civil War in Gettysburg. Courtesy of Gettysburg College Special Collections and College Archives (MS-122_9-5_1963_MarineCorpsBand001).

Portions of chapter 5 originally appeared in "Fighting Civil Rights and the Cold War: Confederate Monuments at Gettysburg," *History News* 71, no. 4 (Autumn 2016): 12–17; they are used here with permission.

For Josiah,
the best gift this time in
Gettysburg has given me

The Civil War is our only "felt" history—history lived in the national imagination. This is not to say that the War is always, and by all men, felt the same way. Quite the contrary.

—ROBERT PENN WARREN, *The Legacy of the Civil War* (1961)

Contents

A gallery of photos begins on page 85.

Acknowledgments

This project was born at the Civil War Institute (CWI) at Gettysburg College, in the classrooms of GC, and on the fields of Gettysburg National Military Park, and it is thus to my colleagues and students that I owe my greatest debts. CWI director Pete Carmichael sat in my office with me as I pondered whether the idea was viable; his astute questions and excellent suggestions helped me realize that there was indeed a story to be told. From day one, Pete has been the project's greatest champion. He has provided invaluable feedback on countless drafts, helped me break the logjam on a key chapter, and made opportunities available that allowed me try out ideas with groups of colleagues, visiting teachers, and conference attendees. Just as importantly, he has encouraged me in moments of frustration, never doubting that the book would see the light of day. Our nearly decade-long professional partnership at CWI continues to energize me, and I am enormously grateful for his friendship and support.

My other CWI colleagues, Ashley Whitehead Luskey and Heather Miller, have likewise buoyed my spirits at difficult junctures. Their interest and support have helped me keep moving forward; I am particularly grateful to Heather for making sense of my research travel receipts and Ashley for answering random questions about 11th Corps battle lines. Also at Gettysburg College, Scott Hancock and Michael Birkner have provided valuable insight and helpful conversation. Scott's public work calling attention to the narratives unexplored on the battlefield landscape has deeply shaped my thinking about both monumentation and the responsibilities of socially engaged scholarship. Last but not least, the students with whom I am privileged to work every day have shaped this work by their insightful questions, critical observations, and passion for putting history to work in the world.

My debts at Gettysburg National Military Park are too numerous to fully enumerate, but Chris Gwinn, Greg Goodell, and John Heiser deserve special thanks. John Heiser always found a way to get me into the park library, even on woefully short notice, pointed me to vital documents, and generously shared his own extensive knowledge of the park's twentieth-century commemorative landscape. Greg Goodell not only welcomed me into the park archives but also made a time-consuming deep dive into the collection to unearth everything that could possibly be of use to me. His advice helped prepare me to productively mine the National Park Service records housed in the National Archives. Despite his busy schedule, Chris Gwinn never failed to respond to out-of-the-blue queries about both battle and postwar details. His research and interpretive programming on battlefield monuments, as well as that of Dan Vermilya, now at Eisenhower NHS, has opened new angles for me to consider, and served as a model of how to pose meaningful questions about Gettysburg's commemorative landscape. I am also grateful to Steven Semmel for citation help at a critical moment.

At the Adams County Historical Society, Andrew Dalton, Tim Smith, and Maria Lynn have gone above and beyond to help me find what I needed and to make collection materials accessible during a pandemic. Tim Smith's unparalleled knowledge of the collection led me to many important sources that I would likely have otherwise never found. Amy Lucadamo, Carolyn Sautter, Ron Couchman, and Devin McKinney at Musselman Library, Special Collections and College Archives (Gettysburg College) could not have been more generous with their time and resources, and have made my work with these collections a joy. Also at Musselman Library, Clint Baugess helped me make sense of Pennsylvania census records and tracked down countless obscure newspaper sources, working miracles despite incorrect citations.

Jonathan Stayer at the Pennsylvania State Archives and Kirk Mitchell of Special Collections, University of South Florida Libraries deserve special thanks for making sources available to me that I would have otherwise been unable to access. In sitting for interviews, Terry Fox, Jean Green, Jim Madison, and Jim Witt gave generously of their time and personal experiences, offering compelling stories and penetrating insight about Gettysburg in the 1960s. I am also indebted to Chanelle Rose, Charles Hughes, and Erin Devlin for their valuable feedback on a 2020 conference paper springing from this project. Mark Simpson-Vos, Cate Hodorowicz, and Jay Mazzocchi, and the rest of the superb team at the University of North Carolina Press, as well as series editor Carrie Janney, have been a joy to work with throughout the course of this project and have immeasurably improved the final product. I owe Carrie Janney and Robert Cook an enormous debt of gratitude for their penetrating criticism of the manuscript; any errors that remain are, of course, my own.

I can never adequately thank all the friends and family who have cheered me, encouraged me, and distracted me over the years of working on this project (particularly during the pandemic stretch). I am fortunate beyond measure. But I have to give special credit to my parents, Jerry and Barbara Ogline, for their lifelong support; to Jen Turner for always being at the other end of the phone line; and most of all, to Sean and Josiah Titus for sharing life with me. Sean, I love you more than ever, even after being quarantined together. Josiah, thank you for understanding the times I couldn't play because I had to write; I love you more than you can imagine.

Abbreviations in the Text

ACCWCC   Adams County Civil War Centennial Commission

AME   African Methodist Episcopal

CCC   Civilian Conservation Corps

CORE   Congress of Racial Equality

CWCC   U.S. Civil War Centennial Commission

DOJ   Department of Justice

GAR   Grand Army of the Republic

GBPA   Gettysburg Battlefield Preservation Association

GCC   Pennsylvania Gettysburg Centennial Commission

GHS   Gettysburg High School

GNMP   Gettysburg National Military Park

KKK   Ku Klux Klan

NAACP   National Association for the Advancement of Colored People

NPS   National Park Service

N-SSA   North-South Skirmish Association

PHRC   Pennsylvania Human Relations Commission

SCLC   Southern Christian Leadership Conference

SCV   Sons of Confederate Veterans

SNCC   Student Nonviolent Coordinating Committee

SUV   Sons of Union Veterans

UDC   United Daughters of the Confederacy

USCT   United States Colored Troops

USIA   United States Information Agency

WCC   White Citizens Council

Gettysburg 1963

Introduction
Using History to Shape the Future

In 1963, Gettysburg prepared for another battle, this one over the meaning of the struggle waged there 100 years earlier. Across the nation, Black citizens courageously risked their livelihoods and, in many cases, their lives to demand equal rights, frequently inciting violent resistance from segregationists. Fear of Soviet dominance gripped much of the nation, and the possibility of nuclear war was imminent. In these tumultuous times, Americans looked to the most famous battlefield of the Civil War for reassurance of their greatness as a people. Unlike the grand battlefield commemorations of 1913 and 1938, in 1963 there were no images of elderly veterans clasping hands across the lines of battle. Though the message of reconciliation and unity remained central to the messaging, the Gettysburg Centennial was not a nostalgic paean to the tragic "brothers' war." Rather, the centennial commemoration was intended to heal a fractured citizenry by extolling the United States as the savior of democracy and advancing a vision of undisputed American supremacy—political, economic, moral, and military—in the global war against Communism.

Gettysburg's 100th anniversary enlisted both the battle and Lincoln's famous Gettysburg Address in the service of the anticommunist crusade, yet Cold War tensions and violent clashes over civil rights continually challenged the message of unity, freedom, and political self-determination animating the commemoration. Vibrant campaigns for equal rights, north and south, shone an unstinting spotlight on the hollowness of "freedom" and the unfinished work of the Civil War. Rather than celebrating the war's legacy as an inevitable march of freedom, African Americans and their white allies used the commemoration to highlight the corrosive effects of racism on a nation that purported to be the world's leading defender of democracy. They were particularly aggressive in refuting the reconciliationist use of the brothers' war trope, which obscured racial injustices and social inequalities plaguing the nation, including the town of Gettysburg itself. For their part, reconciliationists of the Lost Cause vein claimed historical ground to assert that Confederates were freedom-loving Americans entitled to equal space and prestige on the Gettysburg battlefield. Some openly attempted to utilize anticommunist ideology to legitimize massive resistance to civil rights.

1

Yet Gettysburg did not exist solely on the plane of an iconic image in the national and international imagination. It was also a real community with year-round residents, for whom commemoration of the Civil War was part and parcel of day-to-day life. On the local level, the 100th anniversary commemoration powerfully influenced Gettysburg National Military Park's (GNMP's) development, shaped patterns of tourism for years to come, and dramatized the need for drastic action to preserve land threatened by commercial development. The centennial years also profoundly altered the battlefield's commemorative landscape, ushering in a new wave of Confederate monumentation at Gettysburg that would continue for the next fifteen years. Looking back on the centennial anniversary, it is clear that Gettysburg's value as a lens for understanding the intersection of Cold War politics, race in the United States, and Civil War commemoration lies in its multifaceted identity as an idea, a landscape, and a living community. Because Gettysburg was simultaneously all of these things, its centennial anniversary provides a unique vantage point to explore the relationship between politics and commemoration at midcentury on multiple levels and from diverse perspectives.

Though Gettysburg was far from the only important site where commemoration of the Civil War Centennial played out, thanks to Abraham Lincoln's iconic Gettysburg Address, both the battle and the landscape itself are uniquely linked to larger questions of meaning and significance. Historically, Gettysburg has been frequently touted as *the* turning point of the war, and its stature among the visiting public has long towered over that of other Civil War battlefields. For many Americans, both in 1963 and today, Gettysburg *is* the Civil War. Because of this, sustained attention to Gettysburg's role in the larger commemoration is essential. Sizable numbers of Americans experienced the anniversary firsthand; visitation quadrupled between 1950 and 1970, and GNMP saw more than two million visitors during 1963 alone.[1] Countless more followed the news from Gettysburg with interest, donating to centennial battlefield preservation programs, listening to live broadcasts of events from across the field, and poring over the speeches of political leaders who, like Lincoln before them, sought to use history for contemporary purposes.

The Gettysburg anniversary came toward the midpoint of the national commemoration of the war. Supported by substantial public and private funds and spearheaded by a federal commission and forty-four state level commissions, the centennial commemoration of the Civil War was an exercise in Cold War pageantry, designed to inculcate patriotism and strengthen national unity. Many participants thus necessarily skirted controversial issues like slavery, race, draft evasion, and opposition to the war, perpetuating a narrative celebrating martial masculinity and holding up the common soldier of both armies as a unifying model of American heroism. As Civil War soldiers were elevated as models for the nation, the war itself was also deemed essential and purposeful, but not for its emancipationist outcome. Reflecting the foreign policy concerns of the era, the popular narrative of a brothers' war strongly emphasized the conflict's role in making the United States a global superpower. This depoliticized yet politically useful narrative contradicted recent scholarly writing, which increasingly portrayed the war as a revolutionary moment.

Minimizing slavery, Reconstruction, and African American involvement in the war as topics of public discussion ensured that most mainstream centennial commemorations marginalized the voices of Black Americans calling for a historical narrative that would help contextualize contemporary struggles for Black freedom. But as early as April 1961, when plans to commemorate the assault on Fort Sumter nearly imploded over the issue of hotel segregation in Charleston, it became clear that even if the planners wanted to sidestep racial issues, current events would make it impossible to do so. Playing out as it did in a time of increasing Cold War tensions and intensifying struggles to eradicate racial injustice, the Civil War Centennial was deeply intertwined with contemporary politics. This, of course, was not a development specific to the 1960s. From its earliest stirrings during the war itself, the memory of the Civil War has always depended on the present for context and meaning, and all signs suggest that it will continue to do so in future years as well. As David Blight writes in *Race and Reunion*, "as long as we have a politics of race in America, we will have a politics of Civil War memory."[2]

As Pierre Nora has theorized, "sites of memory" such as anniversaries, archives, eulogies, and historic places are a product of the widening split between memory and history. These moments of history, in Nora's words, are "torn away from the movement of history, then returned; no longer quite life, not yet death, like shells on the shore when the sea of living memory has receded." In actively preserving these "moments," modern societies acknowledge that memory no longer occurs naturally: "We buttress our identities upon such bastions, but if what they defended were not threatened, there would be no need to build them." In staging such a broadscale commemoration of the 100th anniversary of Gettysburg, twentieth-century Americans simultaneously acknowledged both the durability and the fragility of the past. While the Civil War clearly continued to exercise a powerful hold on American culture, the traditional mechanisms for connecting to it, such as personal encounters with veterans, battlefield pilgrimages, and interactions with monuments increasingly proved insufficient or impossible, thus necessitating (in the view of many) heightened pageantry and spectacle.[3]

Architects of the Gettysburg commemoration, such as high-ranking National Park Service officials, members of the Pennsylvania Gettysburg Centennial Commission, and the Adams County Civil War Centennial Commission, strove to educate audiences and present a patriotic narrative of consensus. Local business owners sought to strengthen the town's economy by catering to visitors' needs and expectations. Most of the national political leaders who played roles in the commemoration, however, were less interested in historical education and revenue than in using Gettysburg, in the words of Michael Kammen, to "manipulate the past in order to mold the present."[4] Responding to pressures at the local, state, and international level, government officials and politicians across the political spectrum repeatedly attempted to harness the symbolic power of Gettysburg to connect the battle to contemporary struggles to define America's place in the world and the future of Black citizenship in the United States. Three central narratives emerged from these efforts. The first was a states' rights interpretation of the war that branded the intensifying Black freedom struggle as a frontal attack on the liberties of white Americans and the political ideals of the nation; the second a conviction that the best way to honor those fallen at Gettysburg was to work for racial justice in the present; and the third a Cold War–themed call to embrace a consensus version of the Civil War past that could help spread American democracy, capitalism, and technology around the world.

The trajectory of all three of these narratives was rooted in the anniversary's Cold War context. The American civil rights movement was one front in a global struggle waged by the darker-skinned peoples of the world against colonialism, and as such it both benefited from and was severely constrained by Cold War politics. As Nina Silber has effectively demonstrated, Civil War memory was employed as early as the late 1930s to critique fascism, and its use on the world stage swelled during World War II and the subsequent Cold War years, strengthening the patriotic patina of white reconciliation.[5] The political impetus to minimize discussions of race, slavery, and sectional division preceded the Cold War era, but it took on a new urgency as race and political self-determination reemerged as major issues in contemporary politics, on both the national and international stage. The Cold War years also fostered the association of anticommunism with states' rights and traditional race relations, resulting in a kind of open celebration of the Confederate cause on the Gettysburg battlefield not seen in previous decades. Shaped by the Manichean worldview of U.S.-Soviet dualism, however, most proponents of Confederate memory nonetheless identified themselves as patriotic Americans.

In their efforts to forge a usable past, midcentury Americans acted on their visions of Gettysburg's meaning in ways that altered the physical landscape and interpretive orientation of Gettysburg National Military Park and helped fuel resistance to long-established patterns of racial discrimination in the local community. Their choices contributed to forging narratives about the American nation which were employed simultaneously to champion racial equality, legitimize midcentury antigovernment sentiments and activities, and strengthen the U.S. position internationally. This memory-making process was multidirectional, extending downward from political and cultural leaders and high-ranking NPS officials, as well as upward from local business owners, grassroots preservationists, and Black residents seeking a less restricted life. Both Abraham Lincoln's Gettysburg Address and the suffering and perceived devotion to duty and country of the soldiers who fought the battle were broadcast widely as hallmarks of American national character that would save the globe from creeping totalitarianism. Though racial injustice complicated this narrative, the desire to claim the Gettysburg Address as the central philosophical underpinning of American foreign policy helped create space for mainstream civil rights leaders and their white allies to win public and governmental support for limited civil rights reform.[6]

Leading political figures such as Lyndon Johnson, Dwight Eisenhower, and George Wallace used the Gettysburg battlefield during the centennial to interpret the interrelationship between the Black freedom struggle, the Cold War, and the memory of the Civil War in dramatically different ways. Wallace, the leading symbol of southern white resistance to the civil rights movement, argued that states' rights provided the best defense against Communism and "destructive centralization." Former president Dwight Eisenhower infuriated the Black press by calling on Americans to practice "sturdy self-reliance" and reject "paternalistic" assistance from their government, while remaining silent on civil rights. In a speech at the National Cemetery, Vice President Lyndon Johnson offered a direct response to Martin Luther King Jr.'s "Letter from Birmingham City Jail" in which he acknowledged the inappropriateness of white pleas for Black Americans to exercise patience in the face of continuing discrimination. Florida congressman Sam Gibbons addressed the events in Birmingham directly as well, lamenting that racial discrimination (and the damning image of the "snarling police dog") severely undermined the global struggle against Communism. Though they each deployed the image of Gettysburg in different ways, they collectively braided the legacy of the battle into contemporary public debates about race, democracy, political protest, and federalism.

Broadening out beyond those whose stature assured them positions at a speakers' rostrum, this book will also use the lens of Cold War civil rights to explore the diverse ways that local residents and preservation-minded Civil War enthusiasts interacted with the history surrounding them. This attention to local context provides insight into how communities chose to remember their Civil War past in grassroots commemorations such as historical tableaux and large-scale pageants, and how such endeavors intersected with state and national (and at times, international) efforts to define the meaning of the Civil War and mobilize its legacy for present-day action. It also reveals the extent to which the centennial shaped the commemorative landscape that twenty-first-century residents of and visitors to Gettysburg have inherited.

Gettysburg lies only seven miles north of the Mason-Dixon line, and has historically reflected the population demographics and racial codes of a border-state community, uniquely reinforced by a long reliance on Civil War tourism. Despite its beginnings as a Union memorial park, for much of the twentieth century Gettysburg's narrative was primarily defined by the men in gray. The battle was known as the "High Water Mark of the Confederacy," not "the high point of Union defense." Many members of the local community were openly hostile to African American tourists, and life for Black residents was fraught with widespread discrimination in employment, housing, education, and public accommodations. A 1953 survey of race relations in the community noted that the majority of restaurants in town would not serve Blacks, and that the most prominent hotel would serve only those who were nationally known.[7]

Concerned by Gettysburg's long history as a place where African Americans were not accorded the same treatment given whites, the Pennsylvania Human Relations Commission (PHRC) launched a campaign in the spring of 1963 to prevent discrimination against anniversary visitors. PHRC representatives called on local business owners in person to remind them of state law and ask them to post nondiscrimination notices in their windows. Though responses to the PHRC visits were largely positive, anniversary planners feared that the commemoration would be a flashpoint for protest.[8]

Ultimately, organized protest did not materialize, but the commemoration did play a role in breaking down overt segregation in Gettysburg. More broadly, as this book will demonstrate, contemporary racial politics (intertwined with and infused by Cold War principles) profoundly shaped nearly every aspect of the anniversary.

Historians of twentieth-century America have sometimes used the phrase "the Civil War of the 1960s" to refer to an era in which Americans found themselves almost as divided as they were during the 1860s, along lines of race, politics, generation, gender, and region.[9] The phrase "Civil War" is generally applied because of its efficacy in expressing the intensity of civic stress and tension, and because of the bookends that the two decades—neatly spaced 100 years apart—seem to provide. But "the Civil War of the 1960s" is more than a metaphor. As demonstrated so clearly at Gettysburg, memory and commemoration of the Civil War were part and parcel of the struggles of this iconic decade. The desire to make meaning of the Battle of Gettysburg was not new; efforts to remember and commemorate the Civil War began while the conflict was still raging. But the scale and scope of the efforts, the level of involvement from government at all levels, and the broad investment of Americans across geographical lines was remarkable. Recovering the central role of Gettysburg in the centennial commemorations of the Civil War not only deepens our understanding of the era's impact on shaping the modern commemorative landscape but also demonstrates the extent to which race was deeply integrated into the cultural and political frameworks of the Cold War.

CHAPTER ONE

An American Town

Segregation, Civil Rights, and the Color Line in Gettysburg

Flags snapped in the breeze as the white-robed Klan members—5,000 strong—paraded through downtown Gettysburg in the largest and "most colorful" parade in the town's history. A cheering crowd estimated at 25,000 lined the sidewalks, doffing hats and saluting the flags as they passed. Business in the downtown area ground to a halt as employees and customers alike were drawn to the spectacle. Marchers carried open Bibles and miniature schoolhouses (a symbol of the Klan's hostility toward parochial schools) past storefronts decked in red, white, and blue bunting. Testifying to the mainstream nature of the group, only 300 or so, widely assumed to be members of the local chapters, wore hoods. Though not all residents approved, Gettysburg welcomed the enormous Ku Klux Klan rally of September 1925 with open arms, publishing a special commemorative edition of the local newspaper that claimed (erroneously) that "Gettysburg's pulse stopped, while it stood, partly in wonder, partly in awe, but never in fear" of the Knights of the not-so-Invisible Empire.[1]

The Ku Klux Klan has little place in our standard images of Gettysburg, a site of Union victory located far from the cotton, tobacco, and rice fields of the former plantation South. But throughout the twentieth century, the community's iconic status and extensive commemorative landscape regularly made it a stage for dramatizing issues of race and citizenship. As clearly evidenced by the high-profile alt-right gatherings of 2017 and 2020, this role has continued into the twenty-first century as well. Yet Gettysburg has never been a freestanding stage with an audience that empties out at the end of a "performance." Rather, from its earliest days, it has been a living community where players in the drama and onlookers intersect both on and off stage. The debates acted out in Gettysburg may be national (and sometimes even international) in scope, but they have always been simultaneously local, deeply connected to the rhythms and patterns of a real community.

From its earliest days, Gettysburg's populace has included a small African American population for whom the contested nature of Civil War memory has influenced everyday life since 1863. Gettysburg's social and economic structure has been shaped, like every other American community, by demographics, geographical location, political loyalties, size, road networks, and available environmental resources. But it has also been influenced by the battlefield's role in ongoing debates between emancipationist, Unionist, reconciliationist, and Lost Cause memories of the Civil War.[2] Over the course of the century following Lincoln's November 1863 charge to the living to take up the unfinished work of the Union dead, Gettysburg's Black residents struggled for equal opportunity and a new birth of freedom on the ground that gave rise to the phrase.

Though historians have richly documented the twentieth-century northern Black freedom in recent decades, the bulk of these works have focused on large urban centers where sizable Black populations facilitated the creation of sophisticated organizing networks and mass campaigns.[3] Yet not all northern Blacks lived in large cities, and segregation and discrimination limited opportunities and crushed dreams in small towns and minor urban centers as well. Black Gettysburgians battled pervasive discrimination in housing, education, and employment, and were regularly barred from movie theaters, restaurants, and public spaces such as pools, or confined to segregated spaces inside. While some white residents made no secret of their hostile or patronizing attitudes toward their Black neighbors, others used the community's tourist economy as a shield for their own prejudices, speciously arguing that to whatever extent segregation was practiced in Gettysburg, it was only in deference to the sensibilities of white southern visitors.

As was true in many northern communities, the first hurdle Black Gettysburgians faced in their struggle for justice was getting whites to acknowledge the extent of the problem and the depth of racial inequality in the region. Never a high-profile site on the civil rights map, Gettysburg experienced few marches, protests, or coordinated campaigns for racial justice in the first seventy years of the twentieth century. Nevertheless, Black residents used their churches and community groups to nurture a strong sense of collective identity, advocated for better educational opportunities for their children, and by the centennial period had begun to directly challenge segregation in public accommodations, employment, and housing. Though their stories are not always dramatic or transformative, communities like Gettysburg provide vital testimony to the fact that twentieth-century Black freedom struggle was a national phenomenon, playing out in small border-state towns as well as better-known locations such as Montgomery and Harlem. Although large-scale transformation of the social and economic structure that restricted Black advancement did not come to Gettysburg during the centennial period, subtle progress was discernable by 1965.

ESTABLISHED AS A BOROUGH (TOWN) in 1786 and selected as the county seat of the newly formed Adams County in 1800, Gettysburg was known throughout the early and middle decades of the nineteenth century for its farms and orchards, carriage companies, and two institutions of higher learning: Pennsylvania College (founded 1832) and the Lutheran Theological Seminary (founded 1826). In 1860, the town was home to approximately 2,400 people, including a substantial population of German immigrants and more than 200 Black residents, some of whom had been born into slavery in neighboring Maryland.[4] Within three years, however, the community's identity would be forever associated with the battle that raged in and around the town from July 1 to July 3, 1863.

Hoping to relieve the pressure on Virginia, take the war to Northern civilians, and possibly spur Northern opponents of the war to push for negotiations with the Confederacy, Robert E. Lee's Army of Northern Virginia launched an invasion of the North in late spring 1863. Crossing the Pennsylvania border in the final weeks of June, Lee's army pressed northward as far as the outskirts of Harrisburg (the state capital) before falling back to Cashtown to concentrate its forces. The pursuing Union Army, under the command of George Gordon Meade, entered Pennsylvania on June 30, and the two armies promptly clashed at Gettysburg, a border town located at the hub of an extensive network of roads. The battle raged for three days, with devastating consequences for the armies, the local residents, and the landscape alike. Aware that the Confederate Army was seizing Black Pennsylvanians, many of them born free, and sending them south to be sold into slavery, most Black residents fled northward toward Harrisburg, forced to leave their homes and livelihoods behind with no protection. Of the 160,000 men who fought at Gettysburg, 10,000 were killed outright, 11,000 were missing or captured, and more than 30,000 lay wounded in makeshift hospitals, private homes, or on the field itself. Traumatized civilians emerged from their cellars to view a nightmare scene. The landscape was utterly shattered: crops trampled, wells drained or contaminated, fences destroyed, and houses and barns pockmarked with shells, their contents wrecked, scattered, or confiscated for military use. Dead and dying men and horses lay everywhere.[5]

Preservation of the battlefield began almost immediately after the Army of Northern Virginia's retreat. Local attorney David Wills spearheaded the establishment of Soldiers' National Cemetery as a resting place for the thousands of fallen Union soldiers lying in hastily dug graves near their battle lines. Its dedication on November 19, 1863, provided the occasion for Lincoln's Gettysburg Address: the 272 words that made Gettysburg an American icon, ultimately elevating it to a position of nearly unparalleled symbolic significance as the physical manifestation of American ideals. Within a year of the battle, at the instigation of another local attorney, David McConaughy, the Pennsylvania legislature chartered the Gettysburg Battlefield Memorial Association (GBMA) to "hold and preserve, the battle-grounds of Gettysburg . . . as they were at the time of said battle."[6]

By 1895, the GBMA held title to 522 acres of land (all of it along the Union battle lines) and had constructed nearly twenty miles of roads to facilitate access to key spots on the field. Under the GBMA's watch, Union veterans eager to mark the sites where they had fought erected markers and monuments along their lines of battle.[7] Much to the horror of the preservationists, entrepreneurs eager to capitalize on the burgeoning tourist industry constructed a trolley across the battlefield in the early 1890s and opened dance halls and amusement parks catering to tourists. Black employment in the community reached its high point in these years, with many residents finding work in the burgeoning tourist industry as porters, waiters, and livery stable attendants. The expansion of rail lines to Gettysburg and the ensuing competition for passengers resulted in a wide variety of excursion trains featuring reduced fares for veterans and church and civic groups. Some local residents deplored the town's transformation into a tourist mecca, particularly as more working-class visitors flocked to Gettysburg, and condemned the excursions (specifically the alcohol and revelry that accompanied them) as a desecration of good taste and public morality.[8]

Many were particularly disturbed by the large groups of Black excursionists who took the train from Baltimore in these years. Though a good number of Baltimore's Black civic, religious, and fraternal organizations sponsored day trips to Gettysburg between 1880 and World War I, staying overnight was not an option for these guests, since none of the local hotels accommodated Blacks, and the town's first Black boardinghouse did not open until the early years of the twentieth century. The largest and best known of these excursions was the annual Emancipation Day outing sponsored by the city's Black Grand Army of the Republic (the veterans' association serving Union soldiers, sailors, and Marines) posts. Participants in this annual event, held in September in commemoration of Lincoln's preliminary Emancipation Proclamation, toured the battlefield, drank in downtown bars, and danced and ate at Round Top Park, usually a whites-only space but reserved exclusively for

Black visitors this one day of the year. The Grand Army of the Republic (GAR) excursions, which raised funds for the posts' charitable assistance to veterans' widows and orphans, sometimes drew as many as 7,000 participants and sparked hostility among many local whites. Trafficking in deeply rooted racist assumptions about Black inferiority, Gettysburg newspapers frequently portrayed the excursionists as violent, drunken buffoons, and town bars closed to Emancipation Day participants in 1916.[9]

While tourists and veterans made extensive use of the battlefield in the early decades of the twentieth century, they did not have a monopoly on it, and Ku Klux Klan members were quick to grasp the symbolic possibilities of the grounds. Pennsylvania Klan groups made Gettysburg an important component of their activities in the 1920s, which revolved around large open-air demonstrations aimed at recruitment. The strategy proved successful, as state membership grew from 150,000 in 1924 to 300,000 by the end of 1925. Though the original goal of the Second Ku Klux Klan (reborn in 1915) was to reassert white supremacy in the South, it spread rapidly in the north by exploiting labor tensions and ethnic and religious prejudice. In its heyday, the Second Klan was not only much larger than the Reconstruction-era Klan had been, the bulk of its membership was located in northern states. Unlike its predecessor, the Second Klan operated in daylight.[10]

In Pennsylvania, as in many other northern states, the Klan's popularity was fueled by deep-seated hostility toward immigrants, Catholics, Blacks, and Jews. The organization was propelled to new heights by increased Black migration and the rapid growth of ethnic populations in industrial areas. Though it went to great lengths to portray itself as a patriotic Christian outfit committed to the defense of chivalry and public morality, and many members were middle class in social standing, the Klan actively sought out violent conflict. Klansmen frequently carried clubs, blackjacks, and pistols under their robes during parades, and chose their cross-burning sites to maximize the intimidation factor. Over the course of the 1920s, gun battles between Klan members and opposing forces were common, though opponents were much more likely to face prosecution than KKK stalwarts.[11]

Though Klan activity began in Adams County as early as 1923, the spectacle gathering that took place on the battlefield in September 1925 was unprecedented. The Pennsylvania Klan invited members from six states to a mass-scale event that ultimately drew between 20,000 and 25,000 participants. Headquarters were located at the town's premier hotel, the Hotel Gettysburg; attendees unable to secure sold-out hotel accommodations camped on the designated assembly field established along Oak Ridge, site of some of the hardest fighting of the First Day's battle. Given their desire to wield the Civil War as a club against immigrants, the choice of Oak Ridge as an assembly point was symbolically rich in ways that few Klan members likely understood. Their assembly field provided an excellent vantage point to view the location of the July 1 battle lines of the 11th Corps—the Union Army corps best known for its high proportion of German and German American soldiers (many of whom were Catholic). Despite the presence of many experienced officers in the corps, many Northerners viewed 11th Corps soldiers of German descent as unwelcome outsiders in 1863. Their conduct in battle, particularly at Chancellorsville and again at Gettysburg itself, was frequently subjected to nativist-inspired attacks. Yet aside from mistreatment and persecution during World War I, German Americans were generally considered "good Americans" by the 1920s, and Pennsylvania Klan groups did not perceive German immigrants as a threat.[12]

Comparing the scene along Oak Ridge to a Grand Army of the Republic (GAR) or National Guard encampment, the *Gettysburg Times* noted that the KKK camp drew many curious residents and visitors. Over the course of two days, members staged a massive parade, toured the battlefield, held church services and initiation ceremonies, posed for a panoramic photo on the assembly field, and participated in "competitive Klavalier drills" judged by U.S. Army officers. The public response they received likely ensured that leaders felt little doubt that Klan members felt their strategy of using Gettysburg to link their cause to older, martial-themed patriotic traditions had been successful. Symbolically appropriating the battlefield, they presented themselves as modern-day defenders of patriotism and American heritage, seemingly going so far as to suggest a parallel between the armed combat experienced by Civil War soldiers and their own violent clashes with anti-Klan groups.[13]

Across the state, not all town officials took kindly to the idea of the Klan parading through their communities. In Gettysburg, however, the organization seemingly was given free rein. Local merchants began decking their buildings in bunting a week in advance, and scouts reported to their groups that the local climate was friendly. Portraying the Klan as a patriotic organization bringing excitement, pageantry, publicity, and tourist dollars to Gettysburg, the *Gettysburg Times* presented the Klan gathering in a fashion practically analogous to the coverage accorded large-scale veterans' reunions. Opining that the "On to Gettysburg" stickers adorning many of the Klan vehicles were "a splendid advertisement for Gettysburg," the paper went so far as to encourage local residents to open their homes to the Klan members. In its reporting on the parade, the paper began with a Civil War theme that no doubt angered those who opposed the melding of battle and Klan imagery: "Gettysburg capitulated this afternoon to an army of red, white and blue. It surrendered cheerfully and without a casualty." The day after the Klan members departed, the *Gettysburg Times* revealed the economic motivations likely underlying some of the welcome, printing KKK officials' thanks to local business owners for their cooperation and assistance.[14]

Though opponents of the Klan's presence in Gettysburg did not arm themselves with bricks, stones, and firearms (as occurred in some communities), not all local residents welcomed or were willing to ignore the group's rally. Some Gettysburg College students heartily disapproved of the Klan spectacle, editorializing in a campus publication, *The Blister*, that Klan ideology and practices were "repugnant to the idea of democracy." Suggesting that the applauding crowds were not representative of the local community, the authors insisted that disapproval of the Klan's presence was widespread, particularly among "the campus intelligentsia." Drawing on the Gettysburg Address, the students charged Klan members and their supporters with anti-American and unchristian behavior. It is likely that parishioners of Gettysburg's St. Francis Xavier Catholic Church, as well as the town's small African American and Jewish communities, shared these sentiments.[15]

Perhaps capitalizing on an opportunity to demonstrate their commitment to "defend, support, patronize, and attend all Protestant American churches and institutions," and their leadership's desire to position the Klan as a philanthropic organization, members followed up the rally with a highly visible donation to Gettysburg's most prominent Black church. Despite its deep roots and central role in the local Black community, the small size of the congregation and the financial insecurity experienced by so many Black residents kept St. Paul's AME Zion on precarious financial footing. Constantly struggling to meet insurance and mortgage payments, pay their pastor, and make necessary repairs on the building, congregants often turned to fund drives, cash rallies, raffles, and other fundraisers to keep the church solvent. The local newspaper the *Star and Sentinel* reported on October 24, 1925, that Klan members had contacted Reverend R. J. Frazier about making a donation to help pay off the church's mortgage and "received an invitation to attend" a Sunday evening cash rally service.[16]

Marching en masse from their campground along Taneytown Road, the robed and hooded group passed through the heart of the Third Ward, home to the vast majority of Gettysburg's Black citizens. Arriving at the church, they presented Pastor Frazier with $115 — nearly 25 percent of the total sum raised that evening. The *Star and Sentinel's* businesslike take on the story noted that the Klansmen departed at the end of the service singing "Onward, Christian Soldiers," but offered no details on parishioners' response to their presence nor any speculation on the factors that might have compelled either the donation to a Black church or the congregation's response. Nonetheless, the repeated use of passive voice in the article seems perhaps deliberate. Both the statement that the pastor "had been advised some time ago" of the Klan's desire to make a donation and the assertion that Klansmen "received an invitation" to the service obscure specific actions on the part of individuals, hinting at the skewed power dynamics and latent menace inherent in the interaction.[17]

Though the bulk of the Pennsylvania KKK's campaign of violence and intimation was directed against Catholics, some actions were aimed directly at Blacks—such as a 1924 cross burning in Delaware County intended to run Black residents out and a lynching in Beaver County. Klan propaganda relied heavily upon white fears of "race-mixing," and local chapters across the country frequently employed showings of the film *The Birth of a Nation* as a recruitment tool.[18] Despite the *Star and Sentinel*'s portrait of a scene of philanthropic generosity, the scene in the church was charged with intimidation, no doubt leaving many parishioners sickened by the complicity required of them in this charade of goodwill. Members of the Klan delegation, of course, likely viewed their actions as a demonstration of their support for "all Protestant Christian" churches and a way to burnish the KKK's credentials as a community-minded organization. Beyond that, many may have viewed their donation as a statement of support for segregation, a paternalistic contribution to an institution historically perceived by white racists as exerting a "civilizing" influence on Blacks, or simply a way to indicate active surveillance of the Black community.

Black Gettysburgians were already aware that they were being watched closely. Local Klan members had attempted the previous year to intimidate parents and community leaders demanding improved educational opportunities for their children. In the early twentieth century, Gettysburg maintained a segregated school for Black elementary students. In that year, D. William Biggs, B. G. E. Curry, and Richard Thomas led a push to have Black fifth and sixth graders admitted to the all-white Meade School and High Street School. Though the *Gettysburg Times* claimed that conditions at the all-Black Franklin Street School were as good as at the white schools, Biggs, Curry, and Thomas argued that the employment of only a single teacher at Franklin Street made it impossible for her to meet the educational needs of all of her students. Though arguing that the Meade and High Street buildings were already overcrowded and that Franklin Street's enrollment was not out of line for a single-teacher school, the school board agreed to admit the sixth graders. In an attempt to intimidate Blacks into silence, Klan members planted a cross in front of Biggs's home; it was discovered before it was lit, and borough police removed it. Black residents, however, initially stayed the course of their demand, warning that the fifth graders would be waiting at the Meade and High Street doors on the first day of school. Richard Thomas sent a forceful warning to those who planted the cross, telling the *Gettysburg Times* that if it had been lit, the person striking the match would not have made it out of the neighborhood.[19]

Ultimately, the threat to send the fifth graders to the Meade and High Street buildings did not materialize. The *Gettysburg Times* quoted a retired Black minister on the subject, who claimed that the majority of the Black community did not support the position espoused by Biggs, Thomas, Curry, and insisted that "nowhere were the colored children better provided for in terms of education than in Gettysburg." While this rejoinder smacks of the sort of reassuring rhetoric that whites often sought from more conservative Blacks in the face of civil rights activities in their communities, it is also possible that many parents valued the all-Black atmosphere of Franklin Street School. Contrary to widespread opinion, school desegregation was never universally popular among Black parents, even in the 1950s and 1960s. Nonetheless, the episode demonstrates that Gettysburg's Black community had some history of organizing and protest in the face of discrimination and that "the way things were" was not universally accepted. The 1924 events may have played a role — alongside financial concerns — in the school board's decision to close Franklin Street School in 1932.[20]

Scandals among the state leadership and rising numbers of antimask ordinances led to substantial decline in Pennsylvania Klan membership throughout 1926, mirroring a similar trend across the nation. Yet the Adams County chapters remained strong enough to mount a mammoth celebration in Gettysburg over Memorial Day weekend in 1927, presenting themselves as defenders of civic virtue, the Bible, the nation's Protestant churches, and the public school system. Holding battlefield tours and church services side by side with "naturalization" ceremonies, parades, and rallies (including one at the National Cemetery), the group framed their visit as "propelled by the same principles for which men fought and died in the Civil War." Without specifying what those principles might be, they claimed patriotic legitimacy by wrapping themselves in the mantle of the Gettysburg dead. When Klan member Samuel N. Beamer died later that summer, the newspaper coverage of his funeral fueled this conflation, blending description of the Klan rituals at his grave with a detailed account of his childhood interaction with President Lincoln on November 19, 1863.[21]

"It Might as Well Begin in Gettysburg": Black Laborers, Black Leaders, and Gettysburg NMP

The National Park Service (NPS) assumed management of the Gettysburg battlefield from the War Department in 1933. Created in 1916, the NPS was in its early days primarily associated with the natural landscapes of the West, yet by the early 1930s, high-ranking agency officials made a successful case that the Park Service was the rightful custodian of the nation's historic sites and monuments. NPS priorities in the agency's early years of managing the park included increasing the accessibility and usability of the park landscape, providing for the comfort and convenience of visitors, and presenting Gettysburg National Military Park (GNMP) as a multiuse landscape that could appeal to both historically minded visitors and those seeking scenic vistas. NPS management also accelerated Gettysburg's transition from a Union memorial park to a battlefield primarily defined by the actions of Confederate soldiers and known as "the High Water Mark of the Confederacy" rather than the "high point of Union defense."[22]

While the idea of framing the Civil War as a "new birth of freedom" was foreign to GNMP's early NPS managers, they benefited quite directly from the labor of descendants of the Black men and women who experienced the war as an emancipationist event. Park officials went so far as to employ Black laborers serving with the Civilian Conservation Corps (CCC), a New Deal work relief program, to further the development of the battlefield's commemorative landscape as a site of reconciliation. Created to put unemployed youths to work on conservation and outdoor recreation projects, the CCC transformed national and state parks across the nation and played a key role in preparing America's Civil War battlefields for the age of automobile-driven mass tourism. Gettysburg was home to two CCC camps between 1933 and 1942; workers housed at these camps built restrooms, removed nonhistoric tree growth, replaced fencing, reset headstones in the National Cemetery, widened the cemetery gate to accommodate tour buses, and buried telephone wires that marred the historic viewshed.[23]

While the vast majority of CCC workers nationwide were white, African Americans—whose disproportionate poverty rendered them particularly hard-hit by the Depression—fought hard for access to the program, though they were ultimately restricted to 10 percent of the total enrollment. Camps were generally segregated along racial lines, with many of the all-Black camps located in national parks. Company 385-C arrived in Gettysburg in June 1933, with three white officers and 180 Black enrollees, moving into a newly established camp in Pitzer Woods. A second camp in McMillan's Woods, occupied by Company 1355-C, opened later that year. Black workers at camps below the Mason-Dixon line often encountered substantial hostility from local residents, and many white Gettysburgians were also displeased by the enrollees' presence, to the extent that a local congressman asked the CCC director to remove the units. As time passed and the economic benefits and manpower capacities of the camps became clear, local residents ceased to advocate for their removal. The appointment of Black professionals to positions of authority, however, was another matter, and the assignment of anthropologist Louis King to Gettysburg in 1934 led officials to predict chaos and bloodshed.[24]

Angered by the policy of appointing white officers to command positions in Black CCC camps, Black leaders lobbied the White House to appoint Black men to supervisory positions. Aware of the pressure, the white southern liberal Clark Foreman, race relations advisor to Secretary of the Interior Harold Ickes, strategized with Ickes to select a Black man for one of the Interior-appointed "intellectual jobs" in the national park–based camps. Foreman recalled in a 1946 *Reader's Scope* interview that when a vacancy appeared at Gettysburg for an archeologist, few expected that a qualified Black candidate could be located. Foreman alleged that when he submitted Louis Eugene King's name for consideration, NPS officials protested on the grounds that Gettysburg was a segregated community, predicting that the presence of an educated Black man in a position of authority would spark a riot. Foreman's response was to draw on an emancipationist interpretation of Civil War history that gained some traction among political radicals in the 1930s and 1940s. He argued that while his own grandfathers had fought for the preservation of slavery, theirs (they were apparently Northerners) had struggled to win citizenship rights for Black Americans. Assigning Gettysburg a key place in the narrative, Foreman continued, "That war was won at Gettysburg, and by God, if it's got to be fought over again it might as well begin in Gettysburg."[25]

A graduate of Howard University and Columbia University, Louis King finished his Ph.D. work under famed anthropologist Franz Boas in 1932, though he did not formally receive his doctoral degree until much later in life. According to Ira Harrison, King's dissertation, "Negro Life in a Rural Community," was possibly the "first anthropological community study of

African-American life in the United States." His extensive fieldwork in West Virginia applied anthropological techniques to modern society, seeking to objectively document the relationships, cultural practices, and daily experiences of a Black community in a border state. The abysmal job prospects facing Black anthropologists during the Depression closed the doors of the academic community to King, thus bringing him to Foreman's attention in 1934.[26]

Based at Gettysburg from 1934 until the closure of the last CCC camp in March 1942, King conducted an extensive survey of GNMP resources. He also did related work across the mid-Atlantic region of the National Park Service, investigating historically significant buildings across Maryland and Virginia. Clark Foreman used Louis King's success as an illustration of his conviction that "the only way to get rid of discrimination against Negroes is to root it out." Yet because King was employed by the CCC, not the NPS, he lost his job when the agency was abolished in the early days of World War II. Still unable to secure a position in academia, he joined many of Gettysburg's other Black residents in commuting to work at the Naval Supply Depot in Mechanicsburg, Pennsylvania. King remained at the depot for most of his professional life and did not work again in his chosen field until 1969, two years before his death.[27]

Two years after King began his position at Gettysburg, federal officials responded to ongoing pressure from Black leaders by appointing Captain Frederick Lyman Slade, 1st Lieutenant George W. Webb and 2nd Lieutenant Samuel W. Tucker to lead Company 1355-C. Slade was the first Black officer in the nation to command a Black CCC camp. By 1939, the rest of the staff positions in the now-consolidated Gettysburg camp were also filled by African Americans, making Gettysburg an anomaly in an agency that continued to use white officers in almost all other Black camps.[28] The question of why Gettysburg was chosen as a proving ground is an intriguing one. Officials were well aware that patterns of segregation and discrimination were deep-seated in the community. Though (barely) north of the Mason-Dixon line, like many other northern communities, it was hardly a place of opportunity for African Americans.

Employment opportunities for Black residents constricted throughout the first half of the twentieth century, and, as previously noted, the town operated an all-Black elementary school until 1932. Housing opportunities were almost entirely restricted to a subsection of the Third Ward, and the town's largest private cemetery, Evergreen Cemetery, did not accept Blacks for burial. The newly renamed Gettysburg College did not admit Black students, and the borough's other institution of higher learning, the Lutheran Theological Seminary, had not enrolled a Black student since the 1830s, with the possible exception of some summer students. Nonetheless, it is possible that others shared Clark Foreman's belief that Gettysburg's symbolic stature made it the right place to wage the fight to increase opportunity within the CCC.[29]

One of Company 1355-C's tasks was to help construct and lay the gas line to what would become one of the battlefield's most iconic commemorative pieces, the Eternal Peace Light Memorial. With a base of Maine granite boasting the inscription "Peace Eternal in a Nation United" and a column of Alabama limestone topped by an eternal flame, the monument was financed by donations from state governments on both sides of the Mason-Dixon line and dedicated during the last veterans' reunion in 1938. Though deeply rooted in the long history of the veteran as the chief symbol of postwar reconciliation, as historian Nina Silber has argued, the memorial focused less on the experience of battle than on raising "questions about perpetuating war, any war, in a world surrounded by horrific conflict." The dedication address delivered by President Franklin Roosevelt to a crowd of perhaps 200,000 was rooted in the context of the Great Depression, the rising tide of fascism, and the descent of Europe into war. Emphasizing the need for constant vigilance in preserving "a people's government for the people's good," Roosevelt called Americans to wartime unity by lauding Civil War veterans for coming back together under a common flag. Only with such unity, he insisted, could the nation continue to meet the challenge of retaining "that greatest good for the greatest number which this government of the people was created to ensure."[30]

Yet could lasting peace ever be possible without justice? The severing of emancipation from racial justice in the public mind and the triumph of Jim Crow nationwide could not have made it more obvious that the terms of peace had not served Black Americans well. Despite their wartime services and sacrifices, their needs and priorities were again and again deemed tangential to the "greatest good for the greatest number." The cause of racial justice received no attention during the commemoration, and the New Deal emphasis of Roosevelt's words could hardly have failed to remind African Americans—including any CCC members who may have been in the audience—just how fiercely they'd had to struggle for any semblance of fair inclusion in the economic assistance programs Roosevelt obliquely lauded. These men no doubt came away from their assignment to Gettysburg with some significant questions about the limits of emancipation and the price of peace.

In an ironic symbolic twist, the new monument was located on Oak Hill, adjoining the site of the 1925 Klan campground and assembly field. This monument to white reconciliation was built on land that had been claimed fifteen years prior by white supremacists eager to utilize the legacy of the battle to spread their vision of white Christian nationhood. Thus, it is highly likely that many of the town's Black, Jewish, and Catholic longtime residents looked askance at the heralded message of peace and reconciliation. As the years passed, some Klan members adopted the monument itself as a symbol of white supremacy. When the World Knights of the Ku Klux Klan filed for a permit for a demonstration at GNMP in 2006, they requested permission to rally at the Peace Light on the grounds that the monument honored "white unity between North and South."[31]

Racial Segregation, Northern Style

In 1953, a sociology student conducting thesis research concluded that the town of Gettysburg was more segregated in 1950 than it had been in 1900, and that decreased employment opportunities for residents of color were directly correlated with increased poverty and population decline. Racist forms of entertainment persisted into the 1960s, and when the local newspaper, the *Gettysburg Times*, covered stories pertaining to people of color, it frequently employed race as a distinguishing feature in the headlines, even if the stories themselves had little to do with race.[32] Yet Black Gettysburgians persevered in the face of discrimination, creating vibrant neighborhoods, taking pride in their family histories and community traditions, and carving out their own connections to the battlefield and the history of the Civil War.

Donald Becker's investigative research documented the paltry economic opportunities available in Gettysburg for residents of color; in 1953, twenty-one of the borough's fifty-nine employed Black adults worked outside the community. Many of the residents who commuted were employed as civil service workers in Harrisburg (the state capital, thirty-eight miles to the north) or Washington, D.C. (eighty-four miles to the south); others worked at federal installations such as Letterkenny Army Depot (located in Chambersburg, twenty-seven miles to the west) or Mechanicsburg's Naval Supply Depot (thirty-one miles to the north). With the exception of one full-time minister, African Americans who worked locally were predominately employed as laborers, janitors, hotel porters and chambermaids, cooks, and laundry workers. Many young women studied commercial subjects in high school but were unable to secure positions as secretaries or clerks. The employers Becker interviewed provided an assortment of justifications for their refusal to hire Black workers, ranging from claims that Blacks were lazy and untrustworthy to assertions that white employees would not work with them and/or white customers would not interact with them. One employer baldly responded, "They are too dumb to work," and shifting responsibility to others, another asserted that "people in Gettysburg aren't ready for Negroes in offices." This line of reasoning was common in northern communities, where discrimination was readily ascribed to supposed Black failings, and racial justice was expected to wait on white timelines.[33]

As in other northern communities, residential segregation was pronounced, with African American residents, aside from live-in domestics, limited to a segment of the Third Ward along certain parts of S. Washington, Breckenridge, High, and Franklin Streets where Blacks had lived for generations. The neighborhood was tightly knit, with strong community bonds, but residents were nonetheless hemmed in, telling Becker that it was almost impossible to find property anywhere else in the borough. A local realtor confirmed the second point in 1953, openly acknowledging, "There is no attempt on the part of the Negroes to live anywhere else but in the Third Ward. I wouldn't think of placing them anywhere else. The white people wouldn't stand for it, and it would hurt my business. I know all of the realtors feel the same as I do, because we often talk about it. We feel, let well enough alone. After all, there is no point in stirring anything up." As justification for this overtly segregationist practice, he invoked stereotypical characterizations of Black residents as spendthrift troublemakers.[34]

Blacks were generally barred from hotels, motels, and tourist homes. Charging that eleven of the fourteen restaurants in Gettysburg would not serve people of color, Becker also asserted that the town's "most prominent hotel" (presumably the Hotel Gettysburg) served African Americans only if they were nationally recognized or associated with a predominately white group. An integrated party made up of a white faculty wife, a Black housewife, and a Black high school student tested service at the town's six soda fountains during Becker's study; they were seated in all but one and received adequate service in four. The town's two movie theaters, the Strand and the Majestic, maintained segregated seating policies into the 1960s, though Terry Fox, a white man who graduated from Gettysburg High School in 1960, remembers challenges from integrated friend groups asking to sit together. Particularly vivid in Fox's memory is a day when white boys succeeded in gaining access to the balcony, then made so much commotion throwing

M&Ms that management closed the balcony for six months. The boys claimed they had desegregated the theater, as did an older group of girls who had previously sat together on the main floor.[35]

In a variation on the mystique of northern exceptionalism and the widespread practice of denying the extent to which segregation and discrimination were national phenomena, some white elites found it convenient to blame these policies on southern visitors. Eager to defend Gettysburg whites against the charge of racism, a local judge claimed that business owners maintained segregationist policies not due to personal prejudice but out of concern for losing tourist dollars. Drawing on deeply rooted misconceptions about the nature and history of racial segregation in the United States, he asserted that tourists came to Gettysburg from all parts of the country and "the proprietor must make an effort to satisfy the opinions and tastes of all his guests."[36]

Gettysburg closed its Black elementary school in 1932 on the grounds that the small size of the African American population made maintaining separate schools economically unjustifiable, but the desegregated school system did not necessarily provide a welcoming environment for Black students. While the superintendent told Becker in 1953 that any segregation that existed was social in nature, practiced by the students themselves, this assertion was undercut by statements from principals and guidance counselors revealing racist assumptions about Black students' work ethic and intelligence, and testimony from students about friendships that crossed the color line. Many Black students complained that they felt unwelcome in school activities, except for athletics, and that their classrooms did not provide them opportunities to succeed. Some teachers and administrators continued to treat Black students unequally through the 1960s, and students of color were frequently placed in general education classes regardless of their academic abilities.[37]

Becker noted that whenever Black students applied to Gettysburg College, they were always denied, regardless of qualifications, on the grounds that they would be happier somewhere else. The first Black students to study at Gettysburg College participated in the 1950 summer term (which did not require photos in the application process). Becker attested that the two young men were generally accepted by their peers but treated poorly by many members of the faculty. When Walter Langsam took over the presidency in 1952, he mandated that the college open itself to qualified applicants regardless of race, and four years later, Rudolph Featherstone became the first Black student to earn a degree from Gettysburg. Continuing his pioneering trail, Featherstone moved up the hill to the Lutheran Theological Seminary, an equally white institution. It would take another ten to fifteen years, however, for Gettysburg College to make the enrollment and support of minority students a priority; numbers did not exceed fifty until 1971.[38]

Despite the inequities of life in Gettysburg, some Black youths succeeded academically and went on to college, while others pursued opportunities through military service. In 1953, a Black high school student served as secretary of the senior class and president of the GHS National Honor Society chapter. Black residents voted and served on juries without incident, and the crime rate among African Americans was no higher than among whites. Jean Green, who grew up in the Third Ward, did not recall any violence or harassment directed at residents by police, but she was aware that some older members of the community distrusted certain officers.[39]

In the 1950s, the only integrated church in the community was St. Francis Xavier Catholic Church, though pioneering Black worshippers entered other congregations by the following decade. The only Black congregation in Gettysburg with its own church building and called pastor was St. Paul's AME Zion. The St. Paul's pastor occupied a unique and challenging spot in the local social structure. Due to its small size and the limited employment opportunities available to its members, the congregation was frequently strapped for funds. Through the auspices of the Gettysburg Ministerium, local white congregations regularly contributed monies to support the upkeep of the building and the pastor's salary. He or she was often the only member of the Black community included in civic events and could hardly forget that part of his/her salary came from white sources. An anonymous member of the Gettysburg College faculty observed in 1953 that even in the absence of deliberate pressure, these financial ties undermined the pastor's independence and ability to speak his/her mind on "issues which might alarm or antagonize the white community." The professor observed that these constraints impeded his/her capacity to provide the leadership sought by many young Black residents.[40]

This observation was borne out in the late 1940s when a newly called pastor clashed with members of the Gettysburg College Student Christian Association Interracial Committee. Throughout the decade, the Interracial Committee operated an afterschool program for Black children at St. Paul's, hosted holiday parties for young people, and sent cards to Black servicemen during the war. But the pastor who began serving St. Paul's in 1947, perceiving that the students' involvement with the congregation was rooted in paternalism and pity, wanted no part of it, arguing that such relationships propelled Black dependence on whites. He told the students that if they wished to continue the afterschool program, they would need to make it truly interracial by inviting white children to participate. This pastor's tenure in the community was short and his departure somewhat abrupt, with some commentators observing that he was too "ambitious" for Gettysburg. The tension between the student group and the pastor is revealing, suggesting that surface-level "friendly relations" across the color line may have papered over significant resentments, misunderstandings, and divergent priorities elsewhere in the community.[41]

Though little represented, except for behind-the-scenes roles, in the tourist industry and largely absent from the narrative of the war commemorated at Gettysburg, some members of the Black community did carve out their own connections to the Civil War and the commemorative landscape, regularly using the battlefield as a setting for walks and picnics. Black schoolchildren participated in the annual Memorial Day tradition of decorating graves in the National Cemetery. The cemetery, however, had few Black internees. No United States Colored Troops (USCT) units fought at Gettysburg (though Blacks filled supporting roles in both armies), and only two USCT veterans, Henry Gooden and Charles Parker, were ultimately buried in Soldiers' National Cemetery. The vast majority of USCTs buried in Gettysburg were interred in a private cemetery known in later years as Lincoln Cemetery.[42]

Decoration Day (the original name for Memorial Day) was an important holiday in Black communities across the nation, including Gettysburg, and remained a major event on the community calendar well into the twentieth century. Soldiers' graves at Lincoln Cemetery were decorated annually, and the trustees installed a speakers' rostrum to accommodate commemorative ceremonies. Some of these ceremonies, such as the 1933 Memorial Day program, were integrated. Accompanied by the Gettysburg High School band, Black and white veterans' organizations processed to Lincoln Cemetery, schoolchildren strewed flowers on veterans' graves, and Walter Carter—a member of the organizing committee—recited the Gettysburg Address. Within fifteen years, however, commemorative programming at the cemetery virtually ceased, though Black residents attempted to coordinate upkeep of the grounds, and youth organizations did occasional cleanup projects in the cemetery through the 1960s.[43]

When the Western Maryland Railway sponsored a massive pageant in 1952 commemorating Lincoln's November 1863 arrival in Gettysburg, the script called for the involvement of Black liverymen and servants, but no local Blacks wanted to participate, necessitating the casting of a Black man from Baltimore as Lincoln's porter. Donald Becker observed that white residents playing prominent figures in the community were opposed to sharing the stage with Blacks, seeming to ascribe Black residents' hesitancy to volunteer to this opposition. He did not speculate on the question of whether much of the resistance may have sprung instead from Black residents' rejection of a narrative that made space for them only in servant roles. Broadcast widely overseas through the Voice of America, "Mr. Lincoln Goes to Gettysburg" served as inspiration for the large-scale pageants mounted during the centennial years, and its writer and director, theatrical producer Adele Gutman Nathan, would later play an important role in the centennial programming.[44]

As direct action tactics spread across the nation, under the leadership of Adam Myers, a Black postal service employee, a group of residents came together in the late 1950s and 1960s to challenge Jim Crow by testing the color line in public accommodations and churches. Terry Fox recalled swimming at the whites-only Jack's Pool on a day when a Black man possibly associated with this group laid his money on the counter and jumped into the water. According to Fox, "When some of the women at the pool got out when the Black gentleman jumped in the water, I shouted to the women—'it doesn't wash off.'" The tests successfully broke the color barrier, and Jean Green swam at Jack's with an integrated group at least once in the late 1960s. The pool closed in 1968, perhaps in part due to the owners not wanting to deal with the challenges of operating a fully integrated pool.[45]

Given the long history of racist perceptions of Blacks as diseased and overly sexual, integrated swimming was a particularly touchy issue for whites across the nation. Many cities experienced swimming pool riots in the 1950s and 1960s, and several members of the board of directors of the Gettysburg Recreation Association resigned rather than take a position on the prospect of building a public pool in the borough. Renewed attempts in the early 1960s also made no headway, despite frequent identification of a public pool as one of the community's greatest needs, and debate over adding a pool to Recreation Park extended into the early 1980s.[46]

FROM THE KU KLUX KLAN'S appropriation of battlefield land to legitimize its claims to patriotic Americanism and debates over Black entitlement to representation and authority in New Deal relief programs to challenges to racial discrimination in education and public accommodations, the years leading up to the centennial revealed two important realities. First, Gettysburg was a critically important space for twentieth-century Americans to dramatize and debate issues of race and citizenship, concerns that would take on increased resonance as nations around the world lined up in opposing camps for a high-stakes debate over the economic and political system that would define the future. Secondly, though structural inequality remained, the combination of new federal legislation, grassroots action, and concern for the town's image ensured that the explicit and overt segregation so widespread in this border state community as late as the 1950s would not survive the centennial decade. The mid-twentieth-century Black freedom struggle was a national, not regional phenomenon, bringing change not only to southern hamlets and urban centers north and south of the Mason-Dixon line but to small Pennsylvania towns as well.

CHAPTER TWO

The Battlefield Belongs to the Nation

Preservation, Commercialization, and Cold War Tourism

"I hear that Gettysburg is going to be destroyed," fourteen-year-old Eileen Marvin of San Diego, California, wrote to John F. Kennedy in March 1961. "Please, Mr. President, don't let the people destroy Gettysburg. I want my children to see the battlefield that freed the negroes [*sic*] and made America the land of the free."[1] Though unusual for its focus on emancipation, Marvin's letter was only one of many similarly emotional pleas received by the White House that year as alarming news stories about commercial intrusion on the Gettysburg battlefield spread around the nation. As the nation embarked on a four-year commemoration of the centennial anniversary of the Civil War, the struggle over land use in the community marked one component of a multidimensional effort by preservationists, National Park Service officials, business owners, local residents, and southern heritage groups to redefine Gettysburg's physical and interpretive landscape for the next 100 years.

The 1950s and 1960s were a period of rapid change in the community, and this redefinition took many forms. Commercial interests argued that the town's emerging identity as a family vacation destination, the growing local population, and the community's insufficient tax base necessitated further development on battlefield land. Preservationists and some business owners insisted conversely that destruction of battlefield land was a national disgrace, an abdication of locals' obligation to the rest of the world, and, more practically, a threat to the long-term stability of the town's tourist economy. Committed Cold Warriors such as Pennsylvania governor David Lawrence and historian Bruce Catton seized the opportunity to use the community's annual commemorative rituals to criticize Soviet expansionism and call on Americans to reevaluate their definitions of freedom. Members of Confederate heritage groups, finally, sought to transform the commemorative landscape of the battlefield by erecting new "modern" monuments deploying Confederate memory as a weapon of massive resistance and anticommunism.

National Park Service officials seized on the centennial years to achieve the long-realized dream of a freestanding visitor center that would raise the agency's profile with visitors and make Paul Philippoteaux's massive cyclorama painting the heart of park interpretation. Some went so far as to champion a vision of Gettysburg as the primary focus of the centennial anniversary of the war. Rather than a decentralized national commemoration, they argued, Americans would be better served by a coordinated effort to preserve all threatened land at Gettysburg and build a new museum telling the entire story of the war. Though this vision did not triumph, it further solidified the conviction that Gettysburg was the military and spiritual hinge point of the Civil War, an idea and icon that could alleviate international condemnation of American racial abuses and restore the nation's moral supremacy on the world stage.

AS NOTED IN THE PREVIOUS CHAPTER, for all its symbolic power and international reputation as "America's most famous small town," Gettysburg was also a real community, home to a population of nearly 8,000 people (about 97 percent of them white) whose relationship to the Civil War was rarely as straightforward as it might appear on the surface. The proper balance among history, preservation, and economic development was a constant theme in local politics, and for many residents, the battlefield functioned as an extended backyard: a space to hike, picnic, and ride bicycles. While visitors from around the world explored the summits of Little Round Top and Culp's Hill, local children knew how to take the curves on their sleds to get maximum speed and distance. Gettysburg College students went parking at the Peace Light and used the battlefield for fraternity initiation purposes. And in what may have been an annual tradition, local residents rigged up a "ghostly apparition" on Little Round Top to scare passersby during the Halloween season.[2]

In 1960, Adams County was one of the smaller counties in Pennsylvania, but its population was on the rise, increasing by 17 percent over the previous decade. The rate of new construction was higher than the state average, and the youth population was large enough that the Gettysburg High School building first put into use in 1962 was already at capacity by the following year. Perhaps reflective in part of the conservatism of the area, Adams County women bore more children than their counterparts elsewhere, and the divorce rate was lower than the state average. The local economy was primarily dependent on agriculture (particularly orchards and fruit-packing plants) and tourism, and the county's population swelled seasonally with the arrival of large numbers of migrant workers, mostly Black and Puerto Rican.[3]

Traditionally Republican in political loyalties, Adams County was fiercely loyal to its most famous resident, President Dwight D. Eisenhower, who purchased a farm adjoining the battlefield in 1950, which he and his family visited regularly during his two terms in the White House. Eisenhower had a lifelong connection to Gettysburg and once described his 1918 assumption of command of the town's Tank Corp training camp as the proudest day of his life. The Eisenhowers retired to Gettysburg in 1961, and the former president maintained an office downtown, on the Gettysburg College campus. Though John F. Kennedy and Lyndon B. Johnson narrowly carried Pennsylvania in 1960, Adams County went for Vice President Richard Nixon, Eisenhower's second-in-command, by a wide margin, setting a new local record for voter turnout. Votes in Gettysburg borough were even more lopsided, with a total of 2,058 for Nixon and Lodge, and only 1,022 for Kennedy and Johnson.[4]

Thanks to the Eisenhowers' presence in the community and the regular use of the general's farm for diplomatic and political purposes, many national and world leaders visited Gettysburg in these years, including Nikita Khrushchev, Winston Churchill, Charles de Gaulle, and Jawaharlal Nehru. In the space of one weekend in July 1962, the Eisenhowers hosted two major gatherings: a social for attendees of the National Governors' Association Annual Meeting and an "All-Republican Conference" drawing key leaders from across the country to develop a broad-ranging strategy for the midterm elections. King Zaher and Queen Momaira of Afghanistan visited the farm the following year, sparking much curiosity across town about the dress, opinions, and customs of this royal couple.[5]

The regular presence of such high-profile leaders was a distinctive feature of life in Gettysburg in the mid-twentieth century. As a high school student, Terry Fox briefly glimpsed Khrushchev during his visit to town, recollecting in 2019 that the Soviet premier may not have cared much about the battlefield tour Eisenhower provided but was deeply interested in U.S. agriculture and food production. Six years later, Fox was supplementing his income as a teacher with a job as a bellhop at the Holiday Inn when he was charged with attending to former Vice President Richard Nixon. Visiting Gettysburg to strategize with Eisenhower on reorienting the Republican Party in the wake of Barry Goldwater's failed presidential campaign, Nixon sought Fox's "young man on the street" opinion on civil rights demonstrations and escalating U.S. actions in Vietnam.[6]

But it was the Civil War that was truly ever-present in the borough of Gettysburg. The community's Memorial Day traditions revolved around the National Cemetery, the core of the postwar commemorative landscape. By the centennial era, the tradition of children strewing flowers across the graves of more than 3,000 Civil War soldiers was nearly a hundred years old. Begun immediately after the war with residents of the town's newly established home for Civil War orphans, the custom was later taken up by schoolchildren. Local families used the battlefield for a wide variety of recreational purposes, and children sometimes found relics in the course of their play. Many residents were deeply involved in historically themed community organizations, such as the Sons of Union Veterans (SUV), the Gettysburg Civil War Round Table, the Adams County Historical Society (ACHS), or the Gettysburg Battlefield Preservation Association (GBPA). Gettysburg College hosted regular programming on the war under the auspices of the "Civil War Study Group" and, later, the Robert Fortenbaugh Memorial Lecture. Students at the college also forged their own connections to the historic landscape around them, some more lighthearted than others. A nighttime scavenger hunt on the field was central to the initiation process for young men pledging Tau Kappa Epsilon fraternity in the 1960s. Clad in undershirts made of burlap sacks, the pledges were handed a map and a few flashlights and turned loose to collect bricks left by upperclassmen at various locations across the battlefield.[7]

A Family Vacation Destination

The local economy revolved heavily around tourism, boasting a wide range of amenities, educational and otherwise, for a new generation of tourists more likely than their predecessors to undertake vacation travel in family units. With the convergence of the postwar baby boom, the increased standard of living enjoyed by many Americans, and the creation of the interstate highway system, by 1963, more than 40 percent of families were averaging 600 miles per year in vacation travel. Historical sites offered these families educational experiences and an opportunity to inculcate children in the national values deemed under attack in the Cold War years. The ramifications of the travel boom echoed across Pennsylvania; by 1961, the state was third in the nation in tourism revenue, bringing in $1.4 million annually. Historian Jim Weeks has argued that "in a country threatened within and without, responsible parents took their children to Gettysburg for a straightforward lesson in being American . . . parents felt that dipping at the well of the national past edified children and strengthened the family." Yet family vacations could never be solely patriotic, educational experiences. Children clamored for fun and entertainment, and Gettysburg's mid-twentieth-century tourist economy endeavored to appeal to the increasingly diverse desires of the new visitor base.[8]

Vaudeville star Cliff Arquette, most famous for creating the persona of the bumbling bumpkin Charley Weaver, opened Cliff Arquette's Soldiers Museum in 1959, which featured his personal collection of miniature hand-carved soldiers. The National Civil War Wax Museum followed in 1962, presenting the Civil War through thirty-five "moment in time" scenes, including one devoted to John Brown's execution, and an audiovisual presentation depicting highlights of the battle. By 1964, George Rosensteel's Gettysburg National Museum claimed to be "the world's most visited battlefield museum," thanks in large part to the popularity of the Electric Map initially designed on his son Joseph's bedroom floor. Museum publicity capitalized on visitors' confusion over the scope and complexity of the battle, promising a coherent overview in thirty minutes.[9]

Entrepreneur L. E. Smith owned several tourist businesses in the downtown area, including the Lincoln Train Museum, the Lincoln Room Museum, and the Hall of Presidents Museum. Reaching outside the niche of Civil War history, the Hall of Presidents presented itself as an unparalleled entry point to "The Story of America." Located in the historic Wills House, the Lincoln Room Museum provided visitors access to the room where Lincoln spent the night before delivering the Gettysburg Address. Publicity for the museum hailed it as "a must for every American." The Jennie Wade House and Museum, located on the site where the battle's only known civilian casualty was killed while baking bread on July 3, 1863, was less prone to patriotic hyperbole. Rather, it offered visitors a glimpse of the civilian experience of the battle through self-styled "factual dramatization."[10]

Commercial bus tours of the battlefield were first approved by the National Park Service in 1949, and helicopter tours began ten years later. National Heritage Associates held the concession for bus tours by the early 1960s, and the company widely advertised its prerecorded tour as way for visitors to put themselves at the heart of the battle—in air-conditioned comfort, no less. Entrepreneurs eager to capitalize on Gettysburg's national visibility as a heritage tourism destination opened a variety of commercialized historical attractions along the roads leading into town, such as the "World's Largest Horse 'N Buggy Museum" and the "Indian Village," which promised a "visit with real Indians and Indian children in colorful costumes." Excoriating most of the town's commercial attractions as tacky and inauthentic, the magazine *Changing Times* claimed bitterly in 1962 that Lincoln "proved a poor prophet" in his claim that the soldiers consecrated the battlefield beyond the power of others to add or detract.[11]

Many families with children who were confused by the battlefield, or simply worn out by the emotional and intellectual demands of Civil War history, flocked to Fantasyland, a twenty-three-acre storybook park opened in 1959. Park highlights included the world's tallest talking Mother Goose, a Rapunzel's Castle featuring an animated witch, a Santa's Village complete with elves making toys, the frontier-themed Fort Apache, and many life-sized fairy tale scenes. The park was a popular spot for visitors and locals alike and attracted more than 21,000 visitors in its first three weeks of operation. By 1961, Fantasyland's popularity had spurred a competitor of sorts, Fort Defiance Civil War Museum and Frontier Town. Fort Defiance featured a life-sized reproduction of an eighteenth-century blockhouse (complete with reenactors and weapons demonstrations) and promised visitors "Civil War history presented in a most interesting way." Fort Apache, Fort Defiance, and the aforementioned Indian Village all reflected the popularity of the (ethnically/racially problematic) image of the frontier in Cold War America and prefigured the living history approach to historical interpretation that GNMP did not adopt until the 1970s.[12]

As concerns about the commercialization of the battlefield and the celebratory nature of the centennial intensified, Fantasyland attracted some criticism. Kenneth Dick, who cofounded the park with his wife, Thelma, defended the enterprise in a letter to the *New York Times*, stressing that the park was not located on historically significant ground and could not be seen from the National Cemetery or the NPS observation towers. Gettysburg had room for other enterprises besides the Civil War, Dick argued: "Here, my children and yours, who are too small to understand the Civil War, will have something to see and do." Presenting Fantasyland as an addition, not a detraction, to Gettysburg's landscape, Dick invoked his rights as a business owner "in this land of the free."[13]

By the time the National Park Service finally opened its first visitor center in 1962, Gettysburg bore a strong resemblance to tourist destinations such as Niagara Falls or Gatlinburg. A disgruntled visitor wrote the Department of the Interior lamenting that the downtown area had become a farce. "We are firm believers in private enterprise," she insisted, "but here is practiced highway robbery without the benefit of a gun." The presence of the new NPS facility spurred even greater development and the county's inadequate (or entirely nonexistent) zoning ordinances left the National Park Service virtually powerless to stop the encroachment of commercial enterprises around park boundaries. Those decrying the situation seized upon the centennial anniversary as an opportunity to make the case for battlefield preservation before a national audience; a particularly eye-catching article in the *Washington Post* warned that if a reenactment were to be staged in 1963, "some of Pickett's men may be making their charge through a custard stand or souvenir shop."[14]

The Gettysburg Battlefield Preservation Association (GBPA) was incorporated in 1959 in response to two threats: county commissioners' decision to sell the land surrounding the old Poor Farm site and the acquisition of several formerly agricultural parcels on the First Day's battlefield by a company planning to build private homes. GNMP superintendent James Myers deemed this dual threat catastrophic to the battlefield's future, arguing that the land was essential to understanding the First Day's battle. While some local residents stressed the need for more industry and a stronger tax base, others argued against further encroachment on the battlefield on conservation grounds or by arguing that compromising the land tourists came to see would be "killing the goose that lays the golden eggs."[15]

The popular magazine *Parade* ran a story on Gettysburg's preservation woes in January 1961, alongside a special offer: readers could purchase a Civil War portfolio of maps and images, with proceeds to benefit the GBPA. The article noted that of the 3,500 acres of battlefield land considered essential by the NPS (out of 16,000 total), 700 were still in private hands and at great danger of irreversible alteration. In the aftermath of the *Parade* piece, people from around the country sent letters to the *Gettysburg Times* excoriating the county commissioners as "small-minded" and "morally bankrupt." One *Parade* reader argued that "the land may be in Adams County, but the battlefield belongs to the nation." Another drew on the language of the Cold War, deeming the field "a symbol of the freedom of man." A woman who claimed that her husband had grown up in Gettysburg and "played on blood soaked field in a potato sack dress at 4 yrs. old" angrily demanded that Eisenhower divert funds from "European handouts we get no thanks for" to saving the nation's sacred heritage. The letters, however, did not save the property, and a good chunk of the land was ultimately sold to Baltimore developer Morton Klaus, who promptly erected the North Gettysburg Shopping Center on the site.[16]

In response to the House of Representatives' March 1959 decision to strike $1,250,000 earmarked for acquiring battlefield land (including $750,000 intended for Gettysburg) from the Department of the Interior's budget, preservationists launched a campaign to restore funds in the Senate, and newspapers across the country pledged support. A compromise figure was arrived at in June, but GNMP's access to the funds was contingent on the enactment of local zoning laws, and use of any part of the appropriation to purchase the Poor Farm site was explicitly banned. Congressman James Quigley warned the following year that Gettysburg was at risk of losing the money if local governing bodies did not take action on zoning, and events soon bore out his warning. A contentious public hearing on Cumberland Township's proposed zoning law led to repeated claims that the Department of the Interior was trying to ram zoning down local residents' throats and a decision on part of the NPS that making any kind of public statement on the issue was likely to only further inflame the situation.[17]

Recognizing the deep-seated distrust of zoning laws among many township residents and the immediacy of the Poor Farm sale, the newly formed GBPA made the case that the only permanent solution to the problem of commercialization at Gettysburg was outright purchase of threatened lands through private donations. Early leaders of the new group included Dr. Robert Bloom, who spearheaded Gettysburg College's Civil War programs, GNMP historian Frederick Tilberg, and television personality/local museum proprietor Cliff Arquette. Named chairman of the finance committee charged with raising $1 million for land acquisition, Arquette opened the campaign on the airwaves in his persona of Charlie Weaver, encouraging prospective donors to purchase one square inch of battlefield land. Supporters claimed that his efforts reached nearly 100 million Americans, more than half of the nation's population. Nine governors, seven senators, and direct descendants of both Robert E. Lee and Ulysses S. Grant signed on as members of the GBPA advisory board. The group successfully turned its first purchase, a fifty-five-acre tract in the Devil's Den area, over to the National Park Service in April 1962.[18]

Spurred on by the efforts of children in Calumet City, Illinois, the GBPA backed a nationwide initiative by schoolchildren to donate funds for land acquisition at Gettysburg. Funds received by the end of 1962 totaled $4,459, with much of the money raised through bake sales, book sales, and variety shows. GBPA's annual financial report showed an income of $19,507 in 1962; the organization's largest single source of revenue came from the operation of a milk cart at the Gettysburg National Museum. GBPA formally took ownership of eight acres near Oak Ridge near the end of the year and immediately moved to transfer the property to the NPS. Members of the board of directors indicated their determination to make 1963 a banner year for fundraising by voluntarily doubling their personal membership dues.[19]

The NPS Commemorates the Centennial

At the beginning of the centennial period, GNMP maintained thirteen field exhibits, as well as interpretive markers at the Peace Light, the Soldiers' National Monument, the Alabama monument, the Virginia memorial, and the North Carolina monument. Ranger-led tours of the battlefield were generally limited to school groups, military groups, and special visitors; most visitors thus toured the field with a licensed battlefield guide. The park had no visitor center or museum of its own, and its main interpretive device, a massive panoramic painting depicting the climactic moment of Pickett's Charge, was located in a non-climate-controlled temporary building. In the warmer months, park interpreters presented regularly scheduled talks in the inadequate facility, and on Sunday evenings in the summer, they showed films and slides about the national park system. An auto tour route was available to visitors, and the park was in the midst of furnishing General Meade's headquarters at the Leister House with period-appropriate pieces.[20]

Paul Philippoteaux's 1884 cyclorama painting came to Gettysburg in 1913 for the fiftieth anniversary commemoration of the battle. The NPS acquired it in 1942; its role as the keystone of GNMP's educational efforts further reinforced the centrality of the "High Water Mark" narrative to park interpretation and laid the groundwork for many future management decisions. As spiking visitor numbers and stagnant funding across the agency left parks overcrowded, understaffed, and severely limited in amenities and services, NPS director Conrad Wirth won approval in 1956 for a massive public works program in the national parks. Known as "Mission 66," the program's goal was to substantially modernize and enlarge the National Park system by the agency's fiftieth anniversary in 1966. GNMP's top priority for Mission 66 funding was the construction of a new building for Philippoteaux's painting (to be located adjacent to the field of Pickett's Charge, in order to maximize ease of access for visitors) and a freestanding visitor center. Since the park was under a contractual obligation to display the painting, staff members argued that if funding would not stretch to accommodate both a new cyclorama facility and a visitor center, it would be necessary to prioritize the Cyclorama Building.[21]

Civil War parks were a particularly high priority for Mission 66 projects, given the anticipated public interest in the centennial (indeed, attendance at Civil War parks rose by 14 percent in 1961). The Mission 66 Advisory Committee encouraged the NPS to develop an agency-wide program for commemorating Civil War anniversaries, to mitigate against disorganized private efforts, "financially unsound historical dramas," and "more useless memorial shafts." Two opposing viewpoints on how the NPS could best support the commemoration of the war soon emerged. The first advocated for the establishment of a national commission to coordinate commemorative activities over the course of a four-year period, and the second argued that the agency make land preservation and expanded interpretation at Gettysburg the sole focus of its centennial efforts.[22]

NPS director Wirth and northeast regional director Daniel Tobin agreed in 1956 that Gettysburg was the key to the centennial, the place where the NPS should harness the opportunities offered by Mission 66 to focus its efforts. Perhaps influenced by Tobin, Wirth proposed pursuing legislation authorizing the NPS to buy threatened land, create a new interpretive center, and abolish the licensed battlefield guide system. The two leaders were in agreement that the NPS should focus its commemorative efforts rather than dilute them, that Gettysburg was the place to do so, and that doing so effectively would require expanding park interpretation to include substantial coverage of the broader war. This direction was informally approved by the Washington office, and GNMP staff set to work on revising their original museum prospectus to reflect increased attention to situating Gettysburg within the context of the larger war. The edited version included thirty exhibits on Gettysburg (plus the cyclorama) and forty-five devoted to the larger war, including segments on manpower, weapons, and international affairs.[23]

Tobin felt strongly that the nation would be best served by a "one-shot" commemorative observance of the Civil War, and that the establishment of a national commission committed to four years of activities would lead to unseemly celebration of the war, dwindling public interest, partisan debates, and "embarrassing incidents." Far better, he asserted, to leave broad-based commemoration to state and local bodies. The best location for such a one-shot federal commemoration, he asserted, was Gettysburg. He deemed it "appropriate and essential to the dignity of the United States that the official commemoration of the war be on a field of victory for the Union Army." He viewed a northern location as necessary for practical reasons, due to widespread hostility toward the federal government across the South and concerns that "emotions" associated with "the present segregation issue" could be further enflamed by federal involvement in activities on southern battlefields.[24]

Many high-ranking NPS officials, however, disagreed with Tobin's assessment that a one-shot commemoration would best serve the agency's aims. They argued that there was widespread grassroots interest in commemoration across the nation, that the centennial of Gettysburg would not occur until halfway through the commemorative period, and that white southerners were sure to object to a singular focus on Gettysburg. As the tide turned against making Gettysburg the central focus of Civil War centennial activities, significant opposition to the idea of broadened context at the battlefield materialized. Assistant regional director George Palmer argued in December 1956 that visitors came to Gettysburg to learn about Gettysburg, predicting that information about the larger war would be lost on most guests.[25]

Ronald Lee, chief of the Division of Interpretation, laid out his opposition to a broader focus for GNMP's museum the following month, arguing that the idea upended long-established NPS practice of designing museums to aid visitors in understanding the terrain surrounding them. Visitors would not have the energy to explore a large museum, view the cyclorama, and still see the battlefield, Lee asserted, leaving the "real purpose" of their visit to Gettysburg thwarted. Instead, he suggested, exhibits should be limited to providing only necessary background, emphasizing "why the battle was fought, how it was fought, and the importance of that engagement in our national history." Other top-level officials concurred that an NPS museum's central purpose was "to draw the visitor to the field," and the agency must continue to place primary emphasis on the on-site experience. Lee also charged that expanded orientation at Gettysburg ran counter to the priorities for Civil War parks established under Mission 66. So long as each park did as projected and established an adequate museum, a larger one was not necessary.[26]

By early 1957, Daniel Tobin remained the only outspoken voice for a comprehensive museum at Gettysburg, arguing that a successful interpretive experience required historical context. "Battlefields, like many other types of historic remains," he observed, "convey nothing by themselves to the uninformed." While he acknowledged the importance of getting visitors out on the field, he argued that unmediated access to the historic resource was unlikely to produce much in terms of educational value. In order to engage in a constructive and meaningful way with the battlefield, visitors needed an understanding of the conflict as a whole, not just the Gettysburg campaign. To those who insisted that Gettysburg was an inappropriate location for a museum devoted to the entire war, Tobin argued that "it is the Civil War battle whose importance is appreciated by the man in the street." The regional director predicted that future generations would likely view the Gettysburg Address as "the most significant value" associated with the American Civil War, assuring the site's primacy of place well into the future.[27] Ultimately,

Lee's argument triumphed; Tobin's vision of a museum that would contextualize the battlefield by setting it in the context of the larger war would not be realized at Gettysburg until 2008, with the opening of the Gettysburg Museum of the American Civil War.

Interpretive planner John Littleton proposed later in 1957 that the NPS abandon the effort to establish a central space for visitor orientation at Gettysburg and instead construct three smaller facilities. Littleton argued that smaller buildings would meet visitors at disparate points, better serving their needs and eliminating the necessity of marring the landscape with large parking lots. The primary concern underlying the proposal, however, was the National Park Service's visibility and position vis-à-vis the commercial interests competing for visitors' time and attention. Littleton noted in frustration that most visitors "never see the National Park Service, never know who it is that does all the work of keeping the park in such fine condition." Due to the frequency of distinguished visitors touring the field with President Eisenhower, he was particularly concerned about the public relations impact of the NPS's low profile. Littleton hoped that Mission 66 funds might provide an opportunity to rectify the situation. By the end of the year, however, not only did the Washington office not bite on Littleton's proposal, it moved further in the other direction, embracing the model of a one-stop shop for visitor orientation.[28]

James B. Myers was appointed superintendent of Gettysburg National Military Park in 1958. A World War II combat veteran who did graduate work at the University of Virginia, Myers earned a Bronze Star for his performance directing naval gunfire on Okinawa. Two years into his tenure, GNMP released a new master plan utilizing Mission 66 framing to outline the park's future. The plan noted that increasing national interest in the Civil War and the heightened visibility accompanying Eisenhower's association with the area had resulted in a rising visitation trend that might extend past the centennial. In sync with the GBPA's arguments, the report asserted that the town's heightened popularity was "increasing commercial and housing development which, even now, is destroying [Gettysburg's] attractive rural character and detracting from the park itself."[29]

Park historian Harry Pfanz, the plan's author, argued that GNMP must continue to place a premium on acquiring land under threat of development. Furthermore, the park must commit itself to balancing the need to expand visitor comfort facilities and retool park roads for increased traffic with attention to avoiding overdevelopment. Identifying the battle and the Gettysburg Address as the park's primary interpretive themes, Pfanz stressed

GNMP's commitment to restoring park landscapes and buildings to their 1863 appearance and restricting further monumentation on the battlefield, limiting new memorials to "those honoring outstanding persons, units, or groups which participated in the battle."[30] The challenges referenced in this plan—rising visitor numbers, commercialization, development, and a renewed push to populate Confederate battle lines with monuments and memorials—would only intensify throughout the centennial years.

The CWCC and National Commemoration of the War

The decision to go the route of establishing a national commission to coordinate commemorative activities over the course of a four-year period helped pave the way for creation of the U.S. Civil War Centennial Commission (CWCC) in September 1957. Lobbied for by Washington-area business interests, tourism officials, historians, and members of Civil War Round Tables, the commission's rocky track record would bear out Tobin's warning that four years of activities would lead to unseemly celebration, dwindling public interest, partisan debates, and "embarrassing incidents." Consonant with the Eisenhower administration's aims in establishing it, the CWCC repeatedly sought to use the anniversary for Cold War purposes, deploying a particular narrative of Civil War history intended to boost patriotic sentiment and showcase the military heritage, technological superiority, and political culture of the United States for spectators inside and outside its borders. This did not mean, of course, that anniversary architects were able to fully control the parameters of the commemoration, for members of the public always exercise a certain element of control over what narratives they embrace and reject.[31]

Despite the initial enthusiasm for the anniversary, federal funding was limited and the role of the CWCC was defined as a clearinghouse to communicate and coordinate programming planned and funded by state and local bodies. Never missing an opportunity to highlight so-called American virtues, the CWCC encouraged those interested in commemorating the war to proceed in "the true American approach" by organizing locally. The new commission quickly elected Major General Ulysses S. Grant III—the grandson of the Union general—to the chairman's position and appointed businessman Karl Betts, chairman of the District of Columbia Civil War Round Table, executive director. A career military officer and former head of the SUV, Grant embraced the centennial as an opportunity to cultivate patriotism and ward off the spread of "foreign ideologies" in the United States. Though his extremely conservative political views made him popular with many of the commission's members and supporters, they also prevented him from embracing an inclusive vision for the commemoration. Karl Betts's enthusiasm for the centennial was boundless, but his commitment to grand pageantry and broad popular participation and deep aversion to what he deemed "stuffy academic history" would also create issues for the commission down the line.[32]

Hoping to spark a deep emotional connection to the war among members of the general public, Betts championed large-scale battle reenactments, pageants, balls, memorial services, and school programs. He argued that the history of the war offered many avenues for engaging public interest, ranging from ancestral connections and larger-than-life personalities to technological firsts and compelling strategic problems. Escapism, he admitted, played a role in sustaining his own interest in the war, suggesting in 1959 that many Americans might be "seeking an escape hobby, a relief from the worries of the cold war in Berlin and a look back at the hot war of the '60s." The commission's Cold War purpose was crystal clear for Betts. Not only did he see Union and Confederate forces as equal in honor, he believed the war could be used "to prove to the world that we not only know how to fight a war but also how to end it." The reference, of course, alluded to the supposed reconciliation of the postwar years while doubling as a reminder of the nation's military might. In its emphasis on the conflict's role in giving rise to the modern nation, with its advanced technology, strong federal government, and military prowess, the centennial commemorations frequently bore out the truth in Robert Penn Warren's assertion that Americans were too predisposed to regard the Civil War as "part of our divinely instituted success story." Writing in his 1961 meditation on the Civil War's place in the American narrative, *The Legacy of the Civil War*, Warren insightfully observed that it could be easy to fall into thinking "of the dead at Gettysburg as a small price to pay for the development of a really satisfactory and cheap compact car."[33]

Eisenhower extensively employed Cold War language in his proclamation officially opening the anniversary. Framing the war as a "demonstration of heroism and sacrifice by men and women of both sides," the president praised nineteenth-century (ostensibly white) Americans for their "transcending sense of unity and larger common purpose," encouraging the current generation to emulate their example. Not all observers, however, applauded this deployment of Civil War history for patriotic purposes. A host of commentators and left-leaning historians condemned the centennial observance—and particularly the CWCC itself—as money-grubbing, historically inaccurate, racially insensitive, and inappropriately celebratory in tone.[34]

The respected African American historian John Hope Franklin, whose pioneering work on Black history was key to the new scholarly understanding of slavery, emancipation, and Reconstruction emerging during the 1960s, called the centennial a national circus. Franklin questioned why a nation as powerful and ostensibly sophisticated as the United States would "subject itself to ridicule before the entire world with the vulgar reenactment of the Battle of Bull Run." Criticizing the approach to the war as a "glorious game," Dan Wakefield lambasted the centennial in the *Nation* as "the longest, most expensive, most elaborate celebration of tragedy in the history of any civilized country." Lincoln historian Paul Angle ridiculed the crass consumerism of many centennial programs and rebutted the official line that the Civil War's primary legacy was the transformation of the United States into a global symbol of freedom. The young radical historian Jesse Lemisch predicted that "the meaningless pageantry of blue alongside gray" would prove corrosive to the struggle for equal rights.[35]

While many Black Americans were deeply interested in the American Civil War, substantial numbers worried that its commemoration would be at best an exercise in white reconciliation and at worst "an attempt to turn back the clock" by celebrating the Confederate cause. A January 1960 editorial in one of the leading Black newspapers in the nation, the *Afro-American*, criticized the "soft soap and deception" being used by many prominent whites, including President Eisenhower, in their discussion of the war. The paper argued that the "War Between the States" was nothing more than a conceit to placate white southerners who resisted acknowledging "their forefathers as staging a rebellion against the United States to preserve slavery." Historian Lawrence D. Reddick denounced the centennial in April 1961 as an obstacle to the unfolding Black freedom struggle.[36]

National-scale controversy broke out in the winter of 1961 over the CWCC's decision to hold its fourth national gathering in Charleston in April—to coincide with the anniversary of the attack on Fort Sumter—despite the segregation policies that barred Blacks from the city's hotels. In the face of Betts's continued insistence that the national commission had no jurisdiction in the matter and could do nothing to rectify the situation, three state commissions with Black members resolved to boycott the assembly, and civil rights groups such as the NAACP and the Congress of Racial Equality (CORE) began to mobilize their members in protest. The undeniable reality that CWCC was a national commission receiving federal funds propelled a reluctant White House into the controversy. Maneuvering behind the scenes with the assistance of the administration, commission member Bell Wiley finally prevailed on the rest of the group to agree to move the meeting from the Francis Marion Hotel to Charleston's desegregated U.S. naval base. Wiley's solution allowed the event, ultimately deemed "the most disastrous Confederate defeat in South Carolina since 1865," to go forward without protests, but it was wracked by dissention, vitriol, and bad publicity.[37]

In the wake of the Charleston crisis and widespread public criticism of the July 1961 reenactment of the Battle of First Manassas for its commercialism, bad taste, and romanticization of war, Cold War liberals on the CWCC, led by Wiley, maneuvered to dismiss Karl Betts on the grounds that the very survival of the commemoration was at stake. They did not take aim at Grant, despite the fact that he shared Betts's conservative politics and suspicion of professional historians (though the *Afro-American* called on Kennedy to dismiss the commission chairman on the grounds that he had shown himself to be a modern-day Confederate). But Grant refused to go along with the ouster of his junior partner and quickly announced his own resignation. As his successor, Kennedy appointed highly esteemed Civil War historian Allan Nevins, a Cold War liberal committed to a more serious-minded observation of the centennial. James Robertson Jr., a former doctoral student of Bell Wiley, took over the role of executive director, and together the two historians set to work to restore the credibility of the commemoration.[38]

The rapidly approaching anniversary of the Emancipation Proclamation— a political lightning rod— gave Nevins and Robertson little time to regroup. The CWCC commemoration of the proclamation, held at the Lincoln Memorial, moved far away from historical specifics, shifting the focus from the impact of emancipation on American society (which was deemed politicized) to the proclamation's symbolic power as a universal statement of freedom. Cosponsored by the District of Columbia Civil War Centennial Commission, the Lincoln Group of the District of Columbia, and the National Park Service, the ceremony celebrated emancipation as "one event in a worldwide movement . . . for the liberation of the colored peoples of the globe from servitude," but never directly engaged colonialism itself. Attempting to assuage the concerns of southern commissioners that the event would promote civil rights, Nevins stressed that the commemoration would rise "far above petty contentions of the day." Yet in the same breath, he also argued that "in giving it a world-wide significance, we can perhaps at the same time accomplish something for the standing of the United States in the family of nations." Commission staff thus rejected contemporary connections in terms of domestic racial issues as ahistorical and political, yet saw no problem in using the event for the equally contemporary purpose of fighting the Cold War. Indeed, Nevins was confident that the United States Information Agency (USIA) could effectively utilize the program overseas to bolster the nation's public image.[39]

Grassroots Pageantry

Aside from the Emancipation Proclamation event, the CWCC sponsored few programs of its own and thus played only a minor role in the Gettysburg commemoration. Though the governor of Pennsylvania appointed a Gettysburg Centennial Commission (GCC) in 1956 to coordinate plans for commemorating the battle and Lincoln's Gettysburg Address, it was slow to find its footing and the vast majority of the vision and energy driving the Gettysburg centennial in its early years was thus local in origin and focus. The GCC did, however, establish from the outset its commitment to utilizing the anniversary to fight the Cold War, identifying in its first meeting two primary goals for centennial programming: encouraging national unity and "keeping peace through international understanding." Funding challenges beset the commission from the beginning; its operating budget was only $100,000, one-third of the amount originally requested, and its focus was limited to Gettysburg (as opposed to the state's broader relationship with the war), where it planned to mount special programming on July 1 through 4 and November 19, 1963.[40]

Due to the GCC's slow start and exclusive focus on 1963, the prime mover in the early years of the centennial period was the Adams County Civil War Centennial Commission (ACCWCC), established in 1959. Adams County Civil War enthusiasts were confident that the GCC would find its footing in time to adequately commemorate the men who fought at Gettysburg, and thus assigned their own group the responsibility of honoring county residents who served between 1861 and 1865. Aiming to mount at least one major program per year, commission members immediately set to work mapping out a slate of activities that would commemorate the county's role in the war from Fort Sumter to Appomattox.[41]

The ACCWCC kicked off its programming efforts by mounting a large pageant reenacting the events of April 21 and 22, 1861, when the men of the Independent Blues, the first regiment of local men to depart for wartime service, were escorted to the train depot by cheering crowds. Written by a committee of local residents under the direction of Betty Gifford (who had assisted with the 1952 "Mr. Lincoln Goes to Gettysburg" production), the pageant featured a cast of 300, including many prominent local residents in key roles. Sporting sideburns and mustaches, the county commissioners, town council president, and burgess portrayed their 1861 predecessors. The Gettysburg College band filled in for the community band that had performed in 1861, and high school students filled the ranks of the National Cadets, a teenage military group formed with the departure of the Blues. Testimony to the narrowness of the chasm that separated past from present in some cases, Daniel Skelly Jr., the son of the Cadets' captain, portrayed his father.[42]

Reenactors from the North-South Skirmish Association and members of the Sons of Veterans Reserve, the uniformed component of the SUV, represented the soldiers. Residents from around the county played the part of the "cheering crowds," many wearing homemade costumes created with materials purchased by the county commissioners' office to spur public investment in the centennial. The *Gettysburg Times* estimated that more than 3,000 spectators thronged the square to experience the kickoff to the centennial activities.[43]

The ACCWCC mounted two more productions the following year, commemorating a February 1862 flag presentation to the men of the 10th New York Cavalry and J. E. B. Stuart's October 1862 cavalry raids on the towns of Cashtown and Fairfield. Held in the courtroom of the Adams County courthouse, where the New York troops were quartered during their time in town, the pageant featured District Attorney Daniel Teeter in the starring role as the wartime editor of Gettysburg's Democratic newspaper, the *Compiler*. The *Compiler* extensively covered the unit's stay in Gettysburg, and the *Gettysburg Times* accordingly lauded the pageant as one of the most historically accurate ever produced, given the fact that every word of it, except for Teeter's narration, was taken verbatim from the *Compiler*'s coverage.[44]

Held on the Cashtown baseball diamond, the Stuart raid pageant drew participants from veterans' organizations, reactivated Civil War units, and members of local riding clubs. SUV's national commander Major Chester Shriver, a member of the ACCWCC and personal friend of Ulysses S. Grant III, narrated from the podium while the action played out. Looking out over the hills surrounding Cashtown, Shriver connected local history to events playing out on the other side of the globe. "Perhaps here is a lesson for the new nations that are emerging today," he mused, "that they may not blunder into civil war as we did, and be forced to shed brave men's blood to regain their future." Yet the reunion following 1865, he suggested, was the redeeming factor of the war, for it created a nation "far greater than before."[45]

Though tireless in their efforts, the ACCWCC and GBPA were not the only local groups committed to using the centennial to remake Gettysburg. Arguing that making the town appear more historic would bring increased financial gains to downtown businesses, the Gettysburg Junior Chamber of Commerce (better known as the Jaycees) launched a campaign to restore the exterior of the town's downtown business district to its 1863 appearance. Former President Eisenhower, a champion of private, voluntary action as opposed to governmental action, was an important supporter of the project, which was financed by the Jaycees in partnership with the *Saturday Evening Post*. By early 1963, architectural renovations to sixty-four properties were complete, and campaign organizers spearheaded a tree-planting drive to supplement the building work.[46]

The Cold War themes of the commemoration were particularly pronounced in the 1961 Memorial Day ceremonies and the 1962 Dedication Day activities. More than 1,500 local schoolchildren led the Memorial Day procession to the ceremony, where keynote speaker David Lawrence, the governor of Pennsylvania, was joined on the platform by three Soviet veterans. Participants in an Arms of Friendship program devoted to defusing Cold War tensions through maintaining bonds of friendship between American and Russian World War II veterans, the three men were in the midst of a dialogue-themed tour of the United States. One must wonder what they thought of Lawrence's address, which asserted the need to differentiate between the worthiness of a cause and the commitment and courage of those who fight for it.[47]

In order to set up his critique of Communism as antithetical to the exercise of free choice, Lawrence made a case that few wanted to take up when national attention turned to Gettysburg two years later. Identifying slavery as the fundamental cause of the war, he argued—perhaps somewhat erroneously—that few present-day Americans believed that the men of the Army of Northern Virginia were fighting for a just cause. Lest anyone misinterpret his meaning, he continued, "They were seeking to restrict the boundaries of human freedom; they were at odds with their century, with this land's destiny, with our dream of equality for all races and conditions of men." Using this distinction between a good cause and a bad cause, he warned against underestimating the nation's enemies abroad, asserting that "they are brave, skillful, and ruthless; they are dedicated and determined, as convinced in their bad cause as we have come to be in what we hold just and good." It is almost certain that at least some members of the audience balked at this seeming equation of the Confederate cause with totalitarianism.[48]

However, the governor had not yet finished. He proceeded to suggest that the United States should take a lesson from Lincoln and Northern antislavery advocates. While not interfering with Communism in places where it was already rooted, Lawrence argued that the United States should view "the nations of the Atlantic Pact, the troubled countries of Black Africa [and] the lands on the rim of the Asian continent" as free soil and take whatever actions necessary to keep them free from Soviet, Chinese, or Cuban influence. The world must know, Lawrence emphasized, that while not wanting war, Americans did not flinch from the prospect of it and were as ready as their Civil War ancestors had been to sacrifice for the cause of freedom and self-government.[49]

Moving on, Lawrence employed the Cold War lens often utilized by John F. Kennedy to justify the need for civil rights reforms on the grounds that segregation and discrimination frustrated American foreign policy aims and degraded the nation's public image abroad. Referencing the obstruction in Little Rock, the closed schools in Prince Edward County, Virginia, and the mobs and mass jailing confronting Freedom Riders across the South, he argued that "we will hold the allegiance of other peoples or lose their confidence by our own performance in our own society." Though quick to (inaccurately) praise Pennsylvania for having no segregated schools or white supremacist groups, he reminded northerners of the persistence of discrimination in employment and housing across the region. Lawrence charged listeners to take up fighting these forms of racial discrimination as their own contribution to the cause championed by the Union dead. For all his strong words, however, Lawrence did little to further the cause of racial justice — particularly in the realm of fair housing — after his appointment a few months later as head of the President's Committee on Equal Opportunity.[50]

A more Republican interpretation of the commemoration's Cold War purpose found expression later that year in the traditional ceremony marking November 19 as Dedication Day, the anniversary of Lincoln's Gettysburg Address. Senator Everett Dirksen (R-Illinois) delivered the annual address at the National Cemetery, challenging Americans to abandon their fears and timidity, toughen up, and continue to wage the never-finished fight for human freedom. Reflecting Republican opposition to social welfare programs, Dirksen sternly chided those committed to a more expanded and active role for the U.S. government, deeming such proposals dangerous to individual liberties; his exhortations on the subject were similar to those expressed by Dwight Eisenhower throughout the centennial years. Dirksen exhorted his listeners to "assert freedom's cause under God to all the world with the same vigor and purpose which marked the course of [Abraham Lincoln]."[51]

Bruce Catton Connects the Civil War and Cold War

Though Dirksen's speech played an important role in the November 1962 ceremonies, the dominant voice of the observance was that of Bruce Catton, the most popular Civil War historian of the era. Long convinced that the Civil War could impart moral purpose to the Cold War struggle, Catton's public remarks that week revealed a man laboring to process how his growing support for the Black freedom struggle could intertwine with the strain and fear exacted by an event such the recent Cuban missile crisis in shaping his understanding of the contemporary lessons of the war. A major player in centennial programming nationwide, Catton was Gettysburg College's inaugural Fortenbaugh Lecturer in 1962. The college's Civil War programming shifted that year from a pattern of multiday, multipresenter Civil War conferences to a named lecture series featuring an eminent Civil War scholar. More than fifty years later, the Robert Fortenbaugh Memorial Lecture continues to be delivered each fall on the anniversary date of November 19. Catton gave three lectures during his time in Gettysburg, speaking on "The Gettysburg Address—A Revolutionary Manifesto" on November 18, and "The Irrepressible Centennial" and the Emancipation Proclamation on November 19.[52]

Though moderate in his political opinions and deeply committed to Cold War liberalism and the belief that history justified Americans' liberal faith and capacity to lead the world, by 1963 Catton's increasing sympathy with the civil rights movement had begun to shift some of his assumptions about the relationship between the war and the cause of Black freedom. A capacity crowd packed the college's Christ Chapel on November 18 to hear the first of Catton's three addresses, in which he argued that though the original aims of the Civil War were conservative, the conflict quickly took on a revolutionary nature due to the centrality that slavery rapidly assumed in supporting the war aims of both armies.[53]

Catton openly acknowledged that wartime America was hardly prepared for the concept that freedom from slavery would mean "total freedom," noting that "we then looked on America as a sort of exclusive club," where full membership was provided only to white Protestants. He argued that the task Lincoln set for himself at Gettysburg was to expand the definition of freedom and remake the nation as a union open to everyone who sought to belong to it. While briefly acknowledging that 100 years after the war this expanded definition of freedom had still not been realized in every part of the country (including the north), he pointed his audience toward a global context. "We are living now in the middle of a world revolution," he stressed, thus only by working to secure freedom for others across the globe would Americans protect it for themselves. Only then would "our observances of the centennial of the Battle of Gettysburg, the Gettysburg Address, and the whole Civil War" be worth anything. Yet Catton drew specific lines around the definition of freedom. Criticizing the sentiment "Better Red Than Dead" by quoting a line from the spiritual "O Freedom," he questionably employed the voice of an enslaved African American in a critique of the struggles of subordinated people worldwide.[54]

The following morning in his speech "The Irrepressible Centennial," Catton warned listeners to guard against becoming prisoners of the war's romance and the gimmickry and commercialization of the centennial, and thus failing to see the "deep, tragic issues" that precipitated the conflict and resulted in such a profound loss of life. These were slightly ironic words, given that Catton's own enormously popular writings were full of romantic imagery and lyrical language. Historian David Blight has argued that Catton's books made readers "love" the war "in an age when war, with its unfathomable destructiveness, was no longer lovable." Catton's books portrayed men "willing to sacrifice their lives for something larger than themselves—a story with particular resonance in the Cold War era of inhumane, push-button weapons of mass destruction."[55]

Catton encouraged listeners to remember the war as the force that brought about the industrialization of America, eliminated slavery, and propelled the nation to greatness. Criticizing the tendency to minimize the issues at stake in the conflict by focusing exclusively on combat heroics and good fellowship between North and South, he argued that the war was neither a "tournament" of combatants nor a "brothers' war" with no real root cause. Instead, "the Civil War was about something. It was fought for something. And let us never forget that it won something." The Civil War, he stressed, was fought over slavery, and its resolution—emancipation—liberated both Blacks and whites alike. Though Catton believed deeply in the power of Civil War history as a unifying force, in this speech, he refused to allow the goal of unity to keep him from criticizing attempts to use the memory of the war to impede progress on civil rights.[56]

Marking Confederate Space

Despite GNMP's new master plan explicitly calling for the limitation of new memorials on the battlefield, the centennial period brought an intense acceleration of Confederate memorialization along West Confederate Avenue. The first of five major Confederate monuments erected along the avenue between 1961 and 1965—and the one that symbolically paved the way for the others—was commissioned by the state of Georgia, which dedicated identical battlefield monuments at Antietam and Gettysburg in September 1961. The Gettysburg monument—a 16-foot column of Georgia blue granite—was located roughly 100 yards south of the West Confederate Avenue observation tower, near the spot where Georgia divisions massed to attack on July 2. The United Daughters of the Confederacy (UDC) was the primary driving force behind the erection of both monuments, with Gertrude Kibler of Atlanta serving as chair of the Georgia Centennial Committee. Both of these projects proceeded more quickly than usual, with only minimal review by the National Park Service. The abbreviation of the timeline was likely due in part to the committee preemptively inviting former President Eisenhower and CWCC chairman Grant to the dedication ceremonies before permission was in hand.[57]

The Georgia delegation at the Gettysburg dedication ceremony included high-level UDC officials, state governor Ernest Vandiver, and representatives of both the Sons of Confederate Veterans (SCV) and the Southeast Georgia Brigade (made up of the descendants of Union soldiers who moved south after the war). The ceremony for the first state monument dedicated at Gettysburg in more than thirty years (and the fourth erected by a formerly Confederate state) referenced the Cold War as openly as Governor David Lawrence had done in his speech at the cemetery four months earlier, but unlike Lawrence, conflated courage and cause. Much attention was devoted to balancing national and Confederate symbols; the band played both the "Star-Spangled Banner" and "Dixie," and UDC leaders led the group in two pledges of allegiance, the first to the American flag and the second to the First National Flag of the Confederacy. In his dedication address, Governor Vandiver echoed the oft-expressed idea that the memory of the Civil War could serve as a uniting force for Americans in challenging times. He argued that "never in our history has there been such a need for this nation to present to the world a united front so impregnable that no Communist, no American-Nazi, no agitator group, no lunatic fringe, can even pin-prick our armor of solidarity."[58]

But on what terms would that united front be maintained? By equating the Confederate cause and banner with those of the Union? By embracing the smoldering sentiments inscribed on the state's new monument—perhaps allowed to slip through due to the extreme time crunch under which the approval process took place? The column dedicated read: "WE SLEEP HERE IN OBEDIENCE TO LAW. WHEN DUTY CALLED, WE CAME. WHEN COUNTRY CALLED, WE DIED." The country and laws referenced on the monument were not those of the United States. In most of the other monuments dedicated during the centennial period, approval of inscriptions was handled separately from approval of design. In Georgia's case there was no separate approval process for the inscription, which perhaps at least partially explains why there is no record of concerns being raised about the language.

Vandiver lauded the growing economic and political power of the South, insisting that "we stand upright, full-statured, and equal among the people of the earth." Few attendees likely missed the implicit argument that the (white) South had the right to determine its own destiny, yet Vandiver himself knew both the range and limits of his power as governor to maintain traditional racial politics. Despite campaigning on a slogan of "No, Not One," he had opposed efforts to close the University of Georgia in the wake of court-ordered desegregation in January 1961, and convinced the state legislature to abandon its plans to close K-12 schools as a tool of massive resistance. Yet white Georgians had many avenues available to them to resist, and in the months following the monument dedication, residents of the city of Albany would almost completely stymie the efforts of Black activists to overturn segregation, dealing the civil rights movement a heavy blow. NPS northeast regional director Ronald Lee's speech formally accepting the monument on the behalf of the U.S. government echoed Vandiver's assertion that the memory of the Civil War could serve as a uniting force, calling upon Americans to honor their country's history and "govern ourselves by the historic principles that have made this nation the leader of the free world."[59]

BOTH PRIDE IN AND CONCERN FOR the United States' place in the world hovered in the background of the early centennial years in Gettysburg. Collectively, preservationists, NPS officials, local residents, political leaders and southern heritage groups undertook a process of redefining the community's physical and interpretive landscape for political, economic, and foreign policy purposes. The preservationist cause gathered traction and the Georgia Centennial Committee placed the first of the centennial-era Confederate monuments on the battlefield, paving the way for four more in the next four years and the widespread transformation of West Confederate Avenue by the following decade. Though NPS officials' bold vision of Gettysburg as the rightful focus of the national commemoration of the war did not come to fruition, it further solidified the conviction that Gettysburg was the military and spiritual hinge point of the Civil War, an icon that could restore the nation's moral supremacy on the world stage. By the end of 1962, this idea would take tangible architectural form.

CHAPTER THREE

A Shrine for the Free World

The Cold War Vision of Neutra's Cyclorama Building

The November 19 dedication of internationally acclaimed architect Richard Neutra's Cyclorama Building as Gettysburg National Military Park's first visitor center marked the high point of commemorative activities in 1962. Until its demolition in 2013, the Cyclorama Building would stand as permanent testimony to the influence of Cold War politics on the evolving narrative of Gettysburg and the ways that narrative took concrete form during the centennial years. Far more than simply a facility to orient and service visitors, the building was described in the advent of its dedication as, among other things, a living monument to Abraham Lincoln, a centennial memorial, and Mission 66's central contribution to the Civil War Centennial. The architect held it up as a shrine for the free world and a tool for enhancing national security and supporting the goal of world peace. Others presented it more modestly, as a modern home for GNMP's central interpretive device: Paul Philippoteaux's 1884 cyclorama painting. The wide range of identities and expectations embedded in Neutra's building provide a snapshot of the diverse purposes for which historical memory was employed during the Gettysburg centennial. Accordingly, a close examination of the planning and construction process reveals the extent to which commemoration of this anniversary unfolded in an increasingly global context, charged with supporting the achievement of American foreign policy goals abroad.

MISSION 66 REINVENTED THE NPS FOR VISITORS, expending nearly $1 billion in land acquisition, new construction, and expanded payrolls and giving birth to the modern visitor center, a multipurpose facility devoted to meeting the educational and practical needs of automobile-based visitors. As established in the last chapter, Civil War parks were a particularly high priority for Mission 66 projects. Congress authorized two new Civil War parks (Pea Ridge and Wilson's Creek) during the Mission 66 years and added 3,000 acres to existing ones. Major restoration projects began at Ford's Theatre and Harpers Ferry, and high-profile sites such as Gettysburg, Chancellorsville, Appomattox Court House, and Antietam received new visitor centers.[1]

For all of its accomplishments, Mission 66 also sparked controversy, leading to criticism that the NPS was overdeveloping the parks, prioritizing visitor
access and ease above responsible preservation practice. In Gettysburg, the
decision to locate the new visitor center in Ziegler's Grove was fundamentally
driven by accessibility concerns, not landscape preservation. Though then-
park superintendent J. Walter Coleman acknowledged that a new building would be an intrusion on the historic landscape, the argument that a
visitor center "should be placed where it will do the most good on behalf of
the visitors" carried the day.[2]

As the architectural prospectus for the building took shape, northeast
regional director Daniel Tobin articulated the NPS's original philosophy
toward its design: "I view the proposed Visitor Center not as an incongruous building intruding on the historic scene, but as an appropriate Centennial memorial fully as fitting for prominence in the park as the many and
varied types of commemorative monuments that now dot this great Battlefield." (Ironically, by the early twenty-first century, preservationists would
use the argument that the building was indeed an incongruous intrusion on
the historic landscape to justify its removal.) Others soon added their voices
to the growing consensus that the building should be "of a memorial nature,"
distinct from any other building in the community—or in the NPS itself.[3]

GNMP staff felt strongly that the Cyclorama Building should include a
rooftop observation deck that would allow visitors to connect the painting
to the landscape itself. Their other priorities included a large lobby, restrooms, office space, and a sizable auditorium. Park interpreters insisted
that the program be fully automatic, controlled by a single button in the ticket
booth. Rejecting the idea of a revolving platform for the painting (as employed in Atlanta, home to the nation's other publicly accessible Civil War
cyclorama), assistant regional director George Palmer, suggested simple
swivel chairs instead. In an early manifestation of the idea that the visitor
experience should be participatory, he suggested that controlling their own
chairs would "give the visitors a feeling of personally participating in the presentations as against having it 'dished' out to them." In the final plan, the
building would include the cyclorama gallery, three lounges, an auditorium,
and the park administrative offices.[4]

A Building for Eternity

The contract to design the building was awarded to the Los Angeles–based
firm of Neutra & Alexander in 1958. Richard Neutra was the most critically

acclaimed architect to work with Mission 66, and the two buildings he produced for the NPS during these years—the GNMP Cyclorama Building and the Painted Desert Community—were lauded by critics as stunning works of modern architecture. As work began, Neutra deemed the cyclorama job "the greatest work I've ever undertaken." When challenged as to why the NPS had not selected a local architect for the job, NPS director Conrad Wirth stressed Neutra & Alexander's international reputation and the complexity of the design. High-ranking NPS officials were thrilled with the final product; Ronald Lee praised Neutra at the building's dedication ceremony as one of the world's most creative architects. From the beginning, Neutra embraced a grand vision for the building, framing it as a living monument to Abraham Lincoln and a teaching tool for democracy. In a December 1959 briefing for the subcontractors engaged to work on the project, the architect grandiosely proclaimed that the building "will last forever. . . . It is a building for eternity because it has deeper characters than any of the finest ancient buildings of the world."[5] These words did not prove prophetic; in the wake of a prolonged battle over the structure's architectural significance, the Cyclorama Building was razed in 2013.

Richard Neutra's modernist designs were known for their emphasis on harmony between architectural design and natural settings. Built of reinforced concrete and native stone, the Gettysburg structure was nestled into the hill to reduce its intrusion on the historic skyline of Cemetery Ridge, and the outdoor gathering area was designed to utilize a natural "bowl-like" area. The exterior included a recreation of a dry creek bed full of boulders, fragments of historic fences and broken pieces of a gun carriage. The design also placed a great deal of emphasis on the incorporation of modern technology. In addition to the high-tech equipment employed in the presentation of the painting, the building also featured automatic louvered blinds that self-adjusted as the sun progressed across the sky and buttons that retracted interior and exterior walls alike, opening up the auditorium space for large-scale indoor/outdoor programs. In its prime, the Cyclorama Building was a showpiece for midcentury modernism and space-age design; in its early years, people who worked in it referred to it as the Starship Enterprise. By situating space-age technology at the heart of the battlefield landscape (the building was located at the midpoint between the Angle, Meade's headquarters, and the National Cemetery), the structure embodied a message about the advantages of Western capitalism and the superiority of American political principles as expressed in the Gettysburg Address.[6]

The Park Service's press release for the building's dedication ceremony emphasized "the new era of human freedom which began with President Lincoln's restatement of America's principles" over the graves of the Union dead. In the eyes of those who designed and dedicated the Cyclorama Building, the central reason the Battle of Gettysburg mattered was because it gave Lincoln a platform to make meaning out of suffering. In so doing, he articulated a vision of the United States as the world's shining example of "government of the people, by the people, for the people." At the height of the Cold War, this was an interpretation of America's place in the world that was tailor-made for export. Neutra's vision of "technological diplomacy" and international dialogue was, however, somewhat less hawkish than the CWCC's militant claims of American supremacy.[7]

The architect and his team hoped that the Cyclorama Building would become a place for foreign leaders to learn about American democracy and build political ties with the United States, and specifically formulated his design to accommodate an annual program devoted to building peace among nations in a world threatened with atomic annihilation. Neutra envisioned that a different international leader (including some from Communist countries) could be invited each year to share ideas about ways to defuse Cold War tensions and deter nuclear war. Championing his design as "a shrine for the free world," he nonetheless asserted that the world leaders would need to keep their speeches brief "because the building itself is most important and comes first." Architecturally, the structure itself was constructed around a feature that Neutra billed as "a prophetic rostrum." His finished product was a building laden with symbolism and infused with Cold War purpose.[8]

From a design standpoint, Neutra believed that the "drum" of the cyclorama gallery needed to be balanced with as long a "tail" as possible. Architect Fred Esenwein has argued that the placement of the administrative wing (the "tail") served to separate the action on the Third Day's battlefield from the sacred space of the Soldiers' National Cemetery, and that the white of the rotunda was meant to be reminiscent of white marble, signifying the building's identity as a memorial. He has also suggested that the tinted glass in the windows served to evoke the idea of memory—gesturing to historical figures no longer physically present, but nonetheless inscribed on the landscape. Esenwein has intriguingly posited that Neutra's design was a visual realization of interpretive pioneer Freeman Tilden's charge to the NPS to "animate" the agency's resources. Yet the architect's priorities and those of his NPS client did not always line up, as revealed in a 1960 dispute over color in restroom facilities. Implicitly comparing the building to the Taj Mahal, Independence Hall, and the Lincoln Memorial, Neutra & Alexander insisted on a muted color scheme befitting the dignity of the structure. NPS representatives, on the other hand, argued that color-accented exterior doors for the restrooms were an imperative from a visitor services standpoint.[9]

The design team recognized that technology—in the form of the atomic bomb—could destroy the world. Neutra and his compatriots also believed, however, that technology could strengthen national security through attracting allies whose desire for space age technology and fear of nuclear war would lead them to embrace Western political principles such as democracy and capitalism. Many Black Americans, of course, questioned whether a democracy that maintained two-tier citizenship would prove an attractive model to the rest of the world. In a 1962 address at the New York Civil War Centennial Commission's commemoration of the Emancipation Proclamation, Martin Luther King Jr. argued that space-age technology could not obscure the existence of racial injustice. All the superhighways and Telstars in the world would not entice emergent nations in Asia and Africa toward the United States, he insisted, not until the nation began living up to its lofty political principles. "The touchstone is not the sophistication of our industrial devices," King maintained, "but our commitment to freedom and equality. Without faith that we are wedded to these truths, our power and strength become a menace to other peoples and they will maintain their distance until we have justified their confidence."[10]

The contract to construct the building—comprising a circular drum, reflecting pool, spiral ramp, symbolic rostrum, and museum/administrative wing—was awarded to Orndorff Construction Company in October 1959, with the hope that it would be finished in time for the opening of the centennial in 1961. But the process moved more slowly than anticipated. Schedules failed to align; necessary alterations to the design and the architects' insistence on the use of specific materials caused delays; the concrete procured for the project was faulty; the weather frequently proved uncooperative; and the "unique architectural concept" of the structure created substantial challenges for the construction crew. NPS staff frequently expressed their frustration with the slow pace of the project, particularly in light of their need to coordinate the hanging of the painting, plan a dedication ceremony, and execute a move from their current headquarters. Myers noted in irritation in June 1960 that 48 percent of the original contract period had passed, yet the project was only 8 percent complete. The

NPS-appointed project manager frequently alluded in his reports to inclement weather, poor work ethic, and ineffective supervision. The end date for the contract was pushed back several times and costs ballooned.[11]

Conservation work on the Philippoteaux painting, which was cracked and flaking despite previous stabilization efforts, began in 1959 and was carried out by a team headed by NPS preservation specialist Walter Nitkiewicz. Working from a workshop constructed within the old cyclorama facility on East Cemetery Hill, the team removed the painting section by section, facing each with paste and mulberry paper to protect the pigmentation, and secured the whole thing to a new canvas woven on a special loom in Belgium. They then removed the mulberry paper and cleaned the entire painting with turpentine and special cleansing agents. Nitkiewicz experimented with varnishing the painting, but ultimately decided not to proceed with the treatment. It was quickly determined that it would not be practical to replace the missing twelve-foot section lost before the painting arrived in Gettysburg in 1913, and that the conservationists should focus instead on improving the juncture surrounding the existing gap. The question of how to store and transport the enormous canvas was a difficult one, necessitating special equipment built specifically for the purpose. In April 1961, the canvas was rehung in its new climate-controlled home and retouched. This $70,000 restoration project was performed according to the highest conservation standards of the time, although some of the procedures were later deemed to have had a deleterious effect.[12]

Neutra initially suggested that three different prerecorded programs be offered in the cyclorama drum, but NPS officials decided that one would be sufficient. Even with this reduced scope, the plan for a prerecorded program was a departure from the practice in the old Cyclorama Building, where the presentation was provided by a live narrator (a continuation of the original 1880s practice of having a veteran narrate). An early prospectus identified the program theme as "the climax of battle," and encouraged the inclusion of a dramatic reading of the Gettysburg Address as a means of demonstrating the significance of the battle. Staff recommended following the narration with an opportunity for visitors to examine the painting in more detail. By 1960, all concerned were agreed that the program should be "inspirational, mood-setting, and evocative," and that the price of admission should be raised as soon as possible.[13]

Recorded in October 1961 and revised based on audience feedback, the program promised visitors a chance to experience the sights and sounds of battle, including a soundtrack of gunfire and shouts. Another rerecording was made in June 1963 but tabled pending changes to the script. Like most park programming from the centennial era, the early cyclorama programs revolved around the narrative of the High Water Mark, beginning with the moment Confederate forces — described as a "small band of heroes" — broke through the Union lines on July 3. In language sure to gratify many white southerners, Pickett's Charge was repeatedly described as a "glorious defeat" and a "magnificent failure," and the actions of the Union Army were only briefly mentioned. By 1963, the influence of the High Water Mark narrative had moved GNMP far from its Unionist origins. Decades of emphasis on the Army of Northern Virginia's actions on July 3 as the key moment of the engagement had turned the battle into a story of gallantry and heroism in defeat in which the victors were relegated to a secondary role.[14]

Official visits to the park by Department of the Interior officials and members of Congress spiked in fall 1961 as work on the building continued. Coming in at a final price tag of $1,750,000, it formally opened to the public on a regular basis on March 18, 1962, although the work still to be done was substantial enough to warrant delaying the dedication ceremony to the fall. The Sons of Union Veterans deemed the new visitor center "the most beautiful of all National Park Headquarters," and an aide to Pennsylvania governor David Lawrence lauded it as possibly the state's finest public building. More than 1,200 people, mostly local, attended the open house on March 17. Members of the National Park System Advisory Board visited in early May, and 400 attendees from the National Governors' Conference, held nearby in Hershey, came through on July 1. The cyclorama sound and light program began operation three days later, on July 4. Visitation numbers for the battle anniversary month averaged 80,000, nearly 20 percent of those whose attendance was recorded on that battlefield that month.[15]

Just prior to the completion of the building, Daniel Beard, chief of the NPS's Division of Interpretation, assured a high school teacher from Ohio that the new visitor center would greatly improve the average visitor's experience at Gettysburg. The teacher had written to complain that battlefield guides frequently gave presentations that were far too technical for students; in his response Beard assured her that the new exhibits, slide presentation, and cyclorama program would provide all visitors the necessary background to understand the battle. The final version of the slide presentation Beard referenced was a sixteen-minute overview of the three days' fight. The exhibits he praised were located at the base of the painting drum and made up of approximately thirty display cases narrating the story of Gettysburg, and four dioramas depicting aspects of the battle.[16]

The decision regarding how to locate the painting and the museum displays in relationship to each other had been a complicated one. Neutra had pushed back against the original plan to have the displays and the painting structured chronologically, with visitors entering the cyclorama gallery after viewing the events of the Third Day of the battle, and opposed the idea of ending the visitors' experience with the painting. Instead, he proposed positioning the ramp so that the visitor's experience began with the painting (thus offering an easy exit for those uninterested in seeing the rest of the museum), then moved into the dioramas and displays narrating the history of the Gettysburg campaign, and culminated with the Gettysburg Address.[17]

For Neutra, positioning the painting at the beginning of the museum experience would allow it "to emerge out of its darkness to its weird confusion" and render the museum displays a sort of flashback, explaining how the armies arrived on the field of Pickett's Charge. Neutra envisioned that the climax of the visitor's experience would take place around his prophetic rostrum, illuminated by an almost ceremonial spotlight. He enthusiastically noted that "this climactic part of the total space indoors and outdoors will over the decades be hollowed [sic] by the memory of speakers of world stature, who will be heard from the same rostrum from which Lincoln's Address sounds out." On a practical level, while some visitors might see the rostrum in use by one of his envisioned speakers or hear a recording of the address played, the majority would not. Neutra thus advised the Park Service to consider inscribing the text of Lincoln's speech on the wall, but his clients ultimately chose to include only one phrase, "shall not perish from the earth." Neutra told colleagues at an early stage in the project that high-ranking Park Service officials favored his proposed plan for the interior, noting that they were "greatly interested in making this Gettysburg building group such a spiritual center to receive world significant speakers as a good will program of the free world." However, by the time the building opened, the NPS focus shifted away from Neutra's vision of global dialogue, and consequently, more visitors encountered the address through the cyclorama program than through the prophetic rostrum.[18]

Subjects for three of the four dioramas were chosen in December 1959: Confederate general John B. Gordon offering wounded Union general Francis Barlow a drink of water, Confederate and Union troops engaged in hand-to-hand combat on the slope of Little Round Top, and General Meade's late-night council of war. As part of the research process underlying the creation of the diorama depicting the fabled (and possibly apocryphal) Barlow-Gordon incident, Harry Pfanz contacted General Barlow's son Charles in an attempt to answer some key questions about Gordon's story, but Charles Barlow's response made it clear that his knowledge of his father's experience at Gettysburg was limited. Determined to push back against the popular tendency to romanticize the war, regional office staff suggested the inclusion of a quote from Allan Nevins emphasizing the "tragic" nature of the conflict, arguing that attributing the statement to Nevins would help protect the NPS from the anger of "those who might object to our seeming to take the glory out of the war."[19]

The fall of 1962 was a tumultuous time in American history. In September, the violent standoff over desegregation at the University of Mississippi incited sharp criticism from around the world, particularly in the aftermath of the death of a French reporter covering the crisis. Russell Baker, a columnist for the *New York Times*, lampooned Mississippi segregationists in a satirical piece describing the state's secession from the United States, struggle to make it on its own, and subsequent return to the Union, all the while still denouncing the federal government for trampling on states' rights. Baker explained sarcastically that Mississippi had no recourse to the UN, "having walked out of the world organization after the General Assembly rejected its motion to have all African delegates permanently reseated in the rear of the hall," and could not get Soviet aid without "placing the state police under Red Army command."[20]

The following month, the discovery of Soviet missiles in Cuba brought the world closer to nuclear war than it had ever been before. The Soviet military buildup in Cuba was prompted by the desire to give the American people a taste of the close-range nuclear threat that the United States' Jupiter missiles in Turkey posed to the Soviet Union. Other important motivating factors included equalizing the balance of power between the United States and the USSR, and in the wake of the Bay of Pigs fiasco, protecting an ally from potential military invasion. Soviet premier Nikita Khrushchev, who toured the Gettysburg battlefield with Eisenhower in 1959, wrote Kennedy on the climactic day of the crisis: "You are worried over Cuba. You say that it worries you because it lies at a distance of ninety miles across the sea from the shores of the United States. However, Turkey lies next to us. . . . Do you believe you have the right to demand security for your country and the removal of such weapons that you qualify as offensive, while not recognizing this right for us?" Determined to get the missiles out of Cuba and act forcefully enough to forestall another challenge in Berlin, while simultaneously avoiding war, the Kennedy administration instituted a naval blockade to prevent the shipment of military supplies to Cuba and began preparing the armed forces for action.[21]

Gettysburg resident Terry Fox and his dormmates at nearby Shippensburg University crowded into the building's basement to watch Kennedy address the nation at the zenith of the crisis. Fox's fear that if the United States went to war over the missiles, he and his friends—young and single—would be among the first drafted remains clear in his memory today. Aware that he could protect neither the missiles nor the Cuban government in the event of an American attack, Khrushchev ultimately ended the tense standoff by withdrawing the missiles in return for an American pledge not to invade Cuba and confidential assurance that the Jupiter missiles would soon be removed from Turkey.[22]

Four weeks after the highpoint of the crisis, Neutra's Cyclorama Building was formally dedicated before a crowd of some 300 on the anniversary of the Gettysburg Address. This last event in a day full of ceremonies included brief speeches from Chester Shriver, representing the Lincoln Fellowship of Pennsylvania, Lt. Governor John Morgan Davis, GNMP superintendent James Myers, Congressman George Goodling, and a dedicatory address by NPS director Conrad Wirth. James Myers confidently predicted that the new building would be the most-used visitor center in the NPS system by the end of the year. Northeast regional director Ronald Lee welcomed the crowd by stressing the educational value of the new structure. "Today we gather," said Lee, "to dedicate this exceptional building to the interpretation—for future generations—of the meaning of that battle in which those men gave their lives." As noted in the previous chapter, Lee had been the central force behind the effort to keep the museum's narrative focused tightly on Gettysburg, thus ensuring that visitors searching for the "meaning" of the battle would have a harder time understanding it within the broader context of the war.[23]

NPS officials went out of their way to emphasize the building as "the outstanding Mission 66 contribution toward the observance of the Civil War Centennial." The program for the dedication ceremony highlighted the Mission 66 connection and the impetus to invite James Robertson as the official representative of the CWCC lay in a desire to draw broad attention to the agency's "permanent contribution" to the preservation and interpretation of Civil War history. NPS director Conrad Wirth concentrated his remarks on two themes: Lincoln at Gettysburg and the need for continued preservation efforts to protect the community's historic assets. Beyond suggesting that the Gettysburg Address was regularly memorized by children across the globe, Wirth did not allude in any way to Neutra's vision of the building as a key player in Cold War politics, or the idea, popular with his colleagues, that the visitor center itself was a piece of memorial architecture. It was left to Congressman George Goodling to connect the dedication to Cold War politics. Gazing toward the National Cemetery and alluding to Lincoln's words—and likely the events of the previous two months—he warned the audience that "freedom and sacrifice—then as now—are inseparable." In the aftermath of the ceremony, staff and volunteers provided tours of the building, hosted a reception in the lobby, and offered a special showing of the cyclorama program.[24]

Neutra's building was initially very well received. NPS museum specialist John Jenkins prominently featured photos of the building and its exhibits in a presentation on NPS museums for the American Association of Museums 1963 annual meeting. The architectural critic Wolf Von Eckardt praised it lavishly as "quietly monumental but entirely unsentimental," applauding the NPS for its recent advocacy of architectural excellence. Von Eckardt was delighted to see an architect of Neutra's caliber employed on a government project and praised the new visitor center as a manifestation of cultural effectiveness, well suited to its functional purpose of letting the visitor know "at once where he is, why he is there and where the toilet is." The building proved extremely popular with visitors as well, though the design was not universally acclaimed, with some observers characterizing it as derivative of the Guggenheim Museum.[25]

Yet for all the praise it garnered, the much-anticipated building posed challenges from the beginning for those charged with its day-to-day maintenance. Ronald Lee was initially displeased by the quality of the slide presentation, insisting that it was hardly "commensurate with the quality of the building in which it is to be presented—the largest, most costly, and most modern Visitor Center in the National Park System." Issues with the louvers, staircase, and dehumidifier all developed before the end of 1962; the problems with the staircase were serious enough that NPS architects discussed requesting the contractor's bonding company to intervene. Driving rainstorms the following year resulted in serious leaks in the auditorium ceiling.[26]

By the end of the centennial period, even bigger problems associated with the roof and the sliding doors emerged. The reflecting pools had to be removed due to leaks and the jamming of the doors caused by the settling of the foundation effectively destroyed the space's ability to fulfill Neutra's vision of world-renowned speakers addressing indoor/outdoor crowds. Though park staff were relieved to have the structure declared architecturally sound, by 1965, the maintenance department had a significant backlog of deferred maintenance projects, a pattern that over the course of time further eroded the building's ability to function as designed.[27]

In the wake of the visitor center's completion, Gettysburg became a frequent destination point for foreign dignitaries, military officers, and educators affiliated with Cold War diplomatic, readiness, and peace-building programs. The spring of 1963 brought former Secretary of State Dean Acheson and his wife and a Cabinet official from Nyasaland (now Malawi), whose visit was organized by the State Department. The Department of Health, Education, and Welfare international teacher development program brought forty Puerto Rican teachers the following October for a battlefield visit, tour of the visitor center, and viewing of the cyclorama program. The NPS Division of International Affairs facilitated the visits of the assistant secretary of the Hong Kong Colonial Secretariat in July 1965, and twelve Peruvian diplomats the following month.[28]

GNMP RECORDED 1,904,021 VISITORS IN 1962, and ended the year with a landmark new home twenty years in the making.[29] Yet the practical challenges and expensive maintenance costs of Neutra's building soon eroded NPS commitment to the original vision of a functional centennial memorial that would carve out a space for modernism on the battlefield's commemorative landscape and enter into a meaningful dialogue with older architectural forms. The new visitor center quickly shed its symbolic identity and became a utilitarian space. Yet long after the Cold War vision animating the structure's design passed from public memory, the building remained a central player in shaping the park's interpretive programming, visitor services plan, and management of the battlefield landscape.

The original decision to place a modern building on historically significant ground was driven by concern for prioritizing visitor access and belief that the cyclorama painting could be displayed to its best educational effect on the portion of the field that its canvas depicts. For decades, that building's presence in Ziegler's Grove contributed to keeping GNMP's narrative firmly fixed on the concept of the High Water Mark, ultimately becoming one of the biggest obstacles to the park's efforts to restore the battlefield landscape to its 1863 appearance. By the early twenty-first century, the building's intrusion on the surrounding historic landscape would serve as the primary justification for its removal, but at the height of the Cold War, the incongruity was deliberate.

CHAPTER FOUR

1963

All Eyes on Gettysburg

In May 1963, the vice president of the United States, Lyndon B. Johnson, used Gettysburg as a platform to deliver his first major speech in support of equal rights for Black Americans. Standing among the headstones of the National Cemetery, the vice president argued that the nation must remember that justice is a vigil every bit as important as the vigil of peace. Justice, Johnson insisted, "is a vigil we must keep in our own streets and schools, and among the lives of all our people, so that those who died here on their native soil shall not have died in vain."[1] Unexpectedly sworn into office six months later as the nation's thirty-sixth president, Johnson would preside over an unprecedented expansion of civil rights protections for Black Americans. While the roots of this consummate Texas politician's "awakening" on civil rights did not derive from Gettysburg itself, he expertly employed the emancipationist memory of the Civil War to frame racial justice as a moral imperative demanding urgent action on the part of all Americans, white and Black.

Johnson's speech came toward the end of a year of intensifying planning for the July battle anniversary. Though many members of the public clamored for a traditional battlefield reenactment,[2] the Gettysburg Centennial Commission (GCC) instead resolved that those visiting Gettysburg in 1963 should do what Abraham Lincoln himself did in 1863, in the words of CWCC executive director James Robertson: "honor, respect, and remember those who died in the war."[3] Lincoln, of course, reserved his official remembrance and respect for the Union dead alone, but GCC members envisioned a memory that was more expansive in certain ways and more limited in others. Their remembrance extended to Confederate soldiers, their descendants, and contemporary white southerners, but largely excluded emancipation and Lincoln's vision of "a new birth of freedom," and thus, by extension, Blacks.

Throughout the winter and spring of 1963, the GCC laid the foundation for programs of symbolic pageantry that would highlight the shared historical experiences of white Union and Confederate soldiers by celebrating their great sense of duty, their unparalleled display of courage, and their military prowess as elemental to an American military tradition that had no equal in the world. Identifying spreading "understanding of the immense reserves of bravery, of sacrifice, and of idealism which lie in the American character" as their fundamental goal for the commemoration, they were captivated by the idea of a grand patriotic spectacle that would stir participants' historical imagination and rouse their emotions. Such a spectacle, they hoped, would include parades, pageants, and an elaborate sound and light show on the battlefield, and feature prominent national leaders, including the president of the United States, in leading roles.[4]

Many partners and observers wholeheartedly supported these goals. Others, including some local residents — mostly but not exclusively Black — and national figures such as Johnson, embraced a more emancipationist vision. They hoped to see the centennial utilized as a tool for speeding up the process of desegregation on a local level and bringing about a nationwide shift in racial attitudes. Recognizing the ways that the commemoration could potentially prove useful to furthering their own agenda locally and providing additional legitimacy to the cause of Black equality across the United States, they advocated for an observance that would highlight "the social reforms necessary for achieving racial justice and freedom in the cause of international brotherhood and peace."[5] Though this alternate vision could not displace the dominant concept of symbolic pageantry, it did pave the way for speeches, actions, and perspectives that went beyond the narrative of courage and military prowess and provided leverage for the racial justice movement.

IN JANUARY 1962, the GCC issued a formal invitation to President John F. Kennedy to close the centennial activities with a high-profile presidential address from the battlefield. Emphasizing the precedent of previous presidents speaking at Gettysburg during major anniversaries (Wilson spoke in 1913 and Roosevelt in 1938), Chairman Malcolm Hay assured Kennedy that the commemorative program would stress national unity and reconciliation, and "deemphasize the divisiveness of the Civil War." A presidential address from the battlefield had anchored both the fiftieth and seventy-fifth anniversary commemorations, and the commissioners' hopes that Kennedy would continue the tradition were thus high.[6]

To further fulfill their vision of symbolic pageantry, the commissioners turned to Adele Gutman Nathan, the writer/director of the 1952 "Mr. Lincoln Goes to Gettysburg" pageant, charging her with developing multiple theatrical programs for the event and arranging a massive parade. The decision to bring Nathan on board clearly reflected the desire of some commission members to see her restage her 1952 production on the 100th anniversary of the Gettysburg Address. Nathan quickly turned to her old friend Betty Gifford, chairperson of the ACCWCC's Pageant Committee, for help in developing a series of human interest themed "historical vignettes" for performance on July 2 and 3. While Nathan was certainly historically minded, she approached her Gettysburg work from the orientation of the theater. "These people are historians," she told a reporter in March 1963. "They know history. But they don't know show business, and that is what this is."[7]

Scores of local residents, including members of the ACCWCC, poured themselves into preparation for the historical vignettes, commemorative activities focusing on the experiences of townspeople, and the intensifying preservation efforts of the GBPA. Eager to accommodate anniversary visitors, the owners of the Gettysburg National Museum opened a huge new auditorium for the Electric Map. Yet as the summer months drew closer, the projected attendance figures for the July anniversary week sent some local people into panic mode, fearful that the town's infrastructure would be overwhelmed and there would be simply no place to put all the bodies flooding into Gettysburg. Other observers, such as members of the Pennsylvania Human Relations Commission (PHRC), were more concerned about the reception that certain bodies would receive. Would the presence of racial segregation and discrimination in this iconic town embarrass the state—and the nation at large—in the eyes of the world? Would the disillusioning reality that Gettysburg was an American community struggling like any other with issues of race overshadow its power as a symbol of American ideals?[8]

Quiet Does Not Equal Satisfied: The Struggle for Racial Justice in Gettysburg

As 1963 dawned, Black Gettysburgians continued to struggle against segregation and discrimination, and some astutely seized on the publicity generated by the centennial to force concessions from whites. Despite the continued expansion of the town's tourist economy, the Gettysburg labor market remained classified as "one of substantial unemployment," especially among women, who made up less than 40 percent of the total workforce. Significant numbers of Black adults worked in the shoe factory on Fairfield Road and a few held positions in the fruit-packing plants located in the northern part of the county. Employment patterns were otherwise little changed from the previous decade, with many Blacks continuing to commute to jobs outside of town, while a substantial number of those based in Gettysburg worked as dishwashers, cooks, and motel housekeepers. Professional, clerical, and retail positions downtown remained closed to African Americans, and aside from Black community leader Adam Myers, who was employed by the postal service, "you didn't see Black faces working downtown."[9]

Discrimination in employment was a key issue for the Gettysburg Ministerium's Social Action Committee, which identified unfair employment practices as the most significant civil rights issue in the community. The findings of a survey conducted by the committee suggest that while a higher ratio of employed Blacks worked in Gettysburg itself by 1963 than had in the previous decade, unemployment was still high and most of the jobs available did not provide equal treatment or advancement opportunities. According to Adam Myers—the central figure in efforts to overturn local segregationist policies and practices—many employers insisted that they could not change their employment practices because their competitors refused to do so. Myers alleged that these patterns prompted the most highly skilled members of the Black community to move away from Gettysburg, leaving Black youth without professional role models to emulate.[10]

Myers charged in 1963 that whites increasingly encroached on traditionally Black segments of the Third Ward but continued to bar Blacks from pursuing properties in other sections of town. When a Black family secured a house on a previously white block of Breckenridge Street, all the white families soon left, flipping the block. New segments of Gettysburg's residential landscape did not begin to open up to nonwhites until the early 1970s. Barber shops and beauty parlors remained whites-only into the 1960s, on the justification that "Negro hair was too hard on the clippers." Many Black residents traveled nearly forty miles to Harrisburg for a haircut, and lack of access to barber shops became a particularly galling issue for the first Black students at Gettysburg College. For many residents of this generation, Black and white alike, the most prominent memory associated with challenging segregation in public accommodations is that of Adam Myers entering a white-owned barber shop on Chambersburg Street and sitting down in the chair. Though the precise date of this action is unclear, the significance of Myers's stand rippled outward in waves, and the story has assumed a central place in local narratives of civil rights activity in Gettysburg.[11]

While the number of Black-owned institutions in the community was small, Gettysburg's Black American Legion post (Dorsey-Stanton Post #986) was a hotbed of activity. The post sponsored a softball team that played in the community league, hosted weekly dances—as well as a community Thanksgiving dinner and a Christmas party for children—and organized its own Memorial Day activities. Eager to be part of the community life of the Third Ward, some of the college's first Black students frequented the post's dances. Lacking a community of peers on campus, the social space provided by the Dorsey-Stanton Post was a lifesaver for some.[12]

Gettysburg College was still so white in 1963 that when Bruce Gordon, later to serve as president and CEO of the NAACP, arrived on campus, he was the first Black person some of his classmates had ever known. Throughout his time at the college, white classmates frequently asked to touch his hair and skin. Though Raymond Lee (class of '66) recalled later that he had a very limited social life as a student, he nonetheless decided to run for class treasurer in 1962. In what proved "an eye-opening and memorable event" for him, some of Lee's campaign posters were defaced with "KKK." His supporters, however, came to his defense, and he was overwhelmingly elected. Phil Parsons (class of '64) had a similar experience in the fall of 1963, when an essay he had written was defaced with a racial slur and posted in the college cafeteria. In his efforts to describe what Parsons felt at that moment, his friend Edward Southworth reached for a battle analogy, observing that "the fight-or-flight bodily functions he described sounded chemically indistinguishable from those that must have flashed across local battlefields 100 years before."[13]

Some local churches took tentative steps toward grappling with the ever-present issue of race and civil rights. The Gettysburg Presbyterian Church observed Race Relations Sunday in February 1963 by inviting Reverend Joseph Haggler to speak. Haggler, who spearheaded outreach to the county's largely Black and Puerto Rican migrant workers, was pastor of Shiloh Baptist Church and a leading member of Carlisle's Black community. Haggler returned to Gettysburg Presbyterian in August to speak in support of civil rights demonstrations, which he likened to the biblical story of Joshua leading the Israelites in a march around the walls of Jericho. In October, he prodded the Adams County Council of Churches to step away from the sidelines and assume a more active role in the civil rights struggle. NYU anthropology professor Ethel Alpenfeis told an assembly of Lutheran Church Women that the church had a sacred responsibility to stand up for human dignity because "we live on a planet which is basically non-white." Continuing, she invoked Cold War framing to drive home the urgency of the situation: "If

Russia wants to destroy us she only has to put our societies against each other in the area of race."[14]

A handful of local whites began to call out the *Gettysburg Times* for its long-standing practice of identifying people of color by race in headlines, even when race was immaterial to the story. The local ministerial association, the Gettysburg Ministerium, took the initiative to form an interracial Social Action Committee devoted to improving race relations and social conditions in the community. Members of the committee included Adam Myers and Gettysburg College history professor Robert Bloom, who headed the college's Civil War programs, and his wife, Dorothy. The committee pursued their work through presenting at church and community group-sponsored human relations programs, shining a light on discriminatory employment practices, and bringing children together across racial lines for shared play and reading activities.[15]

Myers and Kenneth Smoke, a Gettysburg College psychology professor, addressed the Rotary Club, with Myers focusing on discrimination in Gettysburg and the effects of prejudice upon local Blacks, and Smoke emphasizing the causes of prejudice. Myers and the Blooms spoke to members of the Exchange Club about the need for increased economic opportunities for local Blacks. Myers cautioned members of the Rotary Club not to assume that local Blacks were "satisfied" simply because their pride and commitment to nonviolence kept them from speaking out more directly. He framed his message explicitly in the context of the centennial, warning that the eyes of the nation were focused on Gettysburg and "one incident could bring in outside agitations."[16]

In employing an idea (and phrase) often used by conservative whites to argue that their African American neighbors were content and "agitation" always came from the outside, Myers was likely playing a shrewd game. He well understood that the centennial offered a brief opportunity to shine the spotlight of public opinion (perhaps even global opinion) on racial injustice in Gettysburg. He no doubt knew how much white residents and anniversary organizers feared the specter of direct action protest, concerned that the community's reputation would be tarnished on the national stage, and the Gettysburg Centennial would be torpedoed by the "Civil War of the 1960s" in the same way that the 1961 Charleston event had been. It is highly probable that Myers chose these words carefully to ensure maximum receptivity to his message. In so doing, he made it clear that Black residents were not only—like their white neighbors—profoundly affected by Gettysburg's relationship with the Civil War, but they could also be strategic about harnessing its memory in ways that addressed community concerns and needs.

The continuing presence of segregation and discrimination in Gettysburg, and the larger southcentral Pennsylvania region surrounding it, was public knowledge enough that the Pennsylvania Human Relations Commission launched a campaign in the spring of 1963 to prevent discrimination against battle anniversary visitors. PHRC representatives called on local business owners in person to remind them of the state public accommodations law and direct them to post nondiscrimination notices in their windows. Though the visits were part of a larger statewide campaign to increase compliance with the law, PHRC staffers concentrated on hotels, motels, restaurants and bars in the Gettysburg area because of the centennial commemoration. PHRC executive director Elliott Shirk announced in June that nearly all of the owners of the 248 Gettysburg area businesses visited were cordial to staff members, and that only one (unnamed) establishment refused to post the required notice.[17]

It is difficult to quantify the campaign's impact, but it may have served as an effective warning that local businesses would be in the spotlight, at least through the remainder of the centennial year. When asked by members of the Gettysburg Rotary Club about rumors that civil rights demonstrations were planned to coincide with the July 1–3 commemorative events, Joseph Haggler responded that he doubted it, at least so long as local motels treated patrons of color fairly. He avowed that he knew of a number of people who planned to attend the commemoration who had recently called the motels where they held reservations "to explain that they are Negroes and that they wished to check in advance lest they might suffer some embarrassment." Haggler told the Rotarians that all of these visitors had been assured that they were welcome (or, at least, their money was welcome). Nonetheless, the specter of demonstrations continued to haunt both architects of the commemoration and white Gettysburgians alike.[18]

The effectiveness of the accelerating campaign to eradicate segregation in public accommodations is evident in Mayor William Weaver's official welcome to centennial visitors, carried in the June 27 issue of the *Gettysburg Times*. Weaver made a specific point of assuring visitors that "without exception, their hotel and motel reservations will be honored" and that "everyone will be served in the restaurants as quickly and courteously and well as possible." The PHRC's activities likely played a role in pushing Weaver's hand, and certainly helped to make possible the oft-told story of Adam Myers getting his hair cut in a barbershop that had not previously served Blacks. Jean

Green recalled that the shop had the notice in the window, and when Myers came in, the employee who served him did so in part because he was not comfortable breaking the law in such an overt fashion. Yet the primary force prompting Weaver to make such a direct assurance was almost certainly the widespread fear that civil rights demonstrations would mar the battle anniversary. Segregation in public accommodations had been under attack locally for several years thanks to the initiative of Adam Myers and others, as well as broader social changes. The centennial anniversary, however, provided an unparalleled opportunity to use the expanded publicity provided Gettysburg and the accompanying temporarily heightened concern about global opinion to accelerate the process of change.[19]

Gettysburg residents, of course, did not live in a bubble, cut off from developments elsewhere in the state or across the nation more broadly. Under the leadership of CORE and the NAACP, African Americans in Pennsylvania's largest city spent the summer of 1963 escalating a protest campaign against employment bias in the construction industry. Drawing on the range of direct action tactics employed by the southern freedom struggle, Black Philadelphians mounted union-style picket lines, protest marches, and sit-ins at City Hall. On the other side of the state, the formation of the United Negro Protest Committee (UNPC) in 1963 brought a new level of coordination to Black Pittsburghers' ongoing efforts to combat job discrimination. This grassroots coalition of religious, civic, and civil rights groups launched coordinated protests that summer and fall against a wide range of employers across the city, leading to a range of negotiated hiring agreements. During the battle anniversary week alone, the NAACP announced a new campaign to end segregation in northern schools and put the Tournament of Roses parade on notice that it would no longer accept discrimination in parade operations. Angry Blacks jeered Chicago mayor Richard Daley at a Fourth of July rally and Attorney General Robert Kennedy told the Senate Commerce Committee that private businesses must be subject to the terms of the new civil rights bill.[20]

Residents of Gettysburg did not have to look as far away as Philadelphia or Pittsburgh, though, to see mass direct action. Located less than thirty miles east of Gettysburg, the city of York, Pennsylvania, was home to a Black population that grew 300 percent between 1920 and 1970. As Black migrants flocked to the city in search of better employment and educational opportunities — and a respite from racial terrorism — they found instead the same sort of discrimination in employment and housing that met migrants in most northern communities. While "whites-only" signs were rare, many restaurants, businesses, and entertainment venues refused entrance to

Blacks, and the city's elementary schools were segregated by law until the Supreme Court's decision in *Brown v. Board of Education*.[21]

In the summer of 1963, York was in the midst of a wave of organized protest against police brutality and local government intransigence. Demands for reform, including job training programs and stricter laws to combat discrimination in employment, were broad-based, but the issue that most dominated residents' concerns was police brutality. Too commonly associated in the popular mind exclusively with the south, police brutality was an animating issue for Black communities across the north as well and played a precipitating role in sparking many of the urban revolts of the 1960s and early 1970s. Relations between York's Black community and the police force had been poor for years. Police officers frequently harassed Black men congregating in the street or seen in the company of white women, and the city's 1962 decision to establish a canine corps unleashed a wave of protest.[22]

Mayor John Snyder, a staunch supporter of the corps, regularly walked the streets with his own German Shepherd in what many perceived as an overt attempt to intimidate Blacks. Officers in the canine corps used the dogs on patrol and for crowd control purposes, disproportionately deploying them against Black residents. While the nation commemorated the battle anniversary, dogs mauled two Black men in police custody. The newly formed Peaceful Committee for Immediate Action organized young Blacks around the goal of ending police violence, and marched on City Hall just a few weeks later. More than 300 Blacks and a handful of whites joined the protest, many carrying handmade signs bearing slogans such as "Police Brutality Is NOT a State's Right," "Dogs, Birmingham, and York?" and "End Police Brutality." Well aware of how the city's struggles fit into a broader national context, the group kept up the pressure throughout the summer; its efforts culminated in a capstone rally at Penn Park in October 1963 that drew nearly 1,500 people. Gettysburg's centennial year thus played out in tandem with a period of expanded agitation for civil rights, likely intensifying the concerns of PHRC staff and some local residents that discrimination against anniversary visitors could bring damaging publicity and massive protests.[23]

Preparations for July

As planning stepped up, the GCC opened a Gettysburg office under the direction of its new executive secretary, Louis Simon, a theatrical producer who had previously served in a similar role for the Actors' Equity Association.

Eager to ensure a collaborative relationship with the ACCWCC, Simon promptly asked Betty Gifford to serve as a liaison between the two groups. The commission formally announced the details of its 1963 programs on November 20, 1962, at a sold-out dinner designed to demonstrate that local residents supported the GCC's efforts to provide a program that would reflect well on the town "that is custodian of one of the world's greatest shrines." Organized around the theme "A Nation United," the July anniversary plans were designed to emphasize how the events of 1863 "helped to create the unity that is America's power today."[24]

When William Scranton took office as governor of Pennsylvania in January 1963, he elevated Lt. General Milton Baker to the chairmanship of the GCC and appointed three new members to the body. GNMP superintendent James Myers, who had served as a key advisor to the commission during his four years at the park, was transferred the following month and replaced by Kittridge A. Wing. Wing won approval from both his supervisors and local residents for his efforts to ensure a seamless transition, but the change in personnel during this critical time nonetheless impacted GNMP's ability to exert influence on the plans nearing completion.[25]

The official commemoration was slated to begin July 1 with a ceremony at the Peace Light, and include presentation of two tracts of land to the NPS and the unveiling of a new Battle of Gettysburg commemorative stamp. July 2 would feature a highly theatrical military parade, and July 3 would culminate in a "symbolic re-creation" of Pickett's Charge. The theme for the first day of commemorative activities would be "Our Heritage," the second "Strength Through Unity," and the third, "Reunion at the High Water Mark." Other programming would include rededication ceremonies at monuments and memorials across the field and the historical vignettes developed by Nathan and Gifford. The GCC continued to hang its July 4 plans (with a theme of "Forever Free") on the hope that President Kennedy would address the nation from Gettysburg. When the president ultimately declined the invitation, citing a trip to Europe, the commission scrapped its plans entirely, deciding to end the official commemoration on July 3 instead. Though Kennedy did visit Gettysburg during the centennial year, it was only for a private family tour of the battlefield. When Secretary of the Interior Stewart Udall also declined an invitation for July, Governor Scranton noted in frustration that "the people of Pennsylvania and Civil War adherents everywhere are getting the impression that the Federal Administration doesn't realize that this is America's most important battle."[26]

While this might seem to suggest that perhaps Gettysburg's significance on the national stage had diminished since 1938, the evidence does not support this conclusion. Gettysburg remained as significant as ever, perhaps even more so given the extensive use of Lincoln as a Cold War symbol and the growing tendency to portray the Gettysburg Address as the lodestar of American foreign policy. Kennedy likely declined the invitation not due to the location, but rather because of the politically divisive nature of Civil War commemoration. Despite the GCC's attempts to craft a unifying and uncontentious program, the multiple commemorative visions generated over the course of the anniversary clearly demonstrated that Gettysburg Centennial was never united in spirit or purpose. Both emancipationist and Lost Cause proponents continually challenged the official narrative of reconciliation and national unity. Such volatility undoubtedly troubled Kennedy. In the wake of the 1961 Charleston crisis, the president, who hoped to retain the electoral loyalty of the south without alienating northerners, kept his distance from the commemoration of the war. Given the fact that he had already passed on an invitation to speak at the CWCC's 1962 Lincoln Memorial program, a shrewd observer might have predicted that Kennedy would deem an event at Gettysburg to offer too much political risk for too little potential gain.

As with any major event of this scale, planning for the battle anniversary operated on two levels: programmatic and logistical. GCC members wanted and needed local help on both fronts, and in service of that end invited representatives of local organizations to a March 1963 public meeting to discuss cooperation. In his announcement of the meeting, GCC executive secretary Louis Simon reminded local residents that "the continuing prestige of Gettysburg as a national shrine will be greatly affected for a long time to come by what happens here during a few short days." Fifty-five organizations sent representatives to the meeting; perhaps notably, though other veterans' groups participated, the Black Dorsey-Stanton American Legion Post did not. Attendees elected ACCWCC's Clayton Jester chairman of a committee to coordinate logistics that fell outside the scope of the GCC's responsibility.[27]

Visitors would have to be housed and fed. Public safety and medical needs would need to be anticipated. Traffic and parking would have to be controlled. An adequate water supply would need to be guaranteed, as would sanitary facilities and refuse pickup. The state Health Department added four sanitarians to its Adams County staff in order to meet the expanded responsibility of inspecting restaurants, tourist homes, hotels, and service stations to ensure compliance with state health regulations. The Pennsylvania Civil Air Patrol took on the responsibility of coordinating emergency medical services. Predicting "1,000 casualties a day," they set up an elaborate system of first aid stations and field hospitals with assistance from the Red Cross. The Pennsylvania State Police assumed responsibility for law enforcement and traffic control. Municipal officials investigated alternate water sources. Local officials, however, drew the line at a suggestion that they mark the centennial by changing the name of the county from Adams to Lincoln or Eisenhower.[28]

Gettysburg residents had long resigned themselves to the traffic problems that came with tourism, but the lead-up to the battle anniversary did produce a sarcastic *Gettysburg Times* piece poking fun at the driving habits of visitors. Lampooning tourists' tendency to double park, drive the wrong way around the square, and stop unexpectedly, the article noted drily that "the guide books fail to caution tourists that the motor vehicle is operated the same in Gettysburg as it is everywhere else in the world." Nevertheless concerned about the needs of visitors arriving by car, Gettysburg's municipal leadership applied consistent pressure to the state Department of Highways to finish the Route 15 bypass around the downtown area prior to the centennial year. The contracts for the project were the first in the department's history to require completion not in a certain number of working days, but rather by a specific date: July 1, 1963.[29]

Civil Rights at the Cemetery: Memorial Day, 1963

As the calendar turned toward summer, Vice President Lyndon B. Johnson's keynote address at the annual Memorial Day observance at the National Cemetery provided an advance taste of the symbolic pageantry and national attention that July would bring. Johnson's speech, however, would prove to be an unexpected outlier to the general tone of the official battle anniversary activities, and his presence was far from a preordained acknowledgement of Gettysburg's place in the national pantheon. Depressed by his circumscribed role as vice president and wanting to avoid what he deemed inevitable failure to live up to Lincoln's Gettysburg Address, Johnson wanted to decline the invitation, but his personal secretary ultimately convinced him that Gettysburg provided an opportunity to deliver "a masterpiece to be remembered by." Though he ultimately accepted, Johnson complained in the days leading up to the event that no matter what he said he would be ridiculed—

deemed a bigot if he failed to address the tidal wave of racial demonstrations cresting around the country and lampooned as an opportunist if he attempted to squeeze in a reference or two.[30]

Landing by helicopter on Gettysburg High School's athletic field, Johnson and his daughter Luci were greeted with a nineteen-gun salute from the National Guard. Having indicated a desire to see the children marching in the parade, they were taken directly to a reviewing stand on Baltimore Street. Johnson subsequently joined representatives of the Sons of Union Veterans, the American Legion, and Veterans of Foreign Wars in laying wreaths at the cemetery. As the Gettysburg High School band played "Safe in the Arms of Jesus," 1,800 local schoolchildren carried on the long-established tradition of strewing flowers over the more than 3,000 Civil War graves in the National Cemetery. (Though it would revive toward the end of the century, the practice of decorating USCT graves at Lincoln Cemetery was dormant in the 1960s.)[31]

The ceremony then moved to the speakers' rostrum, where Ambassador John S. Rice, an Adams County native, introduced Johnson to a crowd of some 3,000 people. When the vice president stepped to the microphone, instead of either ducking or shoehorning in civil rights, he made it the centerpiece of his message. After a brief nod to the traditional Memorial Day theme of veterans' sacrifices, Johnson came to the heart of his message: "One hundred years ago, the slave was freed. One hundred years later, the Negro remains in bondage to the color of his skin. The Negro today asks justice. We do not answer him — we do not answer those who lie beneath this soil — when we reply to the Negro by asking 'Patience.'" Americans could no longer pretend that time alone would heal the nation's racial wounds, Johnson argued. Concrete action was necessary. If Americans did not rise to the challenge of eradicating inequality, the vice president warned, the nation's future was at stake. Invoking the Cold War vision of America's special role in the world, Johnson insisted that the price of inaction would be yielding up "our destiny of greatness among the civilizations of history."[32]

For generations, white Americans had asked their Black counterparts for patience in the face of injustice. As the intensity of protest escalated in the 1960s, these calls came with increasing frequency, as whites recoiled from the "incivility" of direct action protests. The Kennedy administration itself — of which Johnson was a representative — had frequently begged Black activists for de-escalation, restraint, and cooling-off periods. In publicly repudiating such calls for patience, Johnson's speech revealed the transformative impact of the protests that had recently rocked Birmingham,

Alabama. In his powerful "Letter from Birmingham City Jail," widely disseminated only a few weeks earlier, Martin Luther King Jr. delivered a stinging rejoinder to white onlookers who counseled delay and moderation. "For years now I have heard the word, 'Wait!' It rings in the ear of every Negro with a piercing familiarity. This 'wait' has almost always meant 'never.'" Framing America's struggle within global context, King continued, "We have waited for more than 340 years for constitutional and God-given rights. The nations of Asia and Africa are moving with jetlike speed toward the goal of political independence, and we still creep at horse and buggy pace toward the gaining of a cup of coffee at a lunch counter." Though Johnson never mentioned King's name, his Gettysburg address must be understood as a direct response to the civil rights leader's charges.[33]

While acknowledging the emptiness of calls for patience, Johnson asked Blacks to maintain faith in the law, seemingly casting aspersions on street protest. "Men may build barricades," he argued, "and others may hurl themselves against those barricades—but what would happen at the barricades would yield no answers." Johnson's listeners likely heard allusions to Birmingham and Jackson in these words, but they may also have thought of events closer to home. As Memorial Day weekend approached, the NAACP-coordinated construction site protests in North Philadelphia had grown increasingly contentious, with picketers engaging in sit-down strikes. More than 300 people walked the picket lines on Memorial Day itself. Drawing on the concept of "what the national interest requires of all its citizens," Johnson pled with Black Americans to use the law to dismantle inequality. Though never directly stated, the Cold War concern that direct action protest exposed the United States to too much negative attention worldwide was inherent in Johnson's framing of legal redress.[34]

Johnson's speech was penned by Horace Busby, one of his regular speechwriters, but was deeply personal. After listening to the vice president think aloud about race in the week preceding his visit to Gettysburg, Busby was so impressed by Johnson's uncharacteristic fluency that his words played an important role in shaping the final draft of the speech. The reasons underlying Johnson's shift toward increasingly forceful support of civil rights in the winter and spring of 1963 are complex. Johnson himself repeatedly insisted later in life that he had always supported civil rights but had been constrained during his congressional career by the opinions of his white constituents, who largely did not. By making him responsible to represent the entire nation, the vice presidency had freed him from these strictures.

As Clay Risen has suggested, however, Johnson was also keenly aware of shifting political currents. He recognized that many white southerners were close to gravitating (or already gravitating) toward conservative Republicanism, and that if given a reason to support the party, African Americans could prove a vitally important new constituency for Democrats.[35]

As Taylor Branch has written, Johnson "knew before leaving the platform that his directness had touched a chord in a tough audience—nearly all whites, with the colors of high school bands scattered among martial units ranging from grizzled World War I veterans to the American Legion Drum and Bugle Corps." Nearly all, but not entirely. Black members of the Dorsey-Stanton American Legion Post marched in the parade and some likely stayed to hear Johnson speak. It is highly likely that some of the members of the crowd thought of this speech when entering the voting booth in November 1964; though Adams County was traditionally Republican country, it went for Johnson that year by a substantial margin. For the rest of his life, the Gettysburg speech would rank as one of Johnson's proudest moments, and he often mailed copies to admirers. Two of the key ideas in this speech—that the promise of emancipation remained unfilled and that the United States would forfeit its special destiny should it fail to solve the problem of racial inequality—would resurface two years later in his most famous piece of oratory, the Voting Rights Address.[36]

Johnson's Gettysburg speech thrilled many Americans around the country, Black and white alike. An editorial in the *Philadelphia Inquirer* praised the vice president for rightfully framing the racial crisis as a national, rather than southern, phenomenon. Nonetheless, many commentators took particular comfort in the fact that a white southerner had spoken so forthrightly on race. An editorial in the *Washington Post* pointed to the speech as an example of the best tradition of the South. Linking Johnson's speech to a likely misunderstood and probably apocryphal story about Robert E. Lee as a civil rights pioneer, the piece argued that the white South had more to offer the country than white supremacy, massive resistance, and attacks on demonstrators. "By his eloquence, by his political courage, by his vision," the writer editorialized, "Vice President Johnson has pointed out for the South the pathway to its future and he has summoned a bemused and lethargic Nation to face the challenge of its own high principles."[37]

In a similar story, Drew Pearson drew on Civil War associations to make a favorable comparison between Johnson's commitment to civil rights and Kennedy's. Pearson argued that the descendant of Confederate soldiers "who fought in the Civil War to prolong slavery" (not a particularly mainstream interpretation of Confederate motivation in 1963) had been far more forthright on civil rights than the president from Massachusetts, "home of the abolitionists who precipitated the Civil War." In his overestimation of abolitionists' influence in northern states, Pearson's simplistic interpretation of the war's causation revealed the widespread durability of what Robert Penn Warren deemed the "Treasury of Virtue" myth. Put simply, the "Treasury of Virtue" historically portrayed the war as "a consciously undertaken crusade so full of righteousness" that it provided northerners of future generations "a plenary indulgence for all sins past, present, and future."[38]

In his call for the entire nation to repudiate discriminatory practices and take action on behalf of racial equality, Lyndon Johnson—a descendant of Confederate soldiers—avoided both the "Treasury of Virtue" and the "Great Alibi" in his National Cemetery speech. Instead, he embraced a limited emancipationist interpretation of the battle's meaning reinforced by foreign policy concerns yet fundamentally rooted in moral concerns. Though Johnson placed limits on "appropriate" protest by criticizing direct action, he forthrightly linked the legacy of the Battle of Gettysburg to racial justice and "a new birth of freedom." Despite its power and widespread resonance, however, Johnson's Memorial Day speech was an outlier to the reconciliationist tone of most spring and early summer programming, which was dominated by local activity and an emphasis on entertainment and boosting visitation.

"That Shows the War Is Over": Reconciliationist Pageantry

In the final weeks preceding the battle anniversary, the pressure of a looming deadline coincided with a period of intensified wrangling in the Pennsylvania state legislature over the GCC's financial solvency. The commission's projected inability to carry out its planned programming with the cash it had on hand prompted three members of Pennsylvania's congressional delegation to make an unsuccessful plea for federal funding in May. After a rancorous partisan debate in which some Democrats accused the commission of "hogwild, irresponsible, and wreckless [sic] spending," the Pennsylvania House finally approved an additional appropriation of $28,000 just days before the July events were scheduled to begin, and the state senate quickly approved the bill.[39]

The U.S. Postal Service's Gettysburg stamp premiered on July 1; advance orders poured into the Gettysburg Post Office at such a volume that the postal service had to add employees to handle the special orders. Nearly one million stamps were sold on the first day of issue, and they continued to be in high demand through the summer; the postmaster estimated that nearly 55,000 more had been purchased by the end of August. The GBPA seized the opportunity presented by the new stamp to raise funds for land acquisition, rolling out a special envelope for collectors. Its February newsletter pled with members to help publicize the envelope, arguing, "if we are to save [these lands] from commercialization, we must do it this year because all eyes will be focused on Gettysburg." This heightened attention ensured that commercialization of the battlefield continued to enrage citizens across the country, many of whom framed their letters of protest to the president, the CWCC, and the National Park Service in the language of international embarrassment.[40]

In the wake of the GCC's failed attempts to create a sound and light program dramatizing the battle, the NPS moved forward with plans to provide visitors a campfire experience instead. Convinced that the success of the program would be largely dependent on situating it in an "undeveloped" portion of the battlefield, GNMP staff chose Pitzer Woods for the new amphitheater. The campfires, which began on July 1, featured the MGM film, *The Battle of Gettysburg*, Civil War songs, and a ten-minute presentation on soldier life. The new program attracted over-capacity crowds, and by Labor Day weekend, attendance figures topped 13,000. A gratified Superintendent Wing deemed the campfire program "the outstanding attraction" of the centennial.[41]

The Jaycees' campaign to boost the historic appearance of downtown Gettysburg culminated in June in a week of "Campaign Gettysburg Sales Days," a Civil War singalong led by Biglerville High School's Centennial Commemoration Choir, and a Civil War drummer boy contest. Participating merchants added a Civil War theme to the advertisements in their shop windows, garbed their front-line staff in period dress, and distributed "Confederate money" to shoppers for use in a special auction. Noting the extent of nineteenth-century facial hair and costuming in the downtown area, a reporter for the *Philadelphia Inquirer* observed (exaggeratedly) that the majority of local residents "have been in Civil War costume since June 15."[42]

The Jaycees' sponsoring partner, the *Saturday Evening Post*, lauded Campaign Gettysburg as a triumph of "commercial democracy," noting favorably that more than 75 percent of the buildings identified for "historical improvements" saw at least some alterations over the course of the campaign. Mayor Weaver publicly thanked the group for giving the town the opportunity "to recreate our proper image" and the Jaycees established a permanent committee for the campaign in November, devoted primarily to encouraging the removal of illuminated signs in the downtown area and providing incentives for local business owners to cooperate with further efforts to promote the community's historical image.[43]

Campaign Gettysburg participants shared a concern for architectural and landscape preservation with GBPA members and NPS staff, and many likely were enthusiastic about the Cold War framing of Gettysburg as a site of patriotic unity and the source of the democratic vision guiding "the free world." This, however, did not mean that either their use of battle narratives or their reasons for remembering the Civil War were identical to those held by NPS officials or GCC members. In addition to their vested economic interest in Civil War history and their strong sense of place, many local residents had strong family ties connecting them to the events of 1861 to 1865. Despite Gettysburg's widespread fame, it was a small town where family relationships were of paramount importance and many inhabitants were directly descended from wartime residents. Despite the passage of time, family stories thus played a key role in shaping local people's understandings of the battle, and the war more broadly, and underlay some of their enthusiasm for historical commemoration.

Fulfilling its pledge to highlight the Civil War service and experiences of local residents, the ACCWCC mounted another pageant on June 27, this one commemorating the capture of Gettysburg by Jubal Early's cavalry and the death of George Washington Sandoe, the first local resident killed during the battle. Featuring more than 600 participants, the program included a parade, a skirmish in the downtown area, the capture of the courthouse, and a scripted scene recreating the delivery of Early's demands to borough council president David Kendlehart. The program strongly emphasized the family connections linking the residents of 1863 to the present-day community. A descendant portrayed Sandoe, and Joseph Kendlehart played the role of his grandfather. Three other members of the Kendlehart family participated as well, and the ranks of soldiers and militiamen were filled with reenactors and members of the Sons of Veterans Reserve. Pageant participants ended the evening with a costumed military ball.[44]

Reflecting its focus on reconciliation, two of the GCC's official guests for the commemoration were Robert E. Lee IV and George Gordon Meade III, great-grandsons of the commanding generals. Lee and Meade were symbolically housed in adjoining rooms at the Gettysburg Auto Lodge. Telling a reporter how Lee and Meade met, shook hands, and headed off to a party, a Lodge clerk insisted, "That shows the Civil War is over." The Hotel Gettysburg furthered this spirit of reconciliation and unity by temporarily adding grits to its menu. When North Carolina governor Terry Sanford and Minnesota governor Karl Rolvaag were spotted eating grits together in the hotel dining room, their comradely enjoyment of traditional southern food made the newspapers, portrayed as further evidence that the bitterness of sectional division was in the past.[45]

Despite the narrative of reconciliation, however, Pennsylvania State Police commanders were not lulled into forgetting the immediate context of the commemoration: a summer of mass demonstrations and racially motivated violence. In assuming the responsibility of law enforcement and traffic control outside GNMP property and providing security details and drivers for visiting dignitaries, including high-profile white supremacist George Wallace, they anticipated disruptions beyond minor traffic violations and episodes of unruly behavior. Borrowing a helicopter to use for aerial direction of traffic (and likely surveillance), the State Police sent a detail of 185 troopers to Gettysburg. The troopers were specifically charged with responding "as gently as possible with any possible racial demonstrations."[46]

COMMEMORATING 1863 IN THE SUMMER OF 1963 ensured that discussions, definitions, and depictions of martial camaraderie, states' rights, and Lincoln's new birth of freedom would be profoundly shaped by the struggle over full citizenship rights for Black Americans. Some local residents, Black leaders, and national political figures, including the vice president of the United States, made determined attempts to use the symbolism of the centennial and the publicity it generated to change public attitudes and secure concessions from recalcitrant whites. As evidenced in George Wallace's high-profile presence throughout the anniversary, though they perceived the nature of the relationship differently, white segregationists were no less convinced of the connections between the commemoration and the issue of civil rights, using Gettysburg to mount their defense of traditional southern mores.

The GCC, however, remained far more concerned with the Cold War than civil rights, clinging to its narrative of sectional reconciliation and national unity. Nevertheless, though Cold War reconciliation undergirded the official battle anniversary program, it did not define every aspect of the event.

Politicians, reenactors, and performers made use of GCC-sponsored activities to send a range of messages, from prosegregationist to openly emancipationist. Participants, likewise, did not simply absorb the commemoration's messaging wholesale, but rather made decisions about where and how to participate (and what ideas to embrace) that ensured a variety of different takeaways about the connections between 1863 and 1963.

The April 22, 1961, Independent Blues pageant was the first large-scale grassroots event of the centennial period. With a script written by a committee of local residents under the direction of Betty Gifford, the pageant depicted the April 1861 departure of the first regiment of local men to leave for wartime service. It featured a cast of 300, including reenactors associated with the North-South Skirmish Association and many prominent local residents in key roles. Courtesy of Adams County Historical Society.

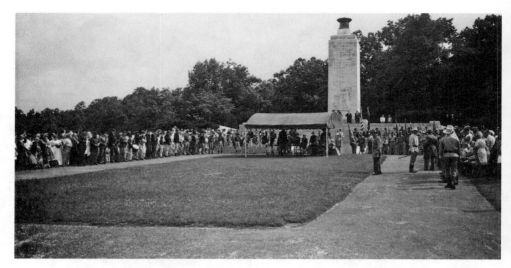

The official 1963 commemorative activities sponsored by the Gettysburg Centennial Commission opened with a July 1 ceremony at the Eternal Peace Light featuring formal representatives of twenty-seven of the twenty-nine states that had troops at Gettysburg. A crowd of at least 2,000 braved the sweltering heat to view the opening ceremonies, which included a welcoming address from Pennsylvania governor William Scranton and a wreath-laying ceremony. Courtesy of Gettysburg National Military Park.

George Wallace's participation in the Gettysburg ceremonies came three weeks after his defiant anti-integration "stand in the schoolhouse door," and served to solidify his standing as a national political figure and expand his outreach to voters outside the South. One of the highest profile participants in the commemoration, he was provided an extensive police guard and was warmly received by many attendees. During his time in Gettysburg, he spoke twice at the Alabama monument (pictured behind him), reviewed a parade, toured the battlefield, and gave the keynote address at the dedication of a new monument to South Carolina troops. Courtesy of Adams County Historical Society.

The new South Carolina state monument on Seminary Ridge was dedicated on July 2, 1963, in a combative ceremony featuring speeches by segregationist politicians George Wallace and John May. Openly focused on contemporary politics, the ceremony employed Confederate memory in the service of massive resistance, conflating the Confederate cause with the segregationists' cause. Pictured from left to right are Payne Williams, chairman, South Carolina for Gettysburg Committee; John A. May, chairman, South Carolina Confederate War Centennial Commission; John Amasa Mayo, grandson of John May; John Richardson Russell; and Donald Russell, governor of South Carolina. Courtesy of Adams County Historical Society.

The seven "live action" historical vignettes developed by Betty Gifford and Adele
Gutman Nathan, under the auspices of the Gettysburg Centennial Committee and
the Adams County Civil War Centennial Committee, were among the most popular
(if historically suspect) elements of the battle anniversary commemoration. The
vast majority of the ninety-two cast and crew members were local residents. The
Sharpshooter's Ridge vignette took place among the rocks at Devil's Den and
featured numerous students and faculty from Littlestown High School, including
Jim Witt. Courtesy of Adams County Historical Society.

The July 3, 1963, symbolic reenactment of Pickett's Charge was billed as the culmination of the battle anniversary. Featuring approximately 1,500 reenactors, some of them descendants of soldiers who fought at Gettysburg, the program was not a reenactment per se (by 1963, NPS policy banned reenactments on battlefield land), but rather a highly choreographed meeting of two armies. Playing to an audience of at least 20,000, the symbolic reenactment stressed reconciliation and national unity and portrayed the course of the war as shifting on the fields of Gettysburg. Courtesy of Gettysburg National Military Park.

Gettysburg College hosted a round table on November 18, 1963, on the content and varied impacts of the Gettysburg Address. A follow-up to David Donald's Fortenbaugh Lecture of the previous evening, it featured (from left to right) Philadelphia judge Raymond P. Alexander, U.S. Representative Fred Schwengel, journalist Alistair Cooke, Gettysburg College historian Robert Bloom, and poet Archibald MacLeish. The panelists debated Lincoln's definition of nationalism and speculated on how he would have responded to the racial challenges of 1963. Courtesy of Special Collections/Musselman Library, Gettysburg College, Gettysburg, Pennsylvania.

The U.S. Marine Band led the November 19, 1963, procession from Lincoln Square to the Soldiers' National Cemetery for the cemetery rededication. The Hotel Gettysburg is visible in the background. By the time the procession had reached the cemetery, a crowd of several thousand, including many African Americans, had assembled. Courtesy of Special Collections/Musselman Library, Gettysburg College, Gettysburg, Pennsylvania.

Former president Dwight D. Eisenhower, who retired to Gettysburg in 1961, presided over the rededication of the National Cemetery on the centennial anniversary of Lincoln's Gettysburg Address, November 19, 1963. A passionate student of the Civil War and the honorary chairman of the Gettysburg Centennial Commission, Eisenhower argued that contemporary Americans had an obligation to "give increased devotion" to the cause of democracy and good citizenship. It was his most visible role in the 1963 observances. Courtesy of Adams County Historical Society.

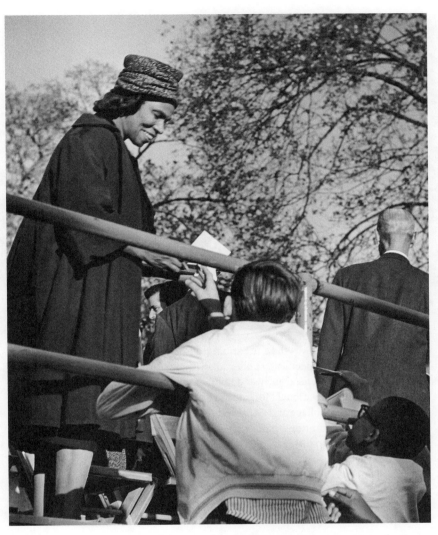

It is very possible that many of the attendees at the ceremony came more to hear Marian Anderson sing than to participate in the rededication of the cemetery. An internationally famed contralto, Anderson had a long symbolic association with Abraham Lincoln and the emancipationist vision of the Civil War. Her performance on November 19, 1963, electrified the crowd and she signed many autographs for young Black fans at the end of the program. Courtesy of Special Collections/ Musselman Library, Gettysburg College, Gettysburg, Pennsylvania.

The Eternal Peace Light was the site of numerous peace actions during the 1960s and early 1970s, many specifically undertaken in opposition to American policy in Vietnam. The largest local antiwar demonstration of the Vietnam War era was this October 15, 1969, National Moratorium to End the War in Vietnam march. More than 500 Gettysburg College and Gettysburg Seminary students, faculty and staff members of both institutions, and local residents participated in a silent march from Lincoln Square to the Peace Light, where they held a short service intended to draw connections between the battlefield of Gettysburg and the killing fields of Vietnam. Courtesy of Special Collections/Musselman Library, Gettysburg College, Gettysburg, Pennsylvania.

CHAPTER FIVE

A Nation Was Born Here
The 1963 Battle Anniversary

When they opened their newspapers during the first week of July, Americans across the country encountered extensive coverage of the battle anniversary. Importantly, these stories did not stand alone; rather, they were enmeshed and embedded in the context of other articles surrounding them. Accounts of the commemoration frequently shared space with pieces on civil rights demonstrations, sectional tensions, arguments over federal/state jurisdiction, and the civil rights legislation currently before Congress. Others bordered articles devoted to national security and/or Cold War developments, thus ensuring that readers absorbed reports from Gettysburg in the context of contemporary events. A handful made the connection even more explicit, as seen in a front-page *Boston Globe* editorial that framed the Gettysburg centennial by comparing the clash of the two armies and the ongoing hostilities between the United States and the Soviet Union.

The *Globe*'s editorial team suggested that the growing scholarly tendency to view the Civil War as an "irrepressible conflict" provided a sobering lens through which to understand contemporary political developments around the world. Just as Lincoln's refusal to countenance additional expansion of slavery prompted the South to go to war, thus the mutual desire of both "Communism and the West" to expand their global influence might spark a hot conflict. Nevertheless, the writers took comfort in the older "blundering generation" line of interpretation (which held that the war had been "blundered into" by misguided politicians). The paper opined that if the Civil War had not been inevitable, it "encourages the hope that a shooting war can somehow be prevented between the world's two competing ideas." The *Globe* ran its story on Gettysburg next to a Ralph McGill column titled "A Negro Tells Why He Hates." The column featured a letter from a Black North Carolinian serving in the air force. Presenting himself as opposed to Black radicalism, the airman nonetheless avowed that the widely circulated photos of dogs attacking protesters in Birmingham had fundamentally altered his feelings toward white Americans, "sparking a consuming hatred which stripped away any feeling of national pride that I might have had."[1]

The *Atlanta Constitution* similarly intertwined its coverage of the Gettysburg anniversary with stories of George Wallace's stand in the schoolhouse door to block desegregation at the University of Alabama and the House Un-American Activities Committee's investigation of former SCLC staff member Jack O'Dell. Columnist Ted Lippman derided Wallace for retreating from confrontation with federal officials in Tuscaloosa then traveling to Gettysburg to proclaim that the fight would continue. The fight was over, Lippman proclaimed. If it had not been, "would George have beat such a hasty retreat from Tuscaloosa?" Arguing that the world would be a better place had the South won the war, Lippman nonetheless alleged that Wallace's posturing damaged his credibility as a leader of southern white resistance. Lest this stance be mistaken for moderation, however, Lippman concluded by claiming that white southerners would be better served by commemorating Captive Nations Week (established in 1953 to raise public awareness of the suffering of nations under Communist control) than the Civil War. If they could not, however, they could at least "milk Northern tourists with battle reenactments and sell them Minie balls." Lippman noted bitterly that "it's good for the pocketbook, even if doesn't do much for the soul."[2]

THE TWO MONTHS PRECEDING the battle anniversary were turbulent ones for the Black freedom movement. Police officers employed fire hoses and dogs against protesters (including children), Wallace stood in the schoolhouse door, and an assassin murdered NAACP leader Medgar Evers in his own driveway. The depths of white brutality on public display in Birmingham, Alabama, the criticism from around the world, and the fear that the scale of the conflict could be replicated in other cities pushed the Kennedy administration to conclude that new federal legislation mandating desegregation of public accommodations could wait no longer. Indeed, in the course of the ten weeks following the crisis in Birmingham, demonstrations broke out in 186 cities across the nation, leading to the arrests of 15,000 people. In mid-May, a small group including Attorney General Robert Kennedy and Burke Marshall, head of the DOJ's Civil Rights Division, began outlining a bill that would focus on public accommodations and school desegregation. Submitted to Congress the following month, the hotly debated Civil Rights Bill was in the forefront of the nation's consciousness as Americans gathered to commemorate their most famous Civil War battle.[3]

The scale of the anniversary program was immense, with the July 3 events drawing nearly 40,000 attendees. A dizzying array of options (some sponsored by the GCC, others arranged by local or outside entities) confronted visitors, ranging from live theater programs, parades, and living history encampments to monument dedications and campfire programs. While many of the various events provided meaningful emotional connections to history or entertaining historical escapism, the GCC-sponsored ones also tended to explicitly utilize battle narratives to champion American supremacy on the world stage and steer away from contentious issues such as emancipation and the legacy of the war. Yet this reconciliationist veneer glossed over inherent tensions between those who planned the anniversary programming and the speakers and attendees alike who brought to it alternative frameworks for interpreting the meaning of the battle.

GCC members hoped to "deemphasize the divisiveness of the Civil War," yet thanks to the disparate views of the speakers invited to participate, ceremonies at the Eternal Peace Light Memorial, the South Carolina monument, and the Florida monument extensively marshalled not only reconciliationist but also emancipationist and Lost Cause interpretations of the battle for contemporary purposes. These included both justifying and opposing the Civil Rights Bill, decrying the impact of American racial abuses on the nation's foreign policy goals, calling for equal justice in housing and education, linking the Black freedom struggle to Communism, and portraying civil rights activists as unpatriotic agitators. By contrast, the July 2 parade, the "Vignettes of History," and the July 3 Pickett's Charge program were more uniformly reconciliationist in tone, using patriotic spectacle and human-scale stories to reinforce the "we are all Americans" message.

Consuming and Proclaiming History:
The *Gettysburg Times* Centennial Edition

The anniversary week began with the publication of a special centennial edition of the *Gettysburg Times*. Publisher Paul Roy structured the edition around historic newspaper accounts of the battle, official proclamations from governors of states that contributed troops in 1863, and a crowd-sourced segment devoted to highlighting local residents' Civil War ancestors. The 546 advertisements that helped pay for the issue provide a fascinating window into Gettysburg's midcentury tourist economy and demonstrate the range of Civil War narratives in widespread circulation in the 1960s. On a deeper level, however, they also reveal the extent to which consumerism itself shaped efforts to draw meaning and lessons from the battle. By the mid-twentieth century, many Americans enthusiastically subscribed to the belief that history not only provided a window into modern national character but that consumer goods provided a means to "reclaiming" essential American values.[4] As entrepreneurs, businesses, and corporations employed narratives of the battle for financial and public relations gain, they played a role in shaping contemporary public memory of the Civil War and helping to elevate the reconciliationist interpretation over alternative narratives. The advertisements in this commemorative newspaper testify to the ubiquity of the Cold War narrative in advertising, a little studied but important arena for forging public memory of the war.

While some advertisements in the centennial edition were indistinguishable from those that might have run in the newspaper each week, the majority were clearly designed to appeal to a centennial audience. A sizable number of the advertisements were historically themed but not specific to the Civil War; many, such as the ad for Bear's Department Store, aimed to awaken a generalized nostalgia for the past in viewers and prompt them to associate their products or services with supposedly historic small-town values of honesty, integrity, and quality craftsmanship. Peoples Drug Store drew on the Whiggish interpretation of history as constantly moving toward greater enlightenment to promise potential customers that "as America has progressed, so have we." Likewise, Teeter Stone, Inc., employed an image of a rocket launch alongside text that thanked the "pioneers of yesteryear who sacrificed and suffered" to lay the foundations for twentieth-century Americans to attain "unbelievable achievements in every field."[5]

Others, however, made specific connections to the battle and the overall history of the war. Dengler Brothers Grocery told readers that the armies came to Gettysburg by chance, not choice, and promised "But you can choose — and eat hearty at bargain prices!" Columbia Gas of Pennsylvania capitalized on the fact that the Eternal Peace Light flame was fueled by natural gas, marshalling the "Strength Through Unity" narrative in their text in order to stress gas's role in "uniting" the American economy. Many employed both Union and Confederate flags and the phrase "we pay honor" to assure visitors of different regional and political loyalties that they were properly respectful of the valor of both sides. Some explicitly embraced the narrative that the Civil War laid the groundwork for the United States to grow into a global superpower. Gettysburg Glass Company's advertisement claimed that the battle "brought unity to our country," a sentiment that would have no doubt perplexed Civil War soldiers. While many lionized the armies of 1863 for fighting for "a cause in which they believed," none attempted to define that cause — testimony to the enduring power of white reconciliation in the popular mind.[6]

The governors' proclamations on the battle are similarly intriguing for the insight they provide into how centennial interpretations of the meaning and legacy of the battle were shaped by politics, geography, and partisan identity. The 1960s were a period of significant political realignment. The Democratic Party fractured internally over the issue of civil rights, with its northern and liberal wings moving further and further away from its traditional southern power base. The Republican Party, for its part, plunged into its own identity-shifting debate over whether the GOP should continue to present itself as the party of Lincoln or pursue the allegiance of disenchanted white southern Democrats by moving in an increasingly conservative direction. Though the wisdom of its swing to the right seemed highly questionable in the wake of massive electoral defeats in 1964, by the end of the decade the long-term viability of the "southern strategy" was evident.[7]

The common ground between the proclamations is significant; almost all began by praising the "courageous" or "honorable" service of soldiers from their state and invoking the "High Water Mark" or "turning point" narrative in some way. Many articulated themes of national unity and reconciliation, embracing the idea that the war had made the United States into the exemplar (and defender) of freedom worldwide. Yet their definitions of freedom and understandings of what was at stake at Gettysburg varied according to region, ideology, and party affiliation. Democrats from northern states and most Republicans were likely to point to equality and human dignity as legacies of the war. Southern Democrats, unsurprisingly, focused intensely on state sovereignty and national endurance.

Pennsylvania governor William Scranton, a progressive Republican, took a reconciliationist line in the first section of his proclamation, opining that "the great wound healed, sutured with bonds stronger than those of sectionalism." Scranton's conciliatory tone was likely influenced, at least in part, by his role as host of the commemoration. Philip Hoff, Vermont's first Democratic governor in a century, stated that the "unity of modern America" was forged "on the anvil of Gettysburg." Orval Faubus, the reactionary Arkansas Democrat, suggested that one of the greatest lessons of the war was that "we must remain united if we are to endure as a nation in this world of turmoil and external dissension." George Romney of Michigan, another moderate Republican, sounded a similar note, arguing that if the nation were to "meet the grim challenges of the Communist world," Americans must "unite behind the principles of freedom and equality which our fathers and their fathers fought to preserve."[8]

South Carolina's Donald Russell, a conservative Democrat, alluded to postwar reconciliation in his observation that "combining the resources of the wonderful people from a wide geographical area, the United States has emerged as the leading democracy of history." Mississippi Democrat Ross Barnett, well known for his white supremacist politics, insisted that the foundation "for the greatest nation in the history of mankind"—not to mention eternal peace—lay in respect for state sovereignty. Moderate Republican John Chafee of Rhode Island, on the other hand, linked American global leadership with the emancipationist interpretation of the Civil War, suggesting that Americans, "as leaders in freedom's cause," needed to be reminded of "this country's firm belief in the fundamental dignity of man."[9]

Some northern governors offered specific interpretations of the battle's meaning fueled in part by Cold War liberals' increasing frustration with the damaging impact of southern white violence on the nation's reputation abroad. Maine's John Reed, a Republican who later became an ally of Lyndon Johnson, deemed its purpose "to establish a free society with equality for all men." Harnessing the myth of the "Treasury of Virtue" to the cause of emancipation and the urgency of the present, Iowa's Harold Hughes, a liberal Democrat, argued that Northern men fell at Gettysburg in defense of the principle of equality. He exhorted readers that "we must continue to pursue this goal if we are to attain the unity we need for those perilous and difficult times." Connecticut's John Dempsey, another liberal Democrat, similarly claimed that Union soldiers fought and died at Gettysburg "in support of liberty, justice and human rights for all men." Karl Rolvaag of Minnesota, a member of the state's Democratic-Farmer-Labor Party, argued that it was at Gettysburg "that a nation was fully born—forged in the heat of battle, tempered with the blood of sacrifice." For Rolvaag, the battle's legacy included freedom of worship, freedom of assembly, and freedom of thought. Should these freedoms ever be lost, he suggested, "those we honor here will be forgotten."[10] This identification of Gettysburg as the site of the nation's birth (or rebirth) was echoed repeatedly throughout the battle anniversary week.

Does Peace Require Justice?
Dueling Interpretations at the Peace Light

Though not an "official" part of the commemoration, the opening act of the anniversary was a June 29 field mass at the Eternal Peace Light sponsored by the University of Notre Dame Foundation. Between 4,000 and 5,000 people, including former President Eisenhower and his wife, Mamie, braved the scorching heat to attend. The ostensible purpose of the mass was to celebrate the life of Father William Corby and place a new interpretive marker in front of his statue. (Corby, the chaplain who famously provided the Irish Brigade a general absolution at Gettysburg, also served as president of the University of Notre Dame.) But the criticism leveled against John F. Kennedy's Catholicism during the 1960 presidential campaign provided a broader backdrop for the event. Organizers openly acknowledged that they hoped to make a statement about "the rapport of the principles of America and of the church." Reverend Joseph Kealy of Gettysburg's St. Francis Xavier Church commented favorably afterward on the "successful display of the patriotism of the members of our church."[11]

The event took on yet another dimension when the scheduled preacher, New York's Francis Cardinal Spellman, had to withdraw and was replaced by the Very Reverend Theodore M. Hesburgh, president of the University of Notre Dame. Standing in the shadow of this iconic symbol of white reconciliation, Hesburgh explicitly invoked an emancipationist understanding of the Civil War. The war, he insisted, was fought for a reason: to win freedom for African Americans. A member of the U.S. Commission on Civil Rights (and permanent Vatican representative to the International Atomic Energy Agency), "Father Ted," as he was widely known, seized the opportunity to urge attendees to become great emancipators in their own communities by taking action to resolve the unfinished business of the Civil War. Condemning racial discrimination in voting, housing, employment, education, and the justice system, he challenged his listeners to take something more than family memories and vacation photos away from Gettysburg. Invoking the spirit of the student protesters who picketed outside Los Angeles dime stores with signs reading "Did They Die in Vain at Gettysburg?" he encouraged his listeners to use their experience on the battlefield to commit themselves to making freedom live for all Americans.[12]

The central theme of Hesburgh's speech was that lasting peace cannot flourish in the absence of justice. One must wonder whether he or any of his listeners thought that evening of the scene concurrently playing out across the Maryland border in the Eastern Shore community of Cambridge. Both peace and justice were in short supply in the town that spent the battle anniversary week under martial law. When the National Guard arrived in Cambridge in the wake of three days of unrest precipitated by violent resistance to civil rights demonstrations, local whites derided the soldiers as "an army of occupation." As speakers and spectators at Gettysburg lauded peace, unity, and harmony, Cambridge residents experienced "peace" only through martial law. The National Guard remained in Cambridge for nearly a year, making their time there "the longest peacetime occupation of a community in the history of the United States," with the exception of Reconstruction. Though it is impossible to know whether Cambridge was on the minds of those who gathered for the Peace Light mass, the symbolism was powerful. As Martin Luther King wrote in "Letter from Birmingham City Jail," the mere absence of tension is a "negative peace." A "positive peace," by contrast, requires the presence of justice. When the Guard first arrived in Cambridge, resident Mabel Booth observed, "I have never seen this place stirred up like this. It has always been quiet. But I'm glad. It was only quiet then because the white man was having his way about things." Despite claims to the contrary at Gettysburg, eternal peace was far out of reach in the America of 1963.[13]

June 30 brought the Gettysburg Fire Company's annual memorial service. The popular Army Field Band and former President Eisenhower headlined the evening program at the high school football field, the kickoff to the usual week of festivities at the Recreation Park. Eisenhower was much in demand as a speaker on Civil War history during the centennial year, yet despite serving as the GCC's honorary chairman, his speech at the fire company event was his only formal role during the summer battle anniversary. Given before an audience estimated at 4,000 to 6,000, Eisenhower's address, "The Meaning of Gettysburg," immediately sparked controversy. The *Washington Post* observed that the former president reiterated his political philosophy of individual self-reliance but steered clear of discussing the big issue of the year: civil rights. Presenting the true meaning of the battle as the preservation of self-government, Eisenhower warned that democracy was vulnerable not only to attacks from external enemies but also to internal rot, brought on by dependence on government largesse.[14]

Proponents of the social safety net found much to dislike in Eisenhower's speech (which *Newsweek* termed "a slam-bang attack on the welfare state") and at least one newspaper pointed out that Eisenhower himself had enjoyed government benefits for the majority of his life. The Black press found the former president's failure to refer in any way to civil rights unforgiveable; the *Chicago Daily Defender* lambasted the speech as "a display of moral insensitivity." The negative reaction from Black leaders may have been magnified by the timing of the speech, which coincided with widespread reviews of E. Frederic Morrow's memoir about his days in the Eisenhower administration, which was sharply critical what he considered the former president's "lukewarm" stand on civil rights.[15] There is little evidence regarding Eisenhower's reaction to this criticism, but he did adopt a somewhat different approach in his remarks at the November activities.

The official commemoration opened at the Peace Light on July 1, where a crowd of 2,000 to 3,000 gathered in spite of the nearly 100-degree heat for a program devoted to "Our Heritage." The elevated platform was packed with governors and appointed representatives of all but two of the twenty-nine states that had troops at Gettysburg; only Louisiana and Tennessee were unrepresented. Pennsylvania governor William Scranton gave a welcoming address and the governors and their representatives laid wreaths honoring the soldiers from their states. The GBPA and the Loyal Legion formally presented land deeds for two newly purchased tracts to a representative of the Department of the Interior, and Postmaster General J. Edward Day dedicated the new Gettysburg commemorative stamp.[16]

In the shadow of a monument predicated in large part on white reconciliation and the erasure of Black Americans, Reverend Lena Parr, pastor of St. Paul AME Zion Church, rose from her seat on the platform to give the invocation opening the ceremony. As discussed previously, St. Paul's was deeply rooted in Gettysburg, and under Parr's leadership, the church offered a wide range of programming. The AME Zion Church was less patriarchal than most other Christian denominations, ordaining women as early as 1948. Still, a female pastor was a rarity in Gettysburg in the 1960s; of the local clergy involved in commemorative activities in these years, Parr was the only African American and the only female. It is likely that her involvement in these programs (and her presence at the Peace Light) derived from the active role she played in the Gettysburg Ministerium.[17]

Only a small remnant of Parr's prayer was recorded, but it is known that she prayed for the nation, the world, and the governors present, and beseeched God that all races would "come together as one." Though these words are reconciliationist on the surface, their inherent assertion of racial equality likely would have horrified white supremacists, including those who shared the platform, who arguably interpreted them as an endorsement of "racial mixing." Parr was undoubtedly well aware of white segregationists' fixation on miscegenation and racial "purity," yet as a Christian minister and a Black woman, she chose to emphasize the liberating potential of the Christian Bible *and* racial integration. Her vision of reconciliation was broader than the GCC's, encompassing not just (white) northerners and southerners but all the peoples of the world. Even though Parr was the only person of color on the platform, a Black woman in a position of influence likely served as powerful testimony to the emancipationist interpretation of the Civil War. Yet many important questions lack reliable answers. As she surveyed the field from the platform, did she think of the Klan's use of this portion of

Oak Hill—and the "gift" her predecessor at St. Paul's had been essentially forced to accept from the group in 1925? How did she feel about sharing a platform with George Wallace? What did the Battle of Gettysburg mean to her on a personal level?[18]

Speaking to reporters in advance of the ceremony, Massachusetts governor Endicott Peabody, a progressive Democrat, argued that the nation had "turned its back on the causes for which the war was fought." Though he deplored the unrest and tension associated with demonstrations, Peabody asserted that they would not cease until the fundamental injustices of American society were redressed. William Scranton's welcome speech hit on some of the same themes, stressing the importance of national unity, the need to eradicate prejudice, and the extent of "freedom's unfinished business." The former Yale history major told the audience that the new birth of freedom called for by Lincoln had been dormant for decades following the war, but was now alive and moving again thanks to the advent of the modern civil rights movement.[19]

Though Scranton, as the host of the commemoration, was careful to also emphasize the reconciliationist themes of national unity and American power, the remarks of some other northern governors during the event reveal an aggressive deployment of northern sectional memory. Peabody argued that "our sons" laid down their lives at Gettysburg in defense of the nation's core principles; the only rightful way to honor their sacrifice was to finally make equality a reality. His words echo Governor John Dempsey of Connecticut's assertion in his gubernatorial proclamation that northern soldiers fought for justice and human rights "for all men." This rhetoric is challenging to precisely categorize. As noted previously, contemporary white southern intransigence clearly played a role in a resurgence of sectional memory among some leading northern politicians and political progressives.[20]

The civil rights movement's influence in revitalizing the idea that the Civil War was fundamentally about slavery and equal opportunity propelled many liberal Democrats and moderate Republicans to buck reconciliationist etiquette and overtly address issues of cause and causation. Yet such statements, which frequently portrayed northerners as righteous crusaders, also revealed more than a hint of the "Treasury of Virtue" myth and its tendency to absolve northerners of all racial sins: past, present, and future. On occasion, this line of argument was even employed to argue that direct action protest was acceptable in the South, but inappropriate and counterproductive in the supposedly free North.[21]

By 1963, the revival of northern sectional memory had reached the White House. Raised on the traditional scholarly narrative of northern venom and southern victimization, John F. Kennedy's understanding of Civil War history had long convinced him that moderation was more effective than coercion. As violent white resistance forced his administration to intervene in crisis after crisis, however, Kennedy began to rethink this assumption. In the wake of the Mississippi state legislature's release of a vituperative and inaccurate report on the desegregation of the state university, the president began to question whether white southerners' accounts of the Civil War era might be similarly unreliable. He told his brother Robert that he "would never believe a book on Reconstruction again." Turning to the works of C. Vann Woodward, Kennedy began see the war years—and their ramifications for political action in the present—differently. Having for years attempted to avoid action on civil rights for fear of alienating white southerners, he told an advisor in the summer of 1963, "I'm coming to believe that Thaddeus Stevens was right. I had been taught to regard him as a man of vicious bias. But, when I see this sort of thing, I begin to wonder how else you can treat them [white southerners]."[22]

William Scranton was a Kennedy Republican, a fiscal conservative who supported civil rights and programs such as the Peace Corps. In his speech at the Peace Light, he stressed the human cost of the battle, urging the audience to resolve in response never "to be torn in two again." Yet while he had a great deal to say about the present, he did not characterize Confederates as defenders of racial oppression and Union troops as liberators. Rather, he identified the problems of racism and racial discrimination as national in scope, insisting that "no American should point his finger at any other." Nevertheless, he robustly championed the United States' political and ideological virtues. In a clear slap at the Soviet Union, Scranton argued that "political freedom without economic freedom is not really freedom at all. . . . We do not believe that man must give up his liberties to fill his belly." While Scranton delivered these lines with Communism in mind, organizers of the following month's March on Washington, which would also draw on the legacy of the Civil War, turned this idea on its head, arguing that without substantial economic redistribution, political and legal reforms in the service of civil rights would never deliver full freedom to American Blacks.[23]

In the summer of 1963, Scranton was widely perceived as a candidate for the Republican nomination for the presidency, and he undoubtedly embraced the opportunities the anniversary provided to boost his profile on the national stage. He issued the formal invitations to the other governors to participate in the commemoration and hosted a luncheon for his colleagues at the Hotel Gettysburg. A columnist for the *Philadelphia Inquirer* found substantial support for Scranton among attendees who identified as Republican. He noted flippantly: "The women go for him just as they went for President Kennedy during his campaign in 1960. Bill is a well put together, handsome guy. And if he should be pitted against Mr. Kennedy in a Presidential contest the combined heart-beat among the gals of the Nation would be sufficient to shake the earth as the cannonading did hereabouts a hundred years ago." Such a match-up never came; as the Republican Party moved to the right over the course of 1964, Scranton lost the nomination to Barry Goldwater and withdrew from electoral politics. But in 1963, many moderate Republicans saw Scranton and Nelson Rockefeller, also a favorite for the nomination, as a balancing force against the extremism of "the Goldwater influence" and an articulate voice for what they deemed "the Lincoln tradition."[24]

In the speeches that followed Scranton's, Postmaster General J. Edward Day provided a new link in the chain of long-lasting connection between antinuclear protest and the Peace Light, contending that "in today's world of a divided Germany, a divided Europe, a divided China, Gettysburg provides a beacon light of hope for reunification. In the face of disappointments and failures in our American efforts for a nuclear test ban treaty and for disarmament, Gettysburg should remind us never to lose heart, because the stakes are so momentous in the effort for peace." John Carver Jr., assistant secretary of the interior, followed up Day's remarks by arguing (indirectly) that the purpose of historical memory was to prompt action in the present. Laying aside his prepared speech, he called on Congress to adopt the Civil Rights Bill on the grounds that Lincoln's Gettysburg Address had defined equality under the law "as the purpose behind the bloody struggle" of the Civil War. Though these words undoubtedly resonated with many in the audience, it is telling that when the eleven state governors participating in the commemoration were introduced from the platform, the crowd reserved its most enthusiastic applause for George Wallace, who arrived in Gettysburg fresh from his obstructionist stand in Tuscaloosa.[25]

Though many critics derided Wallace's action as a publicity stunt, it raised his prestige nationwide, thus ensuring that his visit to Gettysburg coincided with his period of greatest influence as a national spokesman of white resistance. The *Montgomery Advertiser* noted that as the other governors fled the sunbaked scene at the ceremony's conclusion, Wallace signed autographs for twenty minutes, including one—if the reporter's information was correct—for an African American aide to Governor Peabody. Wallace, the great-grandson of a Confederate soldier who may have fought at Gettysburg, toured the battlefield that afternoon with a National Park Service guide, responding to the tour with interest. Unlike many of the other visiting dignitaries, Wallace made a point of attending nearly all of the scheduled events that week, and a reporter noted that he was "a big favorite of the centennial crowds." Crowds mobbed him in the lobby of the Hotel Gettysburg and trailed him around the battlefield begging him to sign their anniversary programs.[26]

Wallace's first stop on the battlefield on the morning of July 1 was a visit to the Alabama monument on West Confederate Avenue, where he laid a wreath. Though the crowd for the ceremony was small, Wallace's presence drew the news media. His message for the reporters gathered translated easily into soundbites: states' rights and constitutionalism, both of which he identified specifically but not exclusively with the South. For all his popularity in his home state, Wallace had political ambitions outside of Alabama, and saw participation in the Gettysburg anniversary programming as an opportunity to begin cultivating a national political following. When asked if he would consider a run for the presidency, his response was that a southern president would be a boon for the nation. Yet he was careful to also emphasize that "we stand [for the defense of the Constitution] among the descendants of brave men who fought for *North and South*." The wording suggests that Wallace wanted to allow room for northerners to count themselves as part of this collective "we"—a first step toward cultivating that national political following.[27]

He sounded the same theme even more directly the following day, telling reporters that Americans across the nation must come together "to save the country from centralized socialist government." Neglecting no opportunity for a meet and greet, Wallace returned to the Alabama monument again the following day, where he spoke with James Van Alen of Newport, Rhode Island, the great-grandson of a Union commander. The politically conservative Van Alen, whose poem "Pickett's Charge" graced the inside of the official centennial program, raved to reporters that Wallace was "100 percent American and it is nice to know someone who is a true American." The *Advertiser* read Wallace's heavy police protection, popularity with attendees, and prevalence in media coverage as evidence that he had become a "protest symbol for Northern whites who are sick of Kennedy and in fear of Martin X" (likely a deliberate conflation of Martin Luther King Jr. and Malcolm X).[28]

Wallace cultivated the reporters who trailed him around the field, maintaining a friendly demeanor and taking time to answer their questions. In an exclusive interview with the *Gettysburg Times*, Wallace argued that his actions in Tuscaloosa were not intended to deny Black students their right to an education but rather to prevent violence and "protect local government," themes that resonated with political conservatives nationwide. He also weighed in on the Supreme Court's controversial 1962 ruling on prayer in public schools, which was unpopular in Adams County. Striking a defiant tone, Wallace vowed to fight enforcement of the decision in Alabama, insisting that "the federal government may send federal troops in and arrest us for praying, but we're going to go right on doing it."[29] For many whites, Wallace's defiance of federal mandates was the root of his appeal, particularly as Congress began deliberations on the Civil Rights Bill, which opponents viewed as nothing short of an all-out assault on states' rights.

Wielding Confederate Memory to Oppose Civil Rights Legislation: The Dedication of the South Carolina Monument

Returning to Washington, D.C., from his Memorial Day visit to Gettysburg, Vice President Lyndon Johnson began to advocate that Kennedy make his own "Gettysburg speech" laying out the moral case for the new legislation. By doing so, Johnson argued, the president would put the force of his office behind the legislation and give Black Americans reason to believe that he planned to fight for it. When informing readers that new legislation was finally in the offing, the *Chicago Daily Defender* connected the dots back to Johnson's Gettysburg speech. Drew Pearson suggested in the *Washington Post* that Johnson's remarks at Gettysburg had increased the pressure on Kennedy to take a public stand. "The speech has now become a sort of Emancipation Proclamation for the Kennedy Administration," he argued, "and some of the White House functionaries are irked that it was the Vice President, not the President, who made it."[30]

Martin Luther King Jr. also made a case for a presidential address on civil rights in a telegram to Kennedy on May 30, as a new groundswell of protest rose across the South. Building on a sustained grassroots boycott of white merchants, sit-ins in Jackson, Mississippi, led to a wave of student actions and the arrest of hundreds of young people. Police in Danville, Virginia, attacked picketers with high-pressure fire hoses and billy clubs; a busload of SNCC activists were imprisoned incommunicado in Winona, Mississippi (emerging days later brutally beaten); and Deputy Attorney General Nicholas

Katzenbach went head-to-head with Wallace in Tuscaloosa. At the height of the University of Alabama crisis, Kennedy's aides suggested that he consider a televised address to the American public. When Wallace stepped aside after a staged confrontation, they deemed the speech no longer necessary, but the president chose to press forward anyway.[31]

Throughout the first two years of his presidency, Kennedy generally spoke of civil rights from a position of Cold War pragmatism that seemed more concerned with the impact of domestic racial upheaval on the image of American democracy abroad than racial injustice itself. This framing angered many Black Americans. In his 1961 State of the Union address, he argued that racial discrimination "subjects us to the charge of world opinion that democracy is not equal to the high promise of our heritage." Later that same year, as Freedom Riders met violent resistance across the Deep South, Kennedy complained that their actions weakened his international standing in the lead-up to a summit with Soviet premier Nikita Khrushchev. Activists responded that they were hardly the ones responsible for embarrassing the nation: "We can't drag the name of the United States in the mud. The name of the United States in already in the mud. It is up to us to get it out."[32]

Though Kennedy certainly framed Wallace's obstruction in Tuscaloosa and the violence in Birmingham in the context of Cold War politics, his June 11, 1963, speech announcing the Civil Rights Bill differed substantially from his previous statements on civil rights. Speaking explicitly to the moral dimensions of racial injustice, Kennedy put the symbolic authority of the White House on the side of the Black freedom struggle, paving the way for a "new public vocabulary on civil rights." Invoking an interpretation of the Emancipation Proclamation employed previously by both Martin Luther King Jr. and Lyndon Johnson (at Gettysburg), he chided the nation for failing to realize the deeper meaning of the edict: full economic and social freedom for African Americans. Black Americans enthusiastically applauded the speech, though some noted that it was long overdue. Distinguished Black scholar John Hope Franklin saw parallels between Kennedy's speech and the Gettysburg Address, observing that Kennedy effectively "reminded his fellow citizens that they had not yet become committed to a new birth of freedom."[33]

The president's speech—and the Civil Rights Bill itself—formed vital background context for the July 2 dedication of a new monument honoring South Carolina troops. The South Carolina Confederate War Centennial Commission appointed television producer Payne Williams to spearhead the state's memorial efforts at Gettysburg in 1961. He and his committee selected a site 300 yards south of the Longstreet Tower, near the spot where

Kershaw's Brigade camped on July 2. As the committee began to finalize its proposed design and inscription, Superintendent Myers advised Williams that "the general rule is that inscriptions shall be a brief historic legend compiled without censure or praise." In one of his first acts as superintendent, Kittridge Wing recommended approval of the proposed design, but the inscription did not reach park staff until early April. South Carolina senator Olin Johnston immediately requested that the secretary of the interior expedite the approval process.[34]

The proposed inscription read: "THAT MEN OF HONOR MIGHT FOREVER KNOW THE RESPONSIBILITIES OF FREEDOM, DEDICATED SOUTH CAROLINIANS STOOD AND WERE COUNTED FOR THEIR HERITAGE AND CONVICTIONS. ABIDING FAITH IN THE SACREDNESS OF STATES' RIGHTS PROVIDED THEIR CREED HERE. MANY EARNED ETERNAL GLORY." Wing's thoughts on the text are unknown, but regional director Ronald Lee was grudgingly accepting. He made no mention of the overt Lost Cause sentiments inherent in the inscription, commenting only that it could be more specifically focused on Gettysburg. Johnston's intervention in the approval process was deemed so effective that when members of the commission charged with erecting a monument to Florida troops wanted to get their plans approved at the last minute, they contacted the senator's office for advice regarding how to most effectively apply pressure within the Department of the Interior.[35]

The argument that discriminatory practices undermined the nation's foreign policy goals failed to resonate with most segregationists, "who were much more interested in preserving their way of life than in what foreign countries thought of the United States." Thus when George Wallace took the podium at the dedication ceremony, he employed the flip side of the Cold War civil rights framework's double edge to brand the Black freedom struggle as subversive. The equation of racial justice with Communism had a long history in the United States. Red-baiting had long proved a successful strategy to destroy the credibility of outspoken Black leaders, even prompting the NAACP itself to expel suspected Communists in the late 1940s in an act of self-preservation. White southerners began to use the Lost Cause as a weapon in this struggle during the 1930s, harnessing condemnation of the "evils" of Reconstruction and the supposed ideals of the Confederacy to the emerging anticommunist crusade.[36]

Like his friend Albert B. Moore, the executive director of the Alabama Civil War Centennial Commission, Wallace believed that the cause of civil rights was communist-inspired and that integration itself was a "manifestation of the red menace," calculated to destroy American democracy. In agreement with Moore that the "Confederate cause" could be used to bolster anticommunism, Wallace thus began his speech at the South Carolina monument by railing against the "dangers of international Communism." Echoing Georgia senator Richard Russell's immediate condemnation of the Civil Rights Bill as a step toward totalitarianism, he painted the Deep South as the nation's last bastion against "destructive centralization" that would destroy constitutional government and individual rights.[37]

The ceremony was defiantly antifederal in tone. Barely three weeks out from the announcement of the Civil Rights Bill, John May stood by the monument and argued that South Carolina troops had fought for principles of self-government enshrined in the Constitution. His insistence that these very principles were currently being misconstrued by those seeking to manipulate the Constitution for "their own selfish use" was no doubt interpreted by many in the crowd as not only a criticism of the legislation itself but a challenge to Kennedy's authority to propose it and Congress's authority to pass it. One wonders what the previous owners of the land upon which the monument was located—the heirs of Valentine Watts—would have made of this argument about self-government. Two of Watts's sons, John and Lloyd, served in the U.S. Colored Troops, a strong indication that they would have defined "the right to self-government" quite differently than John May did.[38]

May served in the South Carolina State House, representing Aiken County, an area transformed during the Cold War by federal dollars in the form of DuPont's Savannah River Plant. Despite his devotion to states' rights, he and his associates did not protest the expansion of federal power in this arena, not so long as it brought prosperity to the region. He was also commander of the South Carolina Sons of Confederate Veterans and chairman of the South Carolina Confederate War Centennial Commission and the Confederate States Centennial Conference, giving rise to his nickname, "Mr. Confederacy." May's devotion to Confederate symbols led him to spearhead the 1962 initiative to place the Confederate flag on the top of the South Carolina State House, where it continued to fly until public outcry in the wake of Dylann Roof's murderous 2015 rampage at "Mother" Emanuel AME Church finally prompted state leaders to remove it.[39]

By 1963, South Carolina had a long history of opposition to campaigns for racial justice and federal protections for Black Americans' civil rights. Two high-profile incidents of racial terrorism in the state—the beating and blinding of World War II veteran Isaac Woodard and the lynching of Willie Earle—played a key role in establishing and guiding the work of Harry

Truman's pioneering President's Committee on Civil Rights. The PCCR's findings led the president to propose new legislation on civil rights in 1948 and the Democratic Party to adopt a strong civil rights plank in its 1948 platform. The inclusion of the civil rights plank prompted the Dixiecrat revolt (which widely popularized use of the Confederate battle flag as a symbol of white resistance) and the nomination of South Carolina governor Strom Thurmond as a third-party candidate in the 1948 presidential election.[40]

This opposition to civil rights and federal authority did not subside in the wake of the Dixiecrats' defeat at the polls. In the weeks leading up to the battle anniversary, white resistance in South Carolina manifested in numerous ways. These included an anti-integration march at the statehouse, a state court ruling closing parks in response to a federal court order to integrate them, and the firebombing of the home of a Black student who had successfully sued for admission to the state university. In inviting George Wallace—the leading spokesman of southern white resistance—to dedicate the monument, the group spearheading the effort made it clear that they saw a clear connection between the Confederate cause and southern resistance to the civil rights movement.[41]

While Wallace and his supporters clearly saw Confederate memory as a weapon in the fight against civil rights, historian C. Vann Woodward had no patience for such use of history. Reflecting on the continuing strength of what Robert Penn Warren memorably termed the "Great Alibi," Woodward scoffed at the way that the narrative of southern victimization enabled "an obscene parody of history" in which "howling mobs become Pickett's immortal heroes and Little Rock is transformed into Gettysburg." Warren put it similarly, questioning rhetorically whether grown men harassing Black schoolchildren could really imagine themselves "at one with those gaunt, whiskery scarecrows who fought it out, breast to breast, to the death?" For Woodward and Warren, no amount of passionate personal identification with the Gettysburg battle narrative could legitimize the idea that twentieth-century defenders of states' rights were a modern-day embodiment of the Confederacy.[42]

In many ways, the South Carolina monument is more of a testimony to how a group of twentieth-century southern whites wanted the world to remember their own defense of "states' rights" than it is a tribute to the soldiers who fought at Gettysburg. But the dedication ceremony also serves as a clear reminder that this interpretation of states' rights had currency nationwide in 1963. The crowd greeted Wallace's assertion that millions of Americans "look to the South to lead in the fight to restore constitutional rights and the rights of states and individuals" with a standing ovation, foreshadowing his later success on the presidential campaign trail with similar language — race-neutral on the surface, but carefully coded.[43]

Wallace's visibility throughout the anniversary undoubtedly contributed to garnering him twenty-three write-in votes in Adams County in the April 1964 Republican primary. R. C. McLaughlin, the owner of a local newsstand, who stopped the governor on his way out of town to shake his hand and pass along his appreciation for "standing up for what you think is right," likely contributed one of them. However, Wallace did not commit to participation in the anniversary programming until late in the game, and the scale of the commemorative activities mitigated against much advance publicity regarding his involvement. The Pennsylvania State Police worried enough about his safety — and the prospect that his presence could spark demonstrations — to assign him a special guard during his time in Gettysburg. Yet no organized protests emerged, and it is highly probable that many people did not even realize that the nation's leading spokesman of white resistance had been in town until he was already gone.[44]

Cold War Civil Rights at the Florida Monument

The more internationalist side of the Cold War Civil Rights narrative held sway in the last official activity of the battle commemoration, the July 3 dedication of a monument to Florida troops, also located along West Confederate Avenue. Made of two upright tablets of granite (the larger standing fourteen feet high), the monument had little ornamentation beyond the state seal and a band of laurel leaves, a traditional symbol of victory, success, and fame. The smaller of the two tablets provided a brief narrative of the brigade's actions and losses, followed by a statement of significance blending traditional Lost Cause rhetoric with Cold War framing: "LIKE ALL FLORIDIANS WHO PARTICIPATED IN THE CIVIL WAR, THEY FOUGHT WITH COURAGE AND DEVOTION FOR THE IDEALS IN WHICH THEY BELIEVED. BY THEIR NOBLE EXAMPLE OF BRAVERY AND ENDURANCE, THEY ENABLE US TO MEET WITH CONFIDENCE ANY SACRIFICE WHICH CONFRONTS US AS AMERICANS."[45]

Though the monument itself shared a certain amount of basic territory with its South Carolina cousin, and John May laid a wreath on behalf of South Carolina, its dedication ceremony was dramatically different, reflecting a profound concern with international politics. The Confederate iconography (flags, music, uniforms) so present at the South Carolina dedication was absent at the Florida one.[46] Keynote speaker Sam Gibbons, a freshman congressman representing Tampa, echoed some of the themes of Johnson's Memorial Day speech, drawing upon the experiences of Florida troops at Gettysburg to argue for a vision of civil rights reform profoundly shaped by foreign policy imperatives.

By the summer of 1963, Cold War liberals had plenty of evidence to support their assertion that racial discrimination was alienating potential U.S. allies in the emerging world and jeopardizing the maintenance of a favorable balance of power between the West and the Soviet bloc. John Dempsey alluded to this concern in his proclamation on the battle, arguing, "If our nation is to maintain and strengthen its position as a leader among free nations, we must present to the world a picture of fifty states solidly united in support of liberty, justice and human rights for all men." New Jersey's Richard Hughes, also a Democrat, struck a similar note, warning that only a commitment on the part of every American to securing basic freedoms for all would "enable the United States to serve as a shining beacon of democracy for the other nations of the world."[47] Representing a state that was a major center of the aerospace industry (fundamentally propelled by Cold War tensions), geographically close to Cuba, and profoundly aware of the importance of public image due to its burgeoning tourist economy, Sam Gibbons shared this internationalist outlook.

In the wake of World War II, a tidal wave of urbanization and suburbanization hit Florida, bringing enormous population growth, economic diversification, and demographic transformation in its wake. No state in the union changed more in the postwar years; within forty years Florida went from one of the poorest in the nation, with the smallest population in the South, to one of the most dynamic and diverse. Florida's metamorphosis into a state that was in many ways less southern, more economically and ethnically diverse, and less solidly Democratic than many of its neighbors, however, did not mean that racial inequality was a thing of the past—or that campaigns for racial justice would not rock communities across the state throughout the 1950s and 1960s.[48]

Some 900,000 northern migrants arrived Florida between 1946 and 1950, leading an observer to note that "the further south you went in Florida, the more it began to feel like the North." With its low taxes, warm weather, and inexpensive land prices, the state quickly became a mecca for elderly northerners. With the establishment of the National Aeronautics and Space Administration (NASA) in 1958, Brevard County, Florida, became the fastest-growing section of the United States; in June 1963, an average of forty-two new residents arrived in the county every day. The majority were not native southerners, and while not necessarily holding progressive views on race, they had diverse political loyalties and little attachment to the Old South. Though generally unenthusiastic about integration, most of Florida's new transplants opposed violence as a tool for maintaining the status quo, and concerns about maintaining the state's tourist-friendly image led elites to shun both direct action protest and violent resistance alike. Determined Blacks and angry whites nonetheless bucked the public relations script in many communities, and an advisor to the U.S. Commission on Civil Rights warned in 1963 that tourist-friendly St. Augustine was "a segregated superbomb aimed at the heart of Florida's economy and political integrity."[49]

None of the state's demographic or political changes, however, rendered Civil War history irrelevant to the state's emerging new identity. Despite the significant percentage of Floridians who had remained loyal to the Union and the presence of northerners in Florida since Reconstruction, identification with the Lost Cause was widespread. On the eve of the Civil War Centennial, only eleven of the state's Civil War monuments (mostly in cemeteries) were Union in association. Though Florida's economic and demographic transformation accelerated during the centennial years, Civil War history continued to exercise a powerful hold on many residents. The postcentennial period gave rise to a veritable boom in Civil War monument building across the state, and all but two of the monuments erected between 1968 and 1997 were traditional Confederate markers. That said, Florida's complex identity as a state in transition profoundly affected its contribution to the wrenching debates over the meaning of Civil War history that played out in Gettysburg in July 1963.[50]

While serving in the state senate, Gibbons played a key role in moving the appropriations bill establishing the Florida Gettysburg Memorial Commission through the state legislature. Though their efforts got a late start, commission members were determined to dedicate the monument during the battle anniversary week. Members of the state's congressional delegation began pressuring the NPS director's office to accelerate the approval process before the official paperwork even reached GNMP staff. When it did, Wing and his staff expressed reservations, noting dryly that the laudatory text "violates the policy of 'no praise' rather flagrantly." Regional director Lee acknowledged the subjectivity of the inscription, yet admitted that it differed little from the one recently approved for the South Carolina monument and observed that it might be useless to object. Given the time constraints, he suspected that the commission had already given the go-ahead to begin carving the inscription. The director's office subsequently approved the inscription and design on June 14.[51]

Later that month, the initial force behind the campaign, Tampa attorney Paul Danahy, wrote Sam Gibbons suggesting three possible directions for his dedicatory remarks. Danahy (a transplanted New Englander) proposed an emphasis on the military significance of the battle, a defense of the constitutionality of secession and the idea "that slavery was a benevolent institution," or the argument that the war "forged a united nation as the bulwark of freedom against our common foe today."[52] Gibbons, however, chose to forge his own oratorical path. He steered the dedication ceremony away from a traditional embrace of Confederate heritage and toward a championing of moderate racial reform as a weapon in the fight against Communism, thus replicating some of the themes in President Kennedy's June 11 speech and repurposing them for use on a Civil War battlefield.

Had he chosen to do so, Gibbons could have undoubtedly spoken movingly of the experience of combat. During World War II, he had parachuted behind enemy lines at Utah Beach and won a Bronze Star for his actions during the 1944 invasion of Normandy. But he said almost nothing about the men in Perry's Florida Brigade, instead devoting his time to arguing that unlike the battle being commemorated, the nation's contemporary conflicts had international significance. The United States could hardly claim to work on behalf of the cause of freedom and equality around the globe without practicing it at home. Gibbons decried the attention-grabbing images of American racism circulating around the world: the "snarling police dog, the fire hose, the electrically-charged cattle prod." He bluntly told his listeners, "We cannot hope to win men's minds in the battle with Communism if America becomes a land in which freedom, equality and opportunity are reserved only for the white man."[53]

One of the factors propelling Kennedy to speak forthrightly on June 11 was concern about international fallout from the crises in Birmingham and Tuscaloosa, namely the strong condemnation issuing from African heads of state who warned that continuing racial abuses in the United States would "seriously deteriorate" U.S.-African relations. Deeply concerned that further deterioration in diplomatic relations could limit U.S. access to African uranium—a key element in building a nuclear bomb—Secretary of State Dean Rusk (who would headline a symposium at Gettysburg in November) sent a circular to all American diplomatic posts stressing the necessity of decisive federal action on civil rights. Kennedy's target audience for the

June 11 speech was clearly global in scope, for all diplomatic posts soon received a copy with instructions from the president regarding how to put it to public relations use in their host countries.[54]

The possibility that alienating the African continent could decrease U.S. advantage in the arms race would likely have resonated ominously in Gibbons's Florida. The Gettysburg commemoration was only nine months removed from the Cuban missile crisis, which gave Floridians a front-row seat to the prospect of nuclear war. Though Soviet premier Nikita Khrushchev had previously threatened the West with nuclear destruction during both the Taiwan Straits and Berlin crises, the Cuban crisis hit home more directly. The standoff terrified Americans from Tampa to Tacoma, but the close proximity of South Florida to Cuba made the crisis resonate particularly intensely in Florida.[55]

Gibbons's Gettysburg speech employed the classic moderate's approach of condemning both sides. While decrying violent attacks on protesters, he also obliquely portrayed civil rights leaders as agitating opportunists seeking monetary and political gain. Taking Lyndon Johnson's concern about street protest a step further, Gibbons argued, "Freedom and equality will be brought about by understanding honestly practiced; education earnestly pursued; and opportunity freely given without discrimination. Our disagreements can no longer be settled by armed conflict as we settled them here a hundred years ago. Our racial conflicts must be removed from the streets and our differences resolved in the true American way in our courts, in our legislative bodies, and at the ballot box." Though able to acknowledge— unlike many of his southern Democrat colleagues—the urgent need for change in America's racial politics, the congressman placed clear limits on the timetable, scope, and tenor of the transformation. He envisioned an elite-managed program of slow and moderate reform achieved through existing political and legal structures, not a grassroots recalibration of American democracy through mass direct action by impoverished and working-class Blacks.[56]

Gibbons's foreign policy–infused conviction that Americans could best resolve their racial conflicts at the ballot box led him to break with many of his southern Democrat colleagues and support the Voting Rights Act in 1965, and to defend the State Department and the United Nations against the conspiracy-driven suspicions of many of his white constituents. His concern about getting protest off the streets, however, did not extend to accepting new laws guaranteeing access to public accommodations and schools. He argued at Gettysburg that the stakes were high, that if moderation failed and extremists gained control (it is unclear whether he meant white extremists or Black radicals), "those who died here and on other American battlefields will then have died in vain." Given the common ground between his speech and Kennedy's June 11 address, and his personal association with the president, some listeners may have heard Gibbons's words as an endorsement of the new legislation. Yet when the bill came to a vote the following summer, he voted against it, as did every member of the Florida delegation with the exception of Claude Pepper, whose liberalism had previously cost him Florida's senate seat in 1950.[57]

Gibbons was not alone in this disassociation. A Harris poll conducted in August 1963 found that nearly 80 percent of white Americans believed that racial discrimination was harming the nation's image abroad. Yet more than 50 percent of those polled indicated that they would object to living next door to a Black family, a third did not want their children to go to school with Black children, and roughly a fourth objected to integrated workplaces and churches. This widespread dissonance between intellectual understanding and action underlay many civil rights activists' frustration with Kennedy's Cold War framing of civil rights issues, prompting demands for the president to state unequivocally that racial discrimination was a betrayal of America's best principles. Kennedy finally took this step in the summer of 1963; Gibbons did not. Nevertheless, his forthright acknowledgement that the rights of citizenship should not be reserved for whites alone and disruption of the equation of honoring the Confederate dead with massive resistance remain notable. Delivering this message at a Confederate monument dedication on a battlefield endowed with symbolic significance as the "High Water Mark of the Confederacy" required its own kind of courage.[58]

IN ADDITION TO THE Florida and South Carolina dedications, many already-existing monuments were rededicated during the "three great days." North Carolina and New Jersey both rededicated their state monuments on July 1, and Virginia followed suit the next morning. The ceremony at the North Carolina monument, sometimes called the "finest piece of sculpture on the battlefield," nearly rivaled the scale of the event at the Peace Light. Despite the Confederate pageantry on display, state senator Hector MacLean—who at the age of eight had pulled the cord for the unveiling of the monument in 1929—devoted his speech to themes of good government, order, and moderation, ideas key to North Carolina's reputation as an enlightened southern state. A reception followed at the Hotel Gettysburg.

Always eager to highlight scenes of alleged fraternity, the *Gettysburg Times* reported that northerners present, such as Endicott Peabody and his aides (perhaps including the African American one who had supposedly requested Wallace's autograph) "enjoyed the 'Dixie' rendition and the rebel yells as much as anyone else."[59]

While George Wallace was railing against "destructive centralization" at the South Carolina monument, his fellow Democrat Richard Hughes was making the case for civil rights at the New Jersey state monument. A reporter for the Harrisburg *Patriot* deemed Hughes's speech the day's strongest statement on civil rights. As governor of New Jersey from 1962 to 1970, Hughes appointed Blacks to public office in substantial numbers, supported fair housing legislation, and acknowledged that the neighborhood school concept perpetuated segregation, yet racial inequality persisted, leading to uprisings in Newark and Plainfield in 1967. Hughes argued for an idealized version of war aims, asserting that the conflict was not waged to "preserve the Union 'lily white' or 'Jim Crow,'" but rather "for liberty and justice for all." Comparing the magnitude of the moral crisis currently confronting the nation to the war, he argued that demonstrations were necessary, justified, and designed to make possible "the ultimate liquidation of the cause of the Civil War." White positions on direct action protest, however, often changed as their proximity to them shifted; some of those who applauded Hughes's words no doubt felt quite differently in the wake of the 1967 uprisings.[60]

The ceremony's focus on civil rights was perhaps unsurprising, given New Jersey's leading role in forcing the issue of the relationship between the centennial and contemporary campaigns for racial justice in 1961. It is possible that many members of the New Jersey Centennial Committee (and maybe Hughes himself) read historian Jesse Lemisch's April 1961 *Nation* piece, which argued that "since the official celebrations will represent a surrender to the Southern view, they must be challenged as ardently as the rest of the structure of segregation of which they are a part." The New Jerseyans may have approached their monument rededication ceremony at Gettysburg with the goal of continuing to do their part. Pointing to Hughes's speech and Scranton's remarks at the Peace Light, a reporter for a Harrisburg newspaper deemed the unfinished business of the war as the central theme of the July 1 activities. The *Washington Post* disagreed, reporting that most of the day's speakers had praised the valor of both North and South and "their dedication to what they thought was right."[61]

Family-Friendly Drama: Parades, Vignettes, and Symbolic Reenactments

Adele Gutman Nathan's elaborate vision for the July 2 "Strength Through Unity" parade revolved around the concept of postwar progress. More than 5,000 contemporary service members marched, in addition to 1,500 reenactors and countless bands and musical groups. The mood was unabashedly celebratory, and some units entered actively into the spirit of dramatic play: a group of Confederate cavalry paraded a grinning "prisoner" and many of the North Carolina units discharged blanks from their weapons. An artillery crew fired a period cannon as air force jets screamed overhead. Floats included a thirty-six-foot-long replica of the Confederate submarine the C.S.S. *Hunley*, a "Ship of State" sponsored by the Gulf Oil Company, and an assortment of modern military scenes. The most popular—judging by the applause it received—was a National Guard float depicting a mobile field bath unit, complete with a soldier taking a shower. The *Washington Post*'s coverage of the parade took a nostalgic angle, telling readers that Gettysburg "treated its Civil War Centennial visitors to some of the fun of small-town living."[62]

ACCWCC Pageant Committee chair Betty Gifford recruited widely for volunteers for the human interest vignettes. Though a sense of community service and a desire to be in on the action likely prompted most local volunteers involved in grassroots commemorative activities throughout the centennial period, some participants were brought into the fold through pressure from above. When a committee member called Littlestown High School asking for assistance with the vignettes, the principal told English teacher Jim Witt, who was active in the school's theater program, that the group needed his help. The young teacher was assigned to the "Sharpshooter's Roost" vignette at Devil's Den and subsequently convinced many of his students to participate.[63]

Though at least one attendee from California wrote to Gifford to volunteer his services, the vast majority of the ninety-two members of the cast and crew were local residents. Witt's friend Roy Maitland was cast as General John Gordon in the Barlow-Gordon vignette primarily because he could supply his own horse. In addition to serving as cast members, local residents also conducted research and wrote the scripts, gathered props, sewed some of the costumes, did makeup, and served as directors. The seven vignettes were designed to capture the attention of visitors through connecting them on an emotional level to the experiences of men in battle. Gifford's commitment to them was such that she soldiered on despite her husband suffering a heart attack that kept him hospitalized through the anniversary week.[64]

NPS officials were less than thrilled with the historical accuracy of the vignettes, which ran between three and six minutes apiece and were restaged repeatedly throughout the morning hours on July 2 and 3. "Life Saved by a Gentleman" featured the familiar but likely embellished story of Confederate general John B. Gordon saving the life of Union general Francis Barlow, and "Friendly Enemies" depicted a historically inaccurate tableau of opposing forces playing cards together after filling their canteens at Spangler's Spring. "Brother Captures Brother" embodied the reconciliationist narrative of the Civil War as a quarrel between brothers, and "A Valiant General—A Noble Man" embraced the larger-than-life image of Robert E. Lee. "John Burns—Venerable Citizen-Warrior" focused on the elderly man who joined Union troops in defending his home, "The Fateful Decision" portrayed Meade's July 2 council of war, and "Sharpshooter's Roost" depicted the action in Devil's Den.[65]

The "Sharpshooter's Roost" cast faced significant challenges. GNMP staff forbade them to cut any underbrush or trample the fields, and reproduction firearms were in short supply. One of the directors ultimately borrowed World War I–era Springfield rifles from a local military post, and the park ranger assigned to direct traffic in Devil's Den convinced the National Guard to loan the group some smoke grenades. Hour after hour, cast members charged back and forth across the road snaking through Devil's Den. During one of the charges, Witt pulled the pin on a National Guard grenade and tossed it between the rocks. Bemused by the cloud of orange smoke immediately ensuing, cast members sidelined the other grenade. Witt recalled that the spectators who poured into Devil's Den throughout the vignette's run were enthusiastic, although "we didn't get any over-the-top raves."[66]

Gifford estimated that more than 50,000 people viewed the 200 vignette performances. While some audience members returned multiple times to specific programs, at least one viewer walked the seven-mile circuit between performance sites to view them all. Civil War reenacting was a hobby born in the decade preceding the centennial, and Jim Witt hypothesized that some of the vignettes' popularity may have derived from the novelty of seeing people wearing period uniforms. His retrospective assessment of the programs—based on participating in "Sharpshooter's Roost" and witnessing "Barlow-Gordon" and "John Burns"—was unequivocal. They were "historically and dramatically miserable," he concluded in 2019, full of historical inaccuracies and devoid of any allusion to the causes and consequences of the battle.[67]

Despite Adele Gutman Nathan's extensive experience in theatrical production, the budget was tight and Witt deemed the vignettes amateur in execution. The GCC, as might be expected, saw things differently, writing in its synopsis of the event for the CWCC that they garnered much praise. The president of the Gettysburg Civil War Round Table proclaimed that the vignettes' cast and crew "did more with a few dollars than the state did with more than $128,000." The *Gettysburg Times* reported that a Shakespearean troupe in the audience deemed the "Brother Captures Brother" vignette professional in quality, and that parents were so unnerved by John Corver's realistic portrayal of General Barlow's injuries that they covered their children's eyes.[68]

GNMP historian Harry Pfanz suggested to James Myers in advance of the centennial that participation of military groups be limited in order to "avoid dealing with eccentrics in Civil War costumes." Reenactor groups quickly won a place for themselves by their enthusiasm and initiative, however, and legacy organizations and "reactivated" Civil War units played a major role in the July 2 parade and July 3 symbolic reenactment of Pickett's Charge. Some units undertook other activities as well; embracing the myth that shoes played a central role in bringing the armies to Gettysburg, the 6th North Carolina paid a prearranged visit to the Gettysburg Shoe Company, where a staff member obligingly offered them fifteen pairs of shoes. Eager to get the last laugh, the company selected a motley assortment of fur-topped boots and women's shoes for distribution to the "soldiers."[69]

To be eligible for campsites and participation medals, units had to register in advance. Union troops, comprising the Sons of Union Veterans, reactivated units, and members of the North-South Skirmishers Association, bivouacked near the High Water Mark monument. Confederate forces camped along West Confederate Avenue at the former CCC camp. Both "armies" opened their bivouac sites for demonstrations of Civil War camp life and campfire singalongs. Anticipating rowdiness, GNMP staff stationed a ranger at each encampment, but few problems materialized and Superintendent Wing praised camp "commanders" for their good order.[70]

Some of the southern reenactors made their political and racial views obvious. When George Wallace visited the Confederate encampment, an autographing mania ensued, with Wallace signing everything from hats and drums to (somewhat ironically) Social Security cards. Many of the reenactors made their support for a "Wallace for President" campaign clear, calling out slogans such as "See you in 64." A reenactor dressed in a Confederate general's uniform clashed with a Gettysburg College staff member overseeing one of the dormitories available for participant use. As the Confederate introduced himself at the door as "General Beauregard," he recoiled at the sight of a Black man exiting the building. When "Beauregard" refused to stay in the same building as a Black man, the staff person responded, "Well, then, you'll have to leave."[71] Though Gettysburg College was far from a pioneering force for racial equality in 1963, guided by state law and its own admissions policy, it rejected the line that many local business owners had held for so long—that catering to tourists meant upholding Jim Crow. The Pennsylvania Human Relations Commission visits and rumors that discriminatory treatment would spark public protests that could derail the anniversary may have also played a role in prompting staff members' determination to uphold the nondiscrimination policy in the face of challenges.

For many members of reenactor groups, the highlight of the commemoration was the July 3 Pickett's Charge program, described by GCC chairman Milton Baker as "an opportunity to interpret the battlefield in a way that will emphasize our present position as a great nation united under a single flag." Though Nathan developed the program scenario, the script itself was penned by playwright Richard Bernstein. The narration, which concluded with the words, "This is high tide for the Army of Northern Virginia," embraced the narrative of the High Water Mark. Walter Abel narrated the events for spectators, and military affairs specialist George Fielding Eliot, playing the role of a war correspondent for the *New York Times*, described the maneuvers as though composing dispatches for his paper. Many of the roughly 1,500 uniformed participants were descendants of Civil War veterans. At least a few were female; the 104th Ohio included eight women in uniform. A handful were children. Though all of the Union units were from northern states, some of the Confederate groups were also comprised of northerners—a testimony to the popularity of Confederate reenacting (and perhaps Confederate ideology) outside the South. Pennsylvania, Maryland, and New York had both Union and Confederate units represented, and, despite the centrality of civil rights to the New Jersey monument rededication, the only New Jerseyans participating in the reenactment wore gray.[72]

Up to 40,000 spectators gathered near the Angle to view the event, posing challenges for the park rangers, state troopers, and Boy Scouts charged with crowd control. Some attendees later complained that they could not hear the narration or see the action, and Park Service staff had to break up numerous conflicts over priority seating for the news media. Despite the repeated assurances that the event would be sober and dignified, newspapers described the crowd's mood as "festive." Clutching hand-sewn flags, the approximately

600 Confederate reenactors, some of them descendants of the original attack force, approached the Angle slowly. They climbed over the fences lining the Emmitsburg Road, pushed back a skirmishing force of Union soldiers, and processed between two rows of speakers broadcasting recorded gunfire and battle sounds. By directive of the NPS, participants were barred from loading their weapons, pointing arms at the enemy, or simulating injury or death. Smoke pots were instead used to provide visual effects.[73]

As they neared the Union line made up of nearly 500 defenders in blue, both sides froze. They then lowered their weapons and clutched each other's hands. Many of the men had tears in their eyes. In the ultimate gesture of unity and reconciliation, the Navy band played the National Anthem while all the participants assembled at attention behind the Angle to salute the flag and recite the Pledge of Allegiance. The crowd quieted at the sight, and many of the spectators were moved to tears. At the conclusion of the salute, however, the *Gettysburg Times* noted that both participants and spectators seemed "at a loss as to what to do with the remainder of the afternoon so many had traveled hundreds of miles to see." Daniel Langan of the *Philadelphia Inquirer* found the event deeply moving, writing that "the ghosts of men who died here a century ago seemed to hover over the battlefield." For eighty-three-year-old Albert Fuger, the ghost most present was that of his father, Frederick Fuger, who as a young man took command of Cushing's Battery after all the officers were killed.[74]

Many members of the crowd likely perceived the event through Cold War lenses, embracing the Union victory at the High Water Mark as the event that prevented the nation from becoming permanently divided, thus providing it the power it would need a century later to counterbalance the Soviet Union on the world stage.[75] Lost Cause devotees, however (whether or not they pledged allegiance to the U.S. flag at the end of the program) likely felt a profound sense of loss and grief. Attendees who held a more emancipationist understanding of the battle or believed that the Civil War could be used to advance the cause of racial justice may have experienced feelings of joy or satisfaction. The percentage of the crowd that may have subscribed to this interpretation is unknown; the Harrisburg *Patriot* claimed that several hundred Black families attended the event, an assertion which cannot be corroborated elsewhere. Organizers, who had been on the lookout for the anticipated racial demonstrations all week, were undoubtedly particularly tense as the Confederates moved out from Seminary Ridge, aware that if a protest were to take place in the midst of the recreated assault, it would garner enormous publicity.[76]

When the GCC canceled plans for July 4 in the wake of Kennedy's decision not to attend, in an attempt to help fill in the gap, the ACCWCC shifted the date of its memorial service honoring county residents who died in the war. The group gathered at the GAR Hall at 4:00 P.M. on the Fourth of July for a service and wreath-laying ceremony. Across town, in a very different gathering, members of the York Action for Peace returned to the Eternal Peace Light Memorial to hold a silent vigil for international peace and "universal abandonment of arms." For these activists, instead of bequeathing the Cold War generation a legacy of patriotic devotion and martial might, Civil War history and battlefield monuments served as a reminder of the horror and destruction of war. Though many tourists were undoubtedly bemused or disturbed by this use of the battlefield landscape, some were supportive, and at least a few joined in.[77]

Disappointed by the prospect of leaving Gettysburg without firing their weapons, some of the reenactor units from Ohio sought permission to use county-owned land near Barlow's Knoll on July 4 for an impromptu reenactment of the First Day's battle. When it was granted, they quickly rounded up some Confederate units, one of which arrived with a cannon in tow. Though positions had to be adjusted, spectators—some of whom were no doubt disappointed by the absence of a traditional reenactment—enjoyed the impromptu skirmish. Reflecting pride in their own contributions, the predominately local audience told reporters that the vignettes and the skirmish were "the best things of the centennial."[78]

THOUGH CERTAINLY SUBSTANTIAL, visitor numbers for the battle anniversary week were lower than anticipated, likely due in no small part to the extreme heat and the absence of presidential involvement. Organizers predicted crowds averaging 40,000 for the first three days of July, but July 3 was the only date to approach hitting that mark. GNMP recorded 404,017 visitors over the course of the month of July, which was a slight decrease from the 404,768 recorded the previous year. Notably, however, nearly 100,000 of them entered the new space-age visitor center. The emergency medical arrangements proved adequate; those coordinating the services concluded with relief that the lower-than-expected numbers kept "casualties" down.[79]

The CWCC's James Robertson commended Louis Simon for a program "worthy of the battle being commemorated." The executive directors of the North Carolina, District of Columbia, and Virginia Civil War Centennial Commissions concurred, and many attendees applauded the GCC for its efforts. A number of the commentators singled out the vignettes for special praise; Simon deemed them "the finest contribution that was made to the entire affair." Nathan was delighted with both the performances and the public's response to them. Though Superintendent Wing told NPS director Conrad Wirth privately that some of the vignettes were historically inaccurate, he acknowledged that they were popular with the public and praised Betty Gifford for her "splendid" contribution to the centennial.[80]

Wing reported that park staff were generally pleased with the execution of the anniversary program, and "at least are very glad to have it over with" without serious accidents or significant damage to park resources. Park historian Frederick Tilberg agreed that things had gone well, though he acknowledged that some observers might have found the anniversary "tame and uninteresting." Likely alluding to the disastrous 1961 Charleston meeting, the ill-fated Manassas reenactment, and the predictions of mass protest, Wirth told a friend, "We are thankful for the more successful aspects of the Centennial. It might have been worse."[81]

The battles in the West might have been more strategically significant than Gettysburg, syndicated columnist Max Freedman acknowledged, but they never touched the nation's soul the way Gettysburg did. Freedman argued that meaningful remembrance of the battle left no room for sectionalism or division, yet acknowledged that the issues animating the conflict "are with us even now." He was optimistic that the Civil War Centennial was playing an important role in deepening public support for civil rights. The *Washington Post* took a similar position; insisting that the centennial's role in the present was to prompt Americans to realize how much action was still necessary to achieve Lincoln's desired new birth of freedom. "Those who share Lincoln's impatience over Meade's slowness of action 100 years ago," it concluded, "can scarcely complain about any undue haste on the part of President Kennedy in asking that certain unfinished business be now attended to."[82]

In the aftermath of the battle anniversary, some Americans were more than ready to be done with Gettysburg. John McClave and Elizabeth A. Woodman both wrote the *Philadelphia Inquirer* to express their frustration with the level of coverage given the anniversary nationwide. McClave implored the nation to let go of its fascination with Gettysburg and "stop fighting the Civil War." Only then, he believed, could Americans truly reunite. Woodman, a supporter of the Test Ban Treaty, worried that what she considered disproportionate attention given to military leaders made Americans too comfortable with war. She argued that it was past time to provide children with other heroes, such as educators, scientists, and artists.[83]

Columnist Don Robertson condemned the commemoration as a "vulgar show," a commercialized desecration of a tragic war. Criticizing the conduct of private business owners and the NPS alike, he deemed both the commemoration and the community itself tasteless. *Newsweek* ran a short piece in mid-July that took a different tack. Instead of criticizing specific choices made by planners, the writer observed that the biggest problem with the Gettysburg commemoration was that it "came at a moment of renewed national friction over the same kind of issues that once separated North from South." Past and present were too intertwined to allow a commemoration free of dissention and discord, and the longevity of racial inequality and battles over federal authority and states' rights itself rendered the lofty sentiments of patriotic unity hollow for some observers.[84]

Though the much-feared "racial demonstrations" did not materialize and press coverage of the event included no mention of overt discrimination against minority visitors, the long shadow of America's "national sin"—racial inequity—nonetheless loomed large over the battle anniversary. Whether at the Peace Light, the fields surrounding the Angle, or the monuments commemorating the actions of men from South Carolina, Florida, and New Jersey, the past was repeatedly invoked in the service of the present. Despite the GCC's hopes to "deemphasize divisiveness" and advance Cold War themes of unity, national purpose, and American greatness, the reconciliationist veneer of its programming glossed over the tensions inherent in the disparate ways the anniversary was being used. Over the course of the battle anniversary week, Gettysburg was simultaneously presented as a justification for intensifying defense of states' rights and white supremacy, a clarion call for racial justice, and an electrifying reminder of both the dangers and the opportunities confronting Americans in the Cold War universe.

A friend teased GNMP's Kittridge Wing that in light of the anniversary's success, perhaps he should come to Washington, D.C., to supervise the U.S. Park Police on the day of the March on Washington. When that day arrived, working outside the framework of official Civil War commemoration, Martin Luther King Jr. powerfully invoked historical memory in the most famous speech of his life. Standing against the backdrop of a memorial erected to honor the memory of the man who spoke so eloquently at Gettysburg of a new birth of freedom, he challenged Americans to confront the realities of their past and present, acknowledge the "urgency of the moment" and "make real the promises of democracy." The battle anniversary was over, but not so the efforts to use Gettysburg to advance the cause of Black freedom.[85]

CHAPTER SIX

The Pen Is Mightier than the Sword

Lincoln's Gettysburg Address

Though men such as Conrad Wirth and Kittridge Wing drew a sigh of relief as July 5 dawned, the Gettysburg centennial was far from over. The battle had been commemorated, but the anniversary of Lincoln's speech loomed large. In the early days of the centennial, the Gettysburg Address anniversary was little more than an afterthought in most planners' minds; arrangements for November took a back seat to preparations for the July events and the bulk of the available funds were expended on the battle anniversary, leaving little left over to draw on to commemorate the address. In retrospect, however, some members of the GCC argued that the November events were the pinnacle of the anniversary year. In a letter to William Scranton, General Edward J. Stackpole insisted that "the commemoration of the Centennial of Lincoln's Memorial Address was of even greater significance than the battle itself." Observing the anniversary of Lincoln's speech required a different kind of approach than the one taken in July, characterized more by lectures, round tables, and policy discussions than costumed impersonation. Clearly anticipating a more cerebral vibe for the November activities, the *Washington Post* predicted that "Gettysburg residents can begin shaving off their beards and taking off their crinolines," and turn their attention instead to commemorating ideas.[1]

Gettysburg's prime position in the national imagination—from 1863 onward—has derived in large part from Abraham Lincoln's iconic refashioning of the battle narrative into a vision for the nation's future. Though initially derided by some, Lincoln's "few appropriate remarks" at the November 19, 1863, dedication of Soldiers' National Cemetery quickly shed their original context as a rallying call for a weary North to press on with the war effort and assumed the status of sacred American scripture. The Gettysburg Address took on an increasingly global prominence during World War II, as the U.S. government began to broadcast it abroad as an exemplar of American political ideas and a universal rallying cry for democracy.[2] By the 1960s, Lincoln's speech had assumed nearly unparalleled stature as an encapsulation of the virtues supposedly cherished by the "free world" and inaccessible beyond the Iron Curtain.

Perhaps buttressed by critiques of the battle anniversary as commercialized and cartoonish, this political context ensured that the November commemorative activities would be less populist and more global in focus. They were also, at least on the official level, more diverse, with esteemed African Americans playing formal roles in the program. In their own distinct ways, Marian Anderson, Judge Raymond Pace Alexander, and E. Washington Rhodes clearly articulated the argument that the ongoing Black freedom struggle was the direct outgrowth of the unfinished work of which Lincoln had spoken.[3] Due in large part to their participation and an accompanying heightened focus on international context and global opinion, the tenor of the November commemoration was more substantive than the battle anniversary and more officially aligned with the emancipationist interpretation of the war. While the vision of civil rights reform espoused was fairly moderate in nature and the need to shore up diplomatic relations abroad provided much of the impetus for the engagement with the idea of a new birth of freedom, the Gettysburg Address centennial nonetheless was more overtly influenced by the civil rights struggle than its July predecessor.

Lincoln and the Gettysburg Address on the World Stage

The Lincoln Fellowship of Pennsylvania (an organization committed to honoring and preserving Lincoln's legacy) began the tradition of commemorating the anniversary of the Gettysburg Address with a ceremony at the Soldiers' National Cemetery in 1938. Reflecting the increasingly vigorous use of the speech for foreign policy and civic revitalization purposes during World War II, Congress formally established November 19 as "Dedication Day" in 1946. The address's premier placement in the pantheon of the nation's most-esteemed documents brought national attention to Gettysburg two years later during the national tour of the Freedom Train. The Freedom Train was one of the highest-profile efforts of the Cold War era to use history to solidify commitment to American ideals such as democracy, freedom, and civil liberties. Coordinated by the newly created American Heritage Foundation (AHF), the Freedom Train brought a collection of 130 key historical documents (including the Gettysburg Address) chosen to highlight the "essence of Americanism" to communities around the nation. Three and a half million people—many standing in line for hours at a time—visited the mobile exhibits during the train's 1948 trek around the United States.[4]

The Freedom Train initiative was initially championed by Attorney General Tom Clark's office as an antidote to what it perceived as Americans' postwar willingness to sacrifice their political heritage for material goods, prosperity, and comfort. The project's narrative of the United States as a "city on a hill" invited Americans around the country to redouble their commitment to democracy and reject intolerance and "alien ideologies." With the support of the AHF, host communities constructed weeks of local programming around the train's visit. Adams County's "Rededication to American Ideals Week" included Armistice Day observances and Religious Freedom Sunday, culminating in the train's visit to Gettysburg on November 19–20, 1948. Tom Clark himself served as the keynote speaker for a program that included a reenactment of the dedication of the National Cemetery, music from the Gettysburg College choir, and a dramatic reading of the Gettysburg Address. Viewed in person by thousands, the half-hour program was also broadcast widely across the airwaves by the Mutual Broadcasting System.[5]

Framed around the theme of American exceptionalism, the Freedom Train ceremony portrayed the United States as the world's shining example of democracy, standing poised in defense of liberty worldwide. Referencing Gettysburg as hallowed ground, Clark asked his audience to consider whether the nation had lived up to Lincoln's words. While briefly alluding to "a historic American emancipation," Clark quickly made it clear that his yardstick for measuring enactment of Lincoln's vision was foreign policy, not racial justice. Clark never mentioned African Americans or civil rights, concentrating instead on "world slavery" and "world emancipation." Clark's framing echoed that employed during the war by Franklin Roosevelt, who frequently used the term "slavery" to describe the despotic actions of Axis leaders. Without identifying Communism by name, Clark encouraged his listeners to draw strength from Lincoln's words, Gettysburg's historic landscape, and the documents on the train to stand firm against "atheistic materialism" and "vicious ideology." Thunderous applause greeted his conclusion that this "quest for world emancipation, for world peace, equality and justice" would be "freedom's last crusade."[6]

Though separating domestic racial issues from American values and international politics was a long-practiced tradition in the United States, it became increasingly difficult to sustain during World War II and in the immediate postwar years. Black activists seized the opportunities provided by wartime to frame local struggles against segregation and discrimination as battles in a global war against white supremacy and racial prejudice. With an eye to the international scene, they employed the language of democracy and antifascism to characterize their efforts, repeatedly drawing attention to the shared ground between Nazism and Jim Crow and utilizing the framework of "Double V" (dual victory against fascism abroad and prejudice at home) to guide their wartime actions.[7]

As the United States sought to shape the postwar world in the image of democracy, capitalism, and anticommunism, domestic racial issues continued to handicap the nation's claims of moral leadership. As violence against returning African American servicemen seeking to exercise the freedoms for which they had fought reached a fever pitch in 1946, the American Crusade to End Lynching stepped up the pressure against the White House. The League for Freedom of the Darker Peoples of the World suggested in 1947 that President Truman send General Douglas MacArthur and his troops to Georgia and South Carolina in hopes that an occupying army that could teach Japan "the fundamental principles of Americanism" might be able to do the same in the American South. But just as discrimination was not limited to the South, neither was Black resentment of widespread use of terms such as "emancipation" and "slavery" to characterize developments abroad with no acknowledgement of their relevance domestically.[8]

While the Truman administration's cautious steps toward civil rights were prompted in large part by a desire to capture the increasing Black vote, it is clear that international factors played a key role as well. Violence against Black servicemen and segregation in the postwar U.S. military complicated the administration's foreign policy agenda. A desire to highlight the negative foreign policy impact of officially sanctioned racial discrimination motivated the Justice Department's repeated attempts to intervene in civil rights cases before the Supreme Court. The recently established President's Committee on Civil Rights' 1947 report concluded that domestic civil rights violations posed a serious obstacle to American attempts to position the nation as the leader of the free world. Thus, in refusing to acknowledge the widespread concern that domestic racial abuses negated the power of postwar propaganda, the speakers at the Gettysburg Freedom Train commemoration made a conscious choice to duck the issue. But the progress of both the domestic freedom struggle and anticolonialism worldwide between 1948 and 1963 ensured that those taking the stage at Gettysburg fifteen years later would be unable to follow suit.[9]

The Lincoln sesquicentennial of 1959 further accelerated the framing of Lincoln and the Gettysburg Address as Cold War assets. Lincoln's growing popularity across the globe as a symbol of freedom and justice undergirded Jawaharlal Nehru's placement of a cast of the sixteenth president's hand on his desk to guide his actions and the Taiwanese government's promotion of the Gettysburg Address's impact on Sun Yat-sen's political principles. In a pilgrimage to Springfield, Illinois, West Berlin mayor Willy Brandt appropriated the "House Divided" speech for application to postwar Germany. Soviet premier Nikita Khrushchev paid honor to the martyred president in a 1959 visit to the Lincoln Memorial, extolling Lincoln for his dedication "to the struggle for freedom." UPI's European news manager, Harry Ferguson, observed in 1962 that "Honest Abe is the #1 American throughout most of Europe; if it's goodwill we're after, he is our man."[10]

The sesquicentennial activities culminated on November 19, 1959. Ceremonies took place around the globe, from Argentina and Italy to Morocco, Taiwan, and Honduras. In Gettysburg, Republican congressman Fred Schwengel, a respected authority on Lincoln, adapted the address to the immediate context of 1959, orating, "now we, too, are engaged in a terrible struggle testing whether that nation, or any combination of nations that love freedom and liberty, can endure." Recounting the story of Khrushchev's reverent visit to the Lincoln Memorial, the congressman alleged that the figure of Lincoln could be the one factor that could bring lasting peace to the world by making the Soviet Union realize that American strength derived not from military power alone but from governing ideals.[11]

Americans Black and white also embraced the Gettysburg Address as the exemplar of their domestic political precepts. Betty Canno prefaced a 1963 letter to the editor of the *Afro-American* calling on whites to take action to correct the injustices in American society with a quote from Lincoln's address. Illinois senator Paul Douglas used a commemorative ceremony to explicitly call on Congress to pass the Civil Rights Act. The National Urban League (NUL), a civil rights organization committed to achieving better employment opportunities for Blacks, began to celebrate November 19 as "Equal Opportunity Day" in the mid-1950s. Branches throughout the nation commemorated the delivery of the Gettysburg Address by mounting a range of programs focused on equal opportunity. From 1956 through the centennial years, the national leadership marked the day by hosting an annual banquet recognizing national leaders in the fields of business and labor for their contributions toward interracial progress. The NUL, whose animating principle has been described as "sell[ing] civil rights to whites," may have seen Equal Opportunity Day as an avenue to capitalize on the Gettysburg Address's iconic place in the American pantheon by directly connecting it to the struggle for racial justice. In his acceptance speech at the 1961 dinner, Walter Wheeler Jr. argued that continued racial injustice made it impossible for the United States to cultivate friendship with people around the world. Attendees could easily seek corroboration of this concern from their fellow dinner guests, many of whom were members of African delegations to the United Nations.[12]

WHEN CWCC EXECUTIVE DIRECTOR JAMES ROBERTSON traveled to Gettysburg in January 1963 to address the Adams County Shrine Club, his acceptance of the invitation was likely driven in part by a desire for a sitdown meeting with GCC members. Robertson came away with the distinct impression that planners were devoting the bulk of their attention and funds to the July ceremonies and had given little thought to the November anniversary. Indeed, GCC's executive director, Louis Simon, was scheduled to end his employment with the group on August 15. When asked to report on the status of the November commemoration, Simon acknowledged that plans were not finalized but would likely follow the model established in 1952 with Adele Gutman Nathan's "Mr. Lincoln Goes to Gettysburg" pageant. Robertson was unimpressed by the commission's intentions to restage the pageant but wary that any commemorative program that the CWCC might mount could be perceived as directly competing with the GCC's efforts. CWCC Chairman Allan Nevins, however, was determined that the CWCC organize its own Gettysburg Address event, one that would connect in some way with the ongoing Black freedom struggle. The CWCC program ultimately took the form of a January 1964 symposium in Washington, D.C., featuring theologian Reinhold Niehbuhr, poet Robert Lowell, and novelist John Dos Passos, among others.[13]

Given the depth of Nathan's involvement with the GCC, it stands to reason that commission members would have looked to her to provide programming for the November anniversary. It is possible that her willingness to serve the commission as "coordinator consultant" was even predicated on the assumption that she would have free rein to restage "Mr. Lincoln Goes to Gettysburg" in November 1963. Yet the pageant was never repeated, and Nathan played no public role in the November events, though she did attend. It seems likely that the precarious nature of the GCC's finances doomed plans to stage such an expensive program, the costs of which were estimated at $61,000.[14]

When the GCC's $100,000 deficit made headlines the previous spring, some Pennsylvanians took the fight to Washington, making a long-shot plea to Congress to create a federal commission to commemorate the two Gettysburg anniversaries. They asked for an appropriation to cover the difference between the $105,000 provided by the state of Pennsylvania and the projected costs of the GCC's programs. In a memo to Kennedy aide Brooks

Hays, William Scranton argued that both anniversaries were inarguably nationally significant, and that the anniversary of Lincoln's address bore international significance. The Gettysburg Address, Scranton insisted, "stands as the most powerful pronouncement of the essence of democracy, as Americans conceive it, ever made." In an effort to establish precedent, Scranton also pointed out that the federal government had appropriated funds to support commemoration at Gettysburg during both the fiftieth and seventy-fifth anniversary years. He noted somewhat desperately that the battle anniversary was only six weeks away, and that the GCC had already pruned its budget to the baseline. Few members of Congress, however, were enthusiastic about the prospect of devoting additional funds to commemorating the memory of a war that had not, despite the lofty predictions of the CWCC, proven to be a unifying force. At the last minute, the state of Pennsylvania gave the GCC an additional $28,000, but the July expenses left only $33,000 to put toward the November events.[15]

Perennially hopeful that Kennedy might agree to play an official role in the Gettysburg commemoration, the GCC issued the president a second invitation, this time for November, but Kennedy again declined, citing travels to Florida and Texas. In his official 1964 report on the commission's activities, Louis Simon dramatically editorialized that the course of American history might have been different had Kennedy chosen to go to Gettysburg rather than Dallas. Scranton also invited U Thant, secretary-general of the United Nations, to speak to the world from Gettysburg on the anniversary. Scranton argued that such a speech would provide an opportunity for Lincoln's "universally respected statement of the philosophy of free government" to reach new audiences around the globe, but Thant passed on the grounds that he was bound to public silence while the assembly was in session.[16]

As planning for November commenced, some local residents continued to make use of the battlefield in ways that defied the notion of sacred ground, or demonstrated the continuing public appeal of reenactments in the face of disapproval on the part of historians and NPS officials. In the span of one week in mid-September, borough police apprehended four college students in the act of stealing GNMP signs and were called to Culp's Hill in response to a stuffed effigy swinging from the tower, which turned out to be symbolic of a high school football rivalry. On September 22, a crowd of nearly 10,000 swarmed the county-owned land along the Harrisburg Road that had been site of the July 4 impromptu reenactment for a "Day in the Life of a Civil War Soldier" program sponsored by the Gettysburg Travel Council.[17]

Concerned about the emergence of new competition for tourist dollars across the state, members of the Travel Council raised their dues in 1963 and redoubled their efforts to purchase billboard space along major highways in advance of the 1964 World's Fair. Estimating that ten million people would travel the Pennsylvania Turnpike on their way to New York City for the fair, council leaders argued that increased billboard space was essential to Gettysburg's continued economic vitality. Motivated perhaps by a drop in downtown visitation in August, which some ascribed to the Route 15 bypass, they also turned to sponsoring their own public events. The September Civil War Soldier program included a sharpshooting competition, an opportunity for visitors to tour Union and Confederate camps, and a reenactment of "no particular battle," designed to demonstrate maneuvers and tactics frequently utilized by both armies. Approximately 450 uniformed reenactors, the majority affiliated with the North-South Skirmish Association, took part in the event.[18]

Perhaps inspired by the popularity of the July vignettes, organizers included staged scenes such as the execution of two deserters by firing squad (complete with ritualized burning of the coffins) and the execution of a spy. Organizers argued that, though not common, military executions made a lasting impression on Civil War soldiers and thus should be included in the program, but it is difficult to reconcile the gravity and horror accompanying wartime executions with the atmosphere of entertainment surrounding the "Day in the Life" program. Indeed, one Union soldier writing after the August 1863 shootings of five deserters in camp near the Rappahannock River noted that "it is a site [sic] that no one need be desirous of seeing." He and his comrades likely would have found the use of staged executions in a tourist event highly disturbing.[19]

GNMP's ongoing efforts to rehabilitate historic buildings to their 1863 appearance extended more expansively to the landscape itself in October when the park was awarded $75,000 for an accelerated public works program to clear 130 acres of land. Superintendent Kittridge Wing billed the project, which prefigured the large-scale landscape restoration efforts introduced at the turn of the twenty-first century, as an opportunity to reclaim the battlefield. At its conclusion in January 1964, crews had removed brush from Little Round Top, the Rose Farm, and the fence lines along the Emmitsburg Road; opened the sightlines from Devil's Den to Seminary Ridge for the first time in fifty years; and cleared the ridge north of Devil's Den. The *Gettysburg Times* noted that the cuts near the Wheatfield allowed visitors to "see these fields now much as Union soldiers saw them in 1863." With this land cleared,

GNMP staff identified additional locations for future cutting, but ultimately the park failed to maintain the cleared areas, and most ultimately reverted to woodlots.[20]

Some of that fall's commemorative events trod on politically sensitive ground. Gettysburg mayor William Weaver found himself on the wrong side of the State Department when he agreed to formally accept a Republic of Ireland flag in tribute to Irish Brigade troops who fought in the battle. Irish Republican Army leader Cathal Goulding, traveling in the United States to solicit financial and political support for the IRA, came to Gettysburg on November 11 in the company of Philadelphia-based members of the American Committee for the Release of Irish Political Prisoners. In addition to presenting a flag to Weaver, the group also laid a wreath at the Irish Brigade Memorial. Many of the members of the committee's Philadelphia branch were also active in the Irish Brigade Memorial Association's annual Memorial Day pilgrimage to Gettysburg, and no doubt saw ritualized commemorative activity as a powerful way to forge a symbolic link between the memory of the Irish Brigade and the IRA. The *Gettysburg Times* noted dryly that Weaver only "learned after arrangements for the presentation had been made that the State Department and the Republic of Ireland take a dim view of the Irish Republican Army."[21]

Delighted by the popularity of the June 30 battle anniversary commemorative newspaper, *Gettysburg Times* editor Paul Roy prepared a special Lincoln edition for November 19 featuring historic newspaper coverage of Lincoln's address, documents associated with the president, and a series of special articles. Civil War Round Tables across the nation sent greetings to readers, and the front page prominently featured salutations from both President Kennedy and former President Eisenhower. Both Kennedy and Eisenhower lauded the address's enshrinement of "government of the people, by the people, for the people" as the centerpiece of the American creed, but their political differences came through in the other aspects of Lincoln's words and life that they chose to stress. Eisenhower focused on Lincoln's rags-to-riches story as an example of the individual opportunity available under the American system. Kennedy, on the other hand, spoke of patriot graves scattered around the globe and a new birth of freedom.[22]

Commemorating the Address

The events of the four-day commemoration were broadly assumed to have worldwide appeal. Local radio station WGET provided complete radio coverage of all of the major programs from November 16 through 19, supplied pickups for other stations' audio and television feeds, and recorded the November 19 rededication of the National Cemetery for distribution to the Voice of America. Though the official program of GCC-sponsored activities did not kick off until the following day, the centennial observance essentially began with the annual Remembrance Day ceremony, featuring the national heads of the GAR's five descendant groups. The Gettysburg College chapel also offered a special Remembrance Day service led by Reverend Paul Empie, who observed that contemporary Americans, who "are among the survivors of two world wars and live in dread of a final and suicidal one find the Gettysburg Address hauntingly contemporary." Noting that all of the Four Freedoms enshrined during World War II were currently in jeopardy across the globe, Empie suggested that as the Civil War generation honored the soldiers who died at Gettysburg, the current generation ought to honor those struggling to assure freedom and justice around the globe.[23]

The official GCC-sponsored centennial observance began on November 17 in Gettysburg College's Student Union Ballroom, with a program devoted to "The International Aspects of the Address," headlined by Secretary of State Dean Rusk. The program had its genesis in a proposal, ultimately abandoned, that the battle commemoration include an International Day, "with a distinguished foreign visitor explaining the meaning of Gettysburg in the terms of world diplomacy from the rostrum at the Visitor Center." The GCC ultimately pursued the idea with the State Department in October, sending a delegation to Washington to meet with Secretary Rusk. Paul Roy, who participated in the meeting, reported that Rusk was immediately enthusiastic about the prospect of highlighting the international impact of the address, noting that he heard about Lincoln all over the world. Finding that his schedule included a window of opportunity on November 17, the secretary of state accepted the group's invitation with the tongue-in-check question of whether he should "confine my remarks to the same length of time as Mr. Lincoln's."[24]

Joining Rusk on the platform were the modern counterparts of the three European dignitaries represented at the 1863 dedication of the National Cemetery: Herve Alphand, the French ambassador to the United States, Sergio Fenoaltea, the Italian ambassador to the United States, and John E. Chadwick, Great Britain's Minister of Commercial Affairs. The enthusiastic crowd of more than 2,100 included hundreds of students, plus "scores of newsmen, photographers, and television crews," and provided the platform party a standing ovation at both the beginning and end of the program. Gettysburg

College president C. A. Hanson introduced the speakers, which also included the lieutenant governor of Pennsylvania, Raymond Shafer. Shafer spoke briefly, arguing that Lincoln's words could not be divorced from the setting in which they were uttered. Referencing the Lincoln Speech Memorial, he claimed proudly that the Gettysburg battlefield was the only place in the world to boast a monument to a speech.[25]

Rusk began his remarks by discussing the contemporary impact of the address worldwide, drawing examples from China, Italy, India, and Germany. He argued that the speech had become the avenue through which America's commitment to freedom and democracy was best known around the world. Taking this line of reasoning one step further, the secretary of state insisted that these Lincolnian commitments to freedom "are the source of our foreign policy." He continued, "They explain our attitude toward colonial questions, our concern about the future of Eastern Europe, and why we are more comfortable in dealing with democracies than with dictatorships. They explain also our concern about our failures here at home to live up fully to our own great commitments." Rusk insisted that this commitment to freedom prompted the U.S. government to support independence for formerly colonized peoples. Referencing the Declaration of Independence, he continued that U.S. policymakers welcomed the rise of new nations around the world to "the separate and equal station to which the Laws of Nature and of Nature's God entitle them."[26]

Rusk did not note the reservations that U.S. government officials held about the rise of some of these new nations to a position of equal status. He also neglected to mention the practical challenges that accompanied the arrival of scores of dark-skinned diplomats in Washington, D.C., a place where the color line still frequently determined access to housing, public accommodations, and schools. The Kennedy administration more openly embraced African independence than the Eisenhower administration had done, but for both, the primary reason for so doing was not memory of the United States' own colonial origins. Rather, officials in both administrations were guided largely by the belief that Africa was "the greatest open field of maneuver in the worldwide competition between the [Communist] Bloc and the noncommunist world."[27]

For Rusk and the agency he led, the diplomatic crises and public relations headaches sparked by nonwhite embassy officials being denied service at restaurants, banned from using restrooms along Maryland highways, and barred from housing in "white" neighborhoods were nearly endless. The scale and scope of the problem, which administration officials feared could affect the success of American policy in the United Nations, necessitated the creation of a new agency within the department's Office of Protocol, the Special Protocol Service Section (SPSS), devoted to preventing racial incidents involving diplomats. The efforts of the SPSS ultimately pushed the State Department, long perceived by many as hostile to Black interests, away from the idea of shielding diplomats from discrimination and toward open advocacy of legislation that would ban racial discrimination in public accommodations.[28]

Rusk then turned his attention to the reality that for many Black Americans, the idea of self-determination was a farce. "The rest of the world is watching closely the struggle for full equality in this country," he observed. "Our failures distress our friends and hearten our enemies." But echoing Kennedy's recent rhetoric placing moral justifications for racial reform above foreign policy ones, he insisted that international opinion was not the primary reason that the nation must jettison discrimination. The main reason, he alleged, was that it was long past time for the United States to complete the work that had begun with the Emancipation Proclamation. Rusk, a native Georgian, had awakened to the injustice of racial discrimination as a young man and had been long committed to small-scale personal actions on the subject. He had refused to join a country club with a discriminatory membership policy, and after moving to Washington, D.C., attempted to have the restrictive covenant on his property removed. When other State Department officials urged him to keep his congressional testimony on the Civil Rights Bill narrowly focused on the foreign policy repercussions of racial discrimination, Rusk refused, clearly calling out racial injustice as a moral issue. When segregationist senator Strom Thurmond tried to get the secretary of state on record as stating that civil rights demonstrations damaged the nation's credibility abroad, Rusk refused to take the bait. Instead, he replied that if he were to be deprived of the rights that Black Americans were routinely denied, he would not hesitate to take similar action.[29]

The secretary of state's receptivity to the invitation to headline the event is testimony both to the centrality of the Gettysburg Address to Cold War diplomacy and Rusk's own conviction that racial discrimination compromised the nation's claim to moral and political leadership on the global stage. The substance of his remarks reveals not only the important ways that the Gettysburg Address centennial was put to contemporary political use but also the extent to which the commemoration of Gettysburg's 100th did help to propel limited racial progress in the 1960s. Rusk closed his speech by observing that the United States possessed a level of global power that the Civil

War generation could scarce have imagined. But the greatest source of that power was not military might; rather it derived from concepts of freedom rooted in the Declaration of Independence and renewed by Lincoln at Gettysburg. "These ideas, these aspirations, are shared today by a great majority of mankind," the secretary of state concluded. "They bind us with others throughout the world." The remainder of the program was devoted to hearing from these others, as represented by the three European diplomats.[30]

Herve Alphand maintained that like all the great orations of history, Lincoln's words were universal, belonging equally to all of mankind. Merging the rallying cry of the French Revolution with Lincoln's address, the French ambassador insisted that France and the United States had always struggled in unison to advance the unfinished work of liberty, equality, and fraternity. This work, he insisted, was as important in the present moment as it had ever been. Acknowledging that the U.S. government was "still struggling against the dark forces of discrimination which Lincoln opposed," Alphand noted (in a self-congratulatory fashion that ignored the bloody realities of France's long struggle with the Viet Minh and the just-ended Algerian War for Independence) that his country had recently recognized twenty new nations in Asia and Africa.[31]

Stressing the excitement with which contemporary Italian patriots such as Mazzini and Garibaldi greeted Lincoln's words, and the presence of Italian volunteers in the Union Army, Sergio Fenoaltea argued that "we men and women of the twentieth century must be grateful to Divine providence for having vested a Nation, inspired by so high an idealism, with so great a strength." The safety and security of the modern world, he commented, depended on the "unique combination of American strength and American idealism." Britain's John Chadwick sounded a similar theme, noting that the Gettysburg Address had become an expression of British ideals as well as American ones. What bound Britain, the United States, and their allies together against present-day foes, he alleged, was their mutual commitment to upholding "the moral and spiritual standard defined by Lincoln in the Gettysburg Address."[32]

Gettysburg College's annual Fortenbaugh Lecture followed that evening. Johns Hopkins University historian David Donald, who had a long history with Gettysburg's Civil War Study Group, delivered an address on "Abraham Lincoln and American Nationalism" in which he identified three concepts underlying Lincoln's focus at Gettysburg: equality, democracy, and nationalism. Donald ruefully noted that the Gettysburg Address posed numerous challenges for any historian attempting to bring fresh eyes to interpreting it.

The first challenge, he acknowledged, was the very familiarity of its words; the second was its extreme brevity. "It is in a literary style so perfect that the historian's words will necessarily appear pompous or flat," he bemoaned. Nonetheless, Donald proceeded to offer some conclusions. The address, he said, was the finest encapsulation of Lincoln's political philosophy, and its purpose was nothing less than justifying "both to his people and to himself, the war as a struggle for equality, democracy, and nationalism."[33]

Gettysburg College hosted yet another program on Monday, November 18: a panel discussion devoted to exploring the content and varied impacts of the address. Noted poet Archibald MacLeish, Congressman Fred Schwengel, Judge Raymond Pace Alexander, and Gettysburg College historian Robert Bloom made up the panel, which drew nearly 900 attendees and was moderated by well-known journalist Alistair Cooke, who condemned white violence in the American South but hesitated to openly embrace racial equality. The Gettysburg High School choir sang several numbers, including one featuring Mary Alice Nutter, a member of one of Gettysburg's most deeply rooted Black families, as soloist. Responding to David Donald's lecture the evening before, the panelists debated Lincoln's definition of nationalism and response to secession. Alistair Cooke also echoed some of the themes of the diplomats' program, speaking expansively about the role of the address in shaping international perceptions of the United States. Britons, he argued, derived their sense of the United States' better angels from Lincoln's speech.[34]

Raymond Pace Alexander, the first African American judge appointed to the Pennsylvania Court of Common Pleas, argued that "had Lincoln lived, the Negro would have been 'raised to full citizenship' a half century or more ago." A lifelong Philadelphian who was deeply influenced by Black history pioneer Carter Woodson, Alexander was the only Black member of his Harvard Law class. Prior to his appointment to the bench, he headed a law firm well-known for its activity on the civil rights front and served as an advisor to the NAACP legal team on *Brown v. Board of Education*. As the Philadelphia NAACP stepped up direct action protests against discrimination in employment, Alexander was increasingly seen by many Black Philadelphians as insufficiently militant, but his statewide reputation as a Black leader remained sterling. The crowd greeted his assertion that Lincoln "would have prevented today's racial problems" with applause. Archibald MacLeish summed up the group's discussion by insisting that were Lincoln to return to Gettysburg in 1963 he would likely be "disappointed by the lack of progress on many fronts" toward his new birth of freedom but would insist that Americans keep trying.[35]

CWCC's James Robertson was the featured speaker at the Lincoln Fellowship's annual November 19 luncheon. Though party to the bitter sectional debates that prevented the commission from achieving its initial goal of boosting national unity, Robertson optimistically claimed that activities such as the November 19 ceremonies "are living proof that the wounds of civil war were not too deep for healing." At the luncheon, a representative of Bethlehem Steel presented NPS director Conrad Wirth a deed transferring ownership of five acres of land north of the National Cemetery, valued at about $75,000, from the company to the NPS. Bethlehem Steel's contribution to battlefield preservation was buttressed by the continuing work of the GBPA, which claimed at the end of the centennial year that it had transferred more than $90,000 worth of land to the National Park Service. Director Wirth used his acceptance remarks to remind local leaders that, in the continued absence of local zoning regulations, private preservation efforts could only go so far.[36]

Whereas the GBPA from its founding had always made the case that the only permanent solution to the problem of commercialization at Gettysburg was outright purchase of threatened lands through private donations, Wirth argued that private action alone was insufficient. Noting that his impending retirement made him more free to speak openly, he reiterated the warning that others had previously offered: that congressional appropriations for land acquisition at Gettysburg National Military Park would remain unavailable until local governing bodies passed zoning regulations. Rooting Gettysburg's historical significance in Lincoln's address, he argued that "it behooves us to get our house in order here within the next few years so that the site of Lincoln's address can be fully protected, so that Gettysburg, which gave one of the most important of ideas to the world, may continue to help those who visit here to understand what occurred here and take away its message." Nevertheless, local governing bodies did not adopt zoning ordinances until 1975, in the aftermath of the preservation crisis surrounding the construction of developer Thomas Ottenstein's mammoth National Tower.[37]

Following the luncheon, attendees joined the procession to the National Cemetery for the rededication, where the large interracial turnout reflected the primacy placed on the event. Classes were cancelled that day for all of Gettysburg's K-12 students, in expectation that teachers and pupils would participate in the commemorative activities. Yet numbers proved so much higher than expected that the GCC put in a last-minute call for additional help with crowd control. Gettysburg College's ROTC cadets were dispatched to the cemetery, including Thomas Gideon Welles, the great-grandson of

Lincoln's secretary of the navy, one of the three cabinet secretaries present for the 1863 ceremonies.[38]

GCC chairman Milton Baker served as master of ceremonies, reading the Kennedy proclamation published in Roy's special edition of the *Gettysburg Times*, and introducing the afternoon's keynote speaker, General Dwight D. Eisenhower, the commission's honorary chairman. Eisenhower, whose speech during the battle anniversary had proven disappointing to many, took a different tack in his November 19 address. Though he still did not make an explicit connection between Lincoln's new birth of freedom and the expanding Black freedom struggle, listeners who saw the two as fundamentally linked could conclude that the connective tissue was present between the lines. At least two newspapers chose to place Eisenhower's presence on the speakers' platform in the company of two distinguished African Americans— newspaper publisher E. Washington Rhodes and singer Marian Anderson— at the center of their coverage of the event. The *New York Times* headline proclaimed, "Negroes Join Eisenhower to Rededicate Gettysburg."[39]

In the weeks leading up to the program, Eisenhower gave an interview in which he affirmed the legal and moral soundness of the Supreme Court's 1954 decision in *Brown v. Board of Education*. The former president's refusal to personally endorse the court's decision while in office infuriated many proponents of civil rights, who argued that his silence encouraged the growth of massive resistance. In the face of a cresting wave of white violence, many supporters of school desegregation, including Chief Justice Earl Warren, perceived Eisenhower's limited statements encouraging white southerners to obey the law as bloodless and inadequate. His refusal to use the bully pulpit to throw the open support of the White House behind the decision played a key role in convincing many onlookers—particularly Blacks—that he was, at best, lukewarm on civil rights. An October 15, 1963, editorial in the *Chicago Daily Defender* summed up the response felt by many to this belated endorsement of the decision: "Too Late, Ike."[40]

The *Defender* blasted Eisenhower for failing to provide moral leadership at a crucial moment, arguing that if he had, his country would have listened. His decision not to speak, the *Defender* argued, bequeathed the nation "a perpetual crisis" that could explode at any time. His belated endorsement counted for little, the paper editorialized, since "his voice today carries neither the weight nor the sonority of national leadership. . . . Eisenhower the private citizen is not Eisenhower the President." Both Eisenhower's opinions and policies on civil rights have been the subject of much debate among historians over the years, many of whom have reached conclusions similar to those of the *Defender*. But David Nichols has argued that focusing on Eisenhower's rhetoric has blinded onlookers and historians alike to the substance of his efforts on behalf of civil rights, particularly as seen in his judicial appointments record and his legislative initiatives. Eisenhower's greatest blind spot, according to Nichols, was that his deep commitment to the separation of powers doctrine left him poorly equipped to understand the growing importance placed on presidential rhetoric, particularly by Americans who could find little redress for their grievances in the nation's political and legal system.[41]

This broader context is vitally important for understanding both what Eisenhower said on November 19 and how contemporary audiences heard it. The address he delivered was in every way a Cold War speech, constructed around the responsibilities and necessary sacrifices of citizenship. Lincoln's faith in the future was justified, Eisenhower maintained, but contemporary Americans had an obligation to "give increased devotion to that cause" that American soldiers had upheld (and by extension, would uphold) in all wars. What was the cause? Eisenhower's answer was duty to country. "True to democracy's basic principle that all are created equal and endowed by the Creator with priceless human rights, the good citizen now, as always before, is called upon to defend the rights of others as he does his own," Eisenhower insisted, "to subordinate self to the country's good; to refuse to take the easy way today that invites national disaster tomorrow." Because Eisenhower never provided a definition of the easy way, multiple interpretations of the speech were — and remain — possible. Some listeners likely heard in this ambiguous wording echoes of his oft-repeated mantras of individual liberty and personal responsibility. Others, particularly those who placed emphasis on the idea of "defending the rights of others" may have discerned echoes of Sam Gibbons's call for white Americans to sacrifice discriminatory practices for their country's good.[42]

Eisenhower was preceded at the podium by fellow Republican William Scranton, who echoed Lincoln in telling his listeners that their presence in this cemetery was for the living, not the dead. "His [Lincoln's] memory to endure has no need of our faint applause," Scranton noted. Rather, the purpose of the ceremony was for mid-twentieth-century Americans to "refresh ourselves at this shrine" and take away from it increased devotion to the cause of human freedom. Yet Edith Evans Asbury of the *New York Times* found it significant to point out that of the three main speakers at the event, only E. Washington Rhodes addressed racial injustice openly and directly. Eisenhower and Scranton referenced civil rights only indirectly, though both did acknowledge that the unfinished work of which Lincoln spoke was still incomplete.[43]

As noted in the previous chapter, Scranton was widely perceived as a potential candidate for the Republican ticket in 1964. He may have deliberately kept his remarks vague as to avoid alienating potential supporters, but if that was his reasoning it likely did not win him any points with activists who were already criticizing his administration's record on civil rights. The same day the governor spoke at Gettysburg, an AP article appeared chronicling the Pennsylvania Equal Rights Council's indictment of his record. Members of the council blasted the Scranton administration for failing to protect Black homeowners from white violence, inadequately funding the state Human Relations Commission, and failing to introduce legislation proposed by the group.[44]

E. Washington Rhodes was one of Philadelphia's most prominent Black Republicans, and his political affiliation—at a time when Black Americans were increasingly identifying with the Democratic Party—no doubt played a role in his selection as a speaker. Rhodes was well aware that his presence on the platform was "as a representative of the American Negro people." No doubt familiar with the ways that many other centennial commemorations had barely acknowledged African Americans as part of the body politic, Rhodes was pleased that Black Americans had been invited to participate in such a significant national occasion. For that reason, he took his responsibility to represent the views and opinions of "the race" quite seriously. As publisher of Philadelphia's oldest Black newspaper, the *Philadelphia Tribune*, and president of the National Newspaper Publishers Association, Rhodes was no doubt as conversant with current events as any of the elected officials on the platform. Arguing that Lincoln's prediction about the unsustainability of a house divided was just as true in 1963 as it had been in 1858, Rhodes insisted that "second-class citizenship with all of its attendant evils must end." Unless people of goodwill took immediate action to dismantle white supremacy, he predicted, "government of the people, by the people, and for the people will soon be endangered beyond repair."[45]

Reflecting the comparatively greater representation of Black Americans in public roles during the November commemoration than the July one, Rhodes was not the only person of color on the platform. The *Afro-American* was quick to point out that "two noted [Black] Americans" joined Eisenhower in the rededication of the cemetery. *Philadelphia Inquirer* columnist John M. Cummings directly tied their presence on the speaker's platform to Lincoln's role as the Great Emancipator, writing (problematically, from the view of history) that "descendants of slaves freed by Lincoln had a conspicuous place on the program." Famed contralto Marian Anderson sang two songs during the ceremony, "Lead, Kindly Light" and "He's Got the Whole World in His Hands." Anderson's long symbolic association with Abraham Lincoln and the emancipationist vision of the Civil War began in 1939, when she performed an outdoor concert on the steps of the Lincoln Memorial after being barred by the Daughters of the American Revolution from using their concert venue. Always seeking opportunities to legitimize the continuing struggle for Black freedom through associating it with Lincoln, NAACP activists played a key role in securing the memorial as a substitute location. Her presence in the National Cemetery particularly electrified the Black members of the crowd; the *Gettysburg Times* noted that when the program ended, "The speakers' platform was thronged by dozens of negro youngsters who scaled the structure and clung to the railing while she autographed their programs and other pieces of paper."[46]

Mourning the President

As it was in every other newspaper in the United States, the assassination of John F. Kennedy was front-page news in the *Gettysburg Times* on November 22. Given the community's unique relationship with Kennedy's predecessor, however, the paper also sought out a statement from Dwight Eisenhower, running word of the former president's "shock and dismay" on the front page as well, directly under its coverage of Lyndon Johnson taking the oath of office. *Gettysburg Times* reporters noted dazedly that the Kennedy family had visited Gettysburg only months earlier, and that the president's statement on the famed address by another martyred chief of state had been read publicly only four days earlier. Gettysburg mayor William Weaver called on residents to observe the official days of mourning declared for the slain president and to attend local worship services to pray for both the nation and the Kennedy family.[47]

After the Bishop of Harrisburg placed all Catholic churches in the diocese in mourning for a month, parishioners of St. Francis Xavier Catholic Church hung black bunting. All schools in the county closed on Monday, November 24, the day of the president's funeral. St. Joseph's Catholic Church held a military mass in Kennedy's honor, and the Gettysburg Ministerium arranged a community memorial service that filled St. James Lutheran Church to near capacity. While the pattern of grief experienced in Gettysburg was in many ways typical of that replicated in communities across the nation, those who had been deeply involved in centennial planning were haunted by the question whether the nation would have been spared such grief if Kennedy had come to Gettysburg, not Dallas. In a letter to Milton Baker, Kittridge Wing asked rhetorically, "If President Kennedy had accepted your invitation to speak at Gettysburg on the 19th, would the national tragedy of his assassination have been prevented?" British minister John Chadwick, who participated in the "International Aspects of the Address" program, noted sadly in a thank-you note to Baker that as he had been preparing his speech he had wondered if Kennedy had "got himself into the sort of political situation" that confronted Lincoln. Writing the day after the assassination, he concluded somberly, "I made a silent prayer that he would not end in the same way."[48]

In two pieces intended to reassure Black Americans that Kennedy's successor was firmly committed to civil rights, the Baltimore-based *Afro-American* drew on Johnson's Memorial Day speech at Gettysburg as proof of the new president's sincerity and resolve. The second of these pieces delved into comparative history, examining the two men named Johnson who ascended to the Chief of State's office in the wake of a presidential assassination. Though also a southerner, Lyndon Johnson, the authors argued, bore no resemblance to the obstructionist Andrew Johnson. Briefly and selectively chronicling his record on race prior to the vice presidency, they avowed that "if there was any remaining doubt as to President Johnson's all-out commitment to the cause of first-class citizenship, it should have been dispelled last May 30 at Gettysburg." Quoting Johnson's National Cemetery speech at length, the article assured readers that he had already taken steps proving that his devotion to the cause would be undiminished as president.[49]

GCC EXECUTIVE SECRETARY LOUIS SIMON packed up the commission's office in the Gettysburg Post Office in mid-December and relocated to Harrisburg for two months to write his official report of the centennial observance. The final report, "Gettysburg—1963: An Account of the Centennial Commemoration—Report of the Commission to the General Assembly," included a narrative history of the commission's work, photos, and full-text reproductions of most of the speeches delivered during the official public events. Simon's open letter to the community of Gettysburg, published in the *Gettysburg Times*, praised residents for their wholehearted cooperation and the town itself as "truly worthy of the high place that an accident of history gave to it."[50]

As they looked back on the year's events, the sense of satisfaction and relief among those involved in their orchestration was widespread. Despite uncooperative weather and lower attendance figures than expected for the battle anniversary, GNMP's visitation numbers for 1963 exceeded the two million mark for the first time in the park's history, totaling 2,041,378. Though stretched, the town's infrastructure did not collapse under the weight of centennial visitation. Coverage of the anniversary nationwide was mostly positive, unmarred by any major emergencies or "embarrassing" racial incidents.[51]

Despite the reality that the GCC devoted the majority of its funds and attention to the July events, the more solemn, internationally focused November commemoration stood out in retrospect as the more important of the two programs. A representative of the Pennsylvania Department of Commerce told commission members in December that the Gettysburg Address centennial observance was the year's signature event. GCC chair Milton Baker argued that the commemoration of Lincoln's address "proved beyond doubt that Gettysburg will be everlasting as a national shrine if it is preserved as a hallowed area of reverence and dignity." In his farewell letter to the local community, Louis Simon acknowledged that the battle commemoration and the address commemoration were fundamentally different occasions, and that the question of which one was "better" was an essentially subjective one. Nonetheless, he concluded: "If ever there were an example of the truth that 'the pen is mightier than the sword,' nowhere has it been more dramatically demonstrated than at Gettysburg in 1963."[52] In its focus on the "pen," the Gettysburg Address centennial offered a vision for the anniversary that was more officially aligned with both the emancipationist interpretation of the Civil War and the increasingly global movement for Black freedom.

CHAPTER SEVEN

Post-100

The Impact of the Centennial Era

Though the national commemoration of the Civil War extended through 1965, centennial zeal waned in Gettysburg after 1963. Charged only with commemorating the 100th anniversary of the battle and Lincoln's address, the Gettysburg Centennial Commission closed its office at the end of the year, and members turned their attention to other commitments. Though GCC's grassroots partner, the Adams County Civil War Centennial Commission, had initially planned to hold at least one major event per year in support of its mission to commemorate the war from Fort Sumter to Appomattox, the group did little after the 1963 battle anniversary and formally disbanded the following year. Americans writ large, however, experienced no similar pullback of enthusiasm for Gettysburg, either as a historical topic of interest or a destination. Even in the absence of high-profile special programming, visitation reached new heights in the final two years of the Civil War Centennial, reaching 2,334,689 in 1965, and GNMP officials predicted that numbers might exceed five million within the following decade.[1]

Gettysburg's increasing popularity with the American public was the great exception to the general rule of declining public interest in the Civil War Centennial. Though some localities mounted successful events throughout the four years of the commemorative period, historians have concluded that the centennial was in decline as early as 1962.[2] Yet throughout the centennial era and beyond, countless Americans threw themselves wholeheartedly into the process of marking various Gettysburg anniversaries and debating the meaning of both battle and address in a rapidly changing world. While many centennial programs captured critics' attention for conflating Confederate heritage and massive resistance, or erasing race and Black freedom from the narrative of the Civil War, the commemorative activities at Gettysburg were more complex and contested. Reconciliationist, Lost Cause, and emancipationist memory intersected in new ways at GNMP, struggling to define Gettysburg's meaning for future generations. Though an extensive wave of Confederate monumentation in the centennial and postcentennial decades testifies to the solidifying of traditional narratives of reconciliation and states' rights during the anniversary years, the emancipationist vision of the Civil War made important gains as well.

Historians and contemporary commentators alike have generally regarded the April 1965 Appomattox commemoration, a low-key ceremony attended by only about 5,000 people, as the last major event of the Civil War Centennial. Though the general mood was quiet and respectful, the playing of "Dixie" elicited a chorus of applause, suggesting that though overt merging of the cause of massive resistance with Confederate commemoration was on the decline in 1965, the centennial had done little to alter the traditional ways that white Americans perceived the history of their Civil War.[3] Yet if the timeline is altered to consider the last major event of the centennial not the Appomattox commemoration but rather Gettysburg's 1965 Dedication Day activities, a somewhat different narrative emerges.

As the ongoing Black freedom struggle and the warming Cold War changed American society in fundamental ways over the centennial period, commemoration of Gettysburg began to reflect greater historical and ideological complexity. As activists for racial justice employed both the Gettysburg Address and the history of the battle itself as ammunition in their struggle to make the nation live up to its creed, official commemorative events became more racially representative. Politicians, diplomats, and architects of U.S. foreign policy made extensive use of Gettysburg in their efforts to prop up the nation's public image and establish democracy as America's leading export. Indeed, the GCC itself argued in retrospect that the pageantry and entertainment value of the battle anniversary mattered less than the Gettysburg Address centennial's emphasis on the ideals of democratic self-governance.

Yet this somewhat more racially inclusive and historically complex narrative was challenged from its infancy by an emboldened Confederate memory demanding additional space on the battlefield for its narratives. A series of decisions by National Park Service officials during and in the aftermath of the centennial furthered the new wave of memorialization transforming the battle lines along Seminary Ridge into full-fledged Confederate memorial space, thus setting up conflict between these two divergent legacies. For Blacks and some whites who lived in the shadow of the battlefield's monuments, including young people on the Gettysburg College campus, racial justice continued to be a pressing issue. Though much of the overt discrimination in public accommodations that had been so common in the 1950s did lessen over the course of the early 1960s, as it did in so many other parts of the country, the color barrier did not dissolve in Gettysburg during the centennial period. It did weaken, however, setting the stage for more substantial change in the following decade.

CROWDS OF ENTHUSIASTIC VISITORS thronged Gettysburg over the 101st battle anniversary, with the local newspaper estimating a crowd of nearly 8,000 at the annual July 2 parade. Not all, however, were happy with the scene that greeted them upon arrival. Alfred Runte, a high school student, was so distressed by the commercialization of the battle-field that he wrote Secretary of the Interior Stewart Udall decrying the presence of neon lights within view of "sacred" battlefield land. Noting that he had last visited Gettysburg in 1960, Runte blamed the centennial anniversary for what he perceived as a significant uptick in development. Retired air force general John Virden concurred, singling out Fort Defiance and Fantasyland for criticism the following year. "Maybe us Rebs do it a little better," he mused in a letter to GNMP's Harry Pfanz. "You must know that we have stood for none of this kind of nonsense at Shiloh, nor at Pea Ridge."[4]

GNMP historian Martin Conway led an anniversary program on July 3, 1964, about the North Carolinians' role in Pickett's Charge. Gazing out at monuments that later generations would find deeply problematic (and many members of earlier generations fiercely resisted), Conway argued that Americans' willingness to allow those who launched a revolution against the government to erect monuments to their struggle "speaks eloquently of the greatness, the magnanimity, the splendor that is the United States of America." One wonders how Conway's words—and the way his audience heard them—were shaped by the events of the previous day. The 1964 battle anniversary coincided with the formal signing into law of the hard-fought Civil Rights Act, a piece of legislation that Lyndon B. Johnson strove to present as a gift from a fully "American" South, not a mandate imposed on the region from without.[5]

The 1964 Dedication Day activities included a ceremony at the visitor center featuring a dramatic keynote address by the Library of Congress's William Coblenz, who argued that the Gettysburg Address's focus on human dignity made it "the greatest single weapon against Communism." Acknowledging that Lincoln certainly did not foresee twentieth-century global politics, Coblenz nonetheless argued that the speech he delivered in Gettysburg's Soldiers' National Cemetery "is the deadliest, the most devastating, the most complete answer to Communism and totalitarianism that has emerged since the Communist Manifesto of 1848."[6]

In 1964, 2,271,105 people visited GNMP, an 11 percent increase over the anniversary year; in 1965, numbers reached 2,334,689. This pattern of sustained popularity differed from that experienced by many other Civil War parks, such as neighboring Antietam, where visitation immediately dipped in the aftermath of the centennial year. Delighted by this heightened public interest, NPS officials sought to find sustainable ways to meet the needs of the expanding visitor population. GNMP opened a nature trail on Big Round Top, installed a series of technologically unreliable "talking interpretive stations" throughout the auto tour loop, continued the popular summer campfire program (attracting an estimated 40,000 attendees over the course of 1964 and 1965), and engaged in a large-scale brush clearing project focused on restoring the historic appearance of the battlefield. These improvements were driven by a long-standing concern for bringing increased visibility to the agency's presence, programs, and activities; NPS officials noted in an internal memo that the campfire program provided "one more way of establishing ourselves in the visitor's eye as the custodian of the battlefield."[7]

GNMP staff confidently predicted that visitation numbers would reach five million within the next ten years; though this was not borne out (attendance dropped substantially by the late 1970s), the park pressed forward with substantially expanded interpretive offerings, including, for the first time, living history programs, and an increasing focus on education. Always concerned about the competition for visitors' attention and time, yet leery of appearing to compete with commercial establishments, in 1973 the NPS finally achieved its long-desired goal of acquiring the Rosensteel family's Gettysburg National Museum, which bordered the park visitor center. With the building came the popular Electric Map and the museum's extensive artifact collection, much of it acquired in the initial days after the battle. Though staff pursued plans to build a new visitor center on the northern border of the battlefield in the early 1970s, the plans came to naught, and the two structures in Ziegler's Grove would continue to house GNMP's visitor services operations into the twenty-first century.[8]

We Shall Overcome: Campaigns for Civil Rights Continue, Both Locally and Nationally

Racial issues began to receive more attention on the Gettysburg College campus in the later years of the centennial. Joseph Washington spoke on Black citizenship in February 1964; a panel discussion featuring local Black activists Adam Myers and Joseph Haggler followed. By 1965, the college had an active Human Relations Forum, which placed a high priority on raising funds to support four students planning to volunteer the following summer with SCLC's Summer Community Organization and Political Education (SCOPE) project, a voter registration campaign modeled on Freedom Summer. Many of the students who were most interested in civil rights issues were associated with the small progressive Christian group closely affiliated with college chaplain John Vannorsdall, who arrived on campus in 1962.[9]

Under Vannorsdall's leadership, Gettysburg instigated a one-week exchange program with historically Black Knoxville College in 1965, as an avenue to building relationships across the color line. Two weeks of exchange programs were held that first year, in November 1965 and March 1966. The Knoxville students visiting Gettysburg were housed in dormitories and fraternity houses, and encouraged to attend classes and campus social events. By the end of the decade, significantly higher numbers of students of color staked out increasingly visible lives on the Gettysburg College campus. These students actively pressured administrators to prioritize recruiting and retaining a larger population of minority students, leading to a significant increase in nonwhite enrollment by the early 1970s.[10]

That said, into the late 1960s, only a small number of fraternities on campus (namely Tau Kappa Epsilon and Alpha Chi Rho) accepted Black and Jewish members; other Greek organizations claimed that their national charters forbade it. Though many of the Black students on campus who pledged a fraternity joined the Tekes, the culture of the Greek system did not sit well with some. Buddy Glover (class of '71) remembered rushing Teke for a week. "I got concerned when they had their pledge box, and had you get up there and sing a song," he reflected later. "All I saw were these white guys trying to get you to sing songs, do this, do that, and they had a Black cook, and it just felt like someone was bringing me to the plantation."[11]

On the day Martin Luther King Jr. was assassinated, some whites on campus cheered; in response, a group of Black students made rounds of the dorms to intimidate white classmates. Cognizant of the tensions unleashed by the assassination, students active in the Knoxville exchange program organized a Peace Week devoted to increasing student awareness of racial discrimination and the Vietnam War. Events included a "Life Ball," a service at the Peace Light, a class strike, and discussions on the draft and "the race issue." Unable to grieve King's death in such a white environment, Glover returned home for a few days to join street demonstrations. Though he initially felt that he could never return to Gettysburg, his mother finally convinced him to do so.[12]

Away from campus, the mood in the Black neighborhoods of the Third Ward was angry and fearful. Though many of her white friends did not seem to understand what had happened, Jean Green's neighborhood grieved as though mourning a family member. In the face of such tragedy, she, like Glover, craved the company of other Blacks. "It was hard to process what might happen next for Black people," Green remembered. Listening to grown-ups say things she had never heard them utter aloud before, she feared for her own physical safety, concerned that white residents might come into the neighborhood to attack Blacks.[13]

Renewed protests against police violence broke out in neighboring York in the final summer of the centennial, sparked by a June 1965 assault on two Black citizens. Demonstrators affiliated with the York NAACP packed the city council's chambers at its next meeting, demanding that the council discontinue the canine corps and hold a hearing on the June incident. In the wake of the council's refusal, picketers surrounded City Hall for a week, activists staged a sit-in at the mayor's office, and the woman involved filed suit against the officer for assault and battery. On the other side of the country, years of tension deriving from police brutality, residential segregation, and discrimination in employment and education exploded that August into six days of uprisings in the Los Angeles neighborhood of Watts, leaving thirty-four people dead, more than one thousand injured, and $40 million worth of property damage.[14]

The Watts riots came only five days after Lyndon Johnson signed the Voting Rights Act. The August 6 ceremony ushered into a law a piece of legislation that broke the logjam that had long derailed attempts to eradicate racial discrimination in voting. The act's three central components were a trigger formula to guarantee the suspension of voting restrictions in areas with unusually low electoral participation, federal registrars to register new voters, and the imposition of a "pre-clearance" requirement on future changes in offending districts. Through these mechanisms, the Voting Rights Act paved the way for large-scale enfranchisement of Black Americans, huge increases in the number of Black elected officials, and the realignment of the nation's two major political parties. The *Chicago Daily Defender* rejoiced in the signing ceremony, billing the Voting Rights Act as "the long awaited sequel to the Emancipation Proclamation." The paper exulted in Johnson's speech at the signing, predicting that certain passages "will echo down the corridors of time with the same fervor and consecration as does Lincoln's Gettysburg Address." But despite its watershed significance in American politics, the Voting Rights Act had virtually no impact on the continuing problems of poverty and discrimination in employment, education, and housing that plagued African American communities across the north. Thus, it could not prevent the rising tide of urban rebellions that crested in the late 1960s. Close to home for Gettysburg residents, the long-simmering tensions in York exploded into full-scale unrest in July 1969, leaving two people dead (one white and one Black) and dozens wounded over the course of six days of armed clashes, made even more severe than they might have otherwise been by police officers openly distributing ammunition to white rioters.[15]

York's uprising has been quantitatively marked the twenty-sixth most severe of the over 500 revolts that swept the country between 1963 and 1972, yet when adjusted for population, it ranks as one of the most dangerous and deadly ones of the era. Jean Green was visiting a friend in the city when the violence erupted. Though the experience terrified her, she also found it somewhat bewildering, recognizing that York residents were experiencing a reality that differed in many ways from her own in small-town Gettysburg. Though Gettysburg borough police geared up to prepare for unrest in town, none materialized, and the *Gettysburg Times* provided residents relatively little coverage of the uprising, focusing instead on the drama of the Apollo 11 moon landing.[16]

Gettysburg and the National Commemoration of the Civil War

In planning the final November 19 exercises of the centennial period, Gettysburg College, the Lincoln Fellowship, and the Sons of Union Veterans invited African American historian John Hope Franklin, an outspoken critic of early centennial activities, to deliver the Fortenbaugh Lecture and the keynote address in the National Cemetery. By 1965, Franklin, the author of such important works as *From Slavery to Freedom*, *The Militant South*, and *Reconstruction After the Civil War*, was professor of history at the University of Chicago. Two years earlier, he had published a critical essay, "The Dilemma of the American Negro Scholar," that powerfully chronicled the ostracism and humiliation regularly faced by Black scholars as they carried out their archival research and speaking engagements, as well as the challenges of balancing scholarship with advocacy and service to the field with service to the race.[17]

In the early 1950s, Franklin assisted the NAACP legal team in preparing its arguments in *Brown v. Board of Education*, an experience that he noted in his "Dilemma" piece leaned more toward the advocacy side of the spectrum than the scholarly side. "I had deliberately transformed the objective data provided by historical research into an urgent plea for justice," he wrote, "and I hoped my scholarship did not suffer." In 1962, he was asked by the Civil Rights Commission to produce a report on the first 100 years of emancipation. The insufficiently celebratory nature of his draft report—which unflinchingly chronicled the devastating impact of racial discrimination on Black Americans—led to a falling out with the commissioners, who had expected a narrative of racial progress that they could use for political purposes. When asked to revise it, Franklin responded that the history documented in his draft was not a pleasant one. To produce the report the commission wanted, "I would be writing a tract and not a history." The commissioners hastily turned elsewhere for a more palatable interpretation of American race relations.[18]

In his November 1965 speech at the National Cemetery, Franklin returned to the theme of using the past for advocacy purposes. He argued strenuously that white supremacists who attempted to use Lincoln quotes on race to justify their own racist sentiments were playing fast and loose with the historical record. Responding directly to the 1964 efforts of the White Citizens' Councils to use excerpts from some of Lincoln's speeches to defend their own ideology, Franklin argued that in their zeal to enlist the sixteenth president, they failed to acknowledge the most important factor in his views on race: that they evolved over the years. Franklin acknowledged that Lincoln's views on race were more typical of his era than his views on slavery were, but argued that "the changes that took place in the last four years of his life regarding . . . racial justice were greater and more significant than the changes on the same subject the Citizens' Councils and their predecessors have undergone in the last 100 years." It was a dangerous practice, he continued, to claim association between historical figures and contemporary causes. When considering Lincoln's legacy in its entirely, he argued that enlisting the sixteenth president in the service of racism and discrimination "is a remarkable distortion of his position and a crude disrespect for his service and memory."[19]

After the event at the cemetery, Franklin was escorted to the college campus, where he spoke informally with students at a reception hosted by Phi Alpha Theta, the history honor society. Jim Madison (class of '66), a member of Phi Alpha Theta who later went on to a distinguished career as a professional historian, commented in retrospect that this encounter with Franklin was transformative for him. Like many of his peers, Madison had never before encountered an African American historian, and thus had never envisioned a Black man in this role. Neither did he know much about the field of African American history, which was not yet well represented in majority-white institutions (there were no courses in Black history available at Gettysburg in 1965). Madison, who later went on to publish several important books on the United States' tortured relationship with race, remembered Franklin as a tremendously impressive figure.[20]

Franklin delivered the college's annual Fortenbaugh Lecture that evening, speaking on the topic of "Lincoln and Reconstruction." Having spoken at the college's inaugural Civil War conference in 1957, he was likely familiar enough with Gettysburg to know that Confederate symbolism was widespread, and that Black residents experienced discrimination in multiple forms. He may have even anticipated the possibility of meeting the kind of discriminatory treatment he highlighted in his "Dilemma" piece. Yet in accepting both invitations to speak, Franklin put into practice his own call for the Black scholar "to use his training, talents and resources to beat down the barriers that keep him out of the main stream of American life and scholarship." His invitation to deliver the lecture was likely due at least in part to the influence of Robert Bloom, who supported the Black freedom struggle and consciously involved Black scholars (in small numbers) in the earliest days of the college's Civil War programming.[21]

The invitation to Franklin can by no means be read as evidence that the emancipationist memory of the Civil War triumphed in Gettysburg by the close of the centennial. Indeed, the new wave of Confederate monumentation that profoundly altered the community's commemorative landscape between 1961 and 1973 testifies to the entrenchment of traditional narratives of reconciliation and states' rights during the anniversary years. Yet that does not suggest that *nothing* changed between 1961 and 1965. People of color such as Franklin, Raymond Pace Alexander, Marian Anderson, E. Washington Rhodes, and Lena Parr played unprecedented roles in commemorative activities during the 100th anniversary, assertively claiming space for Black Americans in Gettysburg in all of its three roles as an idea, a landscape, and a living community. In a departure from previous anniversaries, influential voices for racial justice utilized the community's historic landscape to link the Gettysburg Address to civil rights legislation and call on the nation to honor soldiers' sacrifices by living out a new birth of freedom for *all* Americans

Many commentators welcomed the centennial's end, deeming it a failure. Hollins College historian Louis Rubin argued that the centennial flopped because current events made it impossible to distance reenacting from reality. The anniversary fizzled, he concluded, because the war was not yet over. For his part, retired air force general John Virden blamed the problems on the historians, arguing that after Nevins and Robertson took the helm of the CWCC, "everybody got involved in writing learned papers on 'The Causal Effect of the Ante-Deluvian [sic] Mosquito as Pertains to the Southern Confederacy's Decline in the Civil War' or some other equally pertinent topic and we were all lost from there until the thing came to its merciful demise." Though not taking Virden's view of the historians' efforts, scholars of the centennial have concluded that the most the new leadership was able to accomplish was salvaging some semblance of the project. Matchbooks circulated at the CWCC's final national assembly, held in April 1965 in Springfield, Illinois, bore the message "Thank God It's Finished!" which no doubt resonated with participants on multiple levels.[22]

Nonetheless, the New York Times pointed to some lasting accomplishments for the centennial, such as the Mission 66 initiative, the reconstruction of Antietam's Dunker Church, the restoration of Fort Fisher, Fort Ward, and the Lee Chapel, and the raising of two sunken Civil War ships. Two new Civil War parks—Wilson's Creek and Pea Ridge—came under NPS management during the anniversary years, and already-existing military parks added 3,000 acres of land. The CWCC sponsored the publication of several academic monographs and jump-started the publication of the papers of Jefferson Davis and Ulysses S. Grant. Less recognized, however, is the fact that though the major strands of Civil War memory in 1965 may have been little changed on a national scale from how they had appeared at the turn of the century, in Gettysburg the seeds of a more inclusive, more complex historical narrative had been sown. Due to the intertwinement of Cold War politics and civil rights, the commemoration's enlistment of the battle and the address in the service of the anticommunist crusade ensured a partial reemergence of emancipationist memory.[23]

THE GERMINATION OF THIS NEW NARRATIVE, however, was overshadowed in the immediate postcentennial era by the increased prevalence of Confederate monuments along Seminary Ridge, which ensured that visitors taking driving tours of the battlefield would encounter Lost Cause memory in higher doses than those visiting pre-1961. Between 1965 and 1973, Arkansas, Louisiana, and Mississippi placed monuments to troops from their states along West Confederate Avenue; though Tennessee did not follow suit until the early 1980s, the state's effort had its genesis in the mid-1960s. The UDC and SCV also placed a monument to "the Soldiers and Sailors of the Confederacy" in 1965. In 1960, there were only three Confederate state monuments on the Gettysburg battlefield. By 1973, the battle lines along Seminary Ridge had been transformed into full-fledged Confederate memorial space in which the relatively dispassionate marker tablets of an earlier reconciliationist era were dwarfed by the new testimonials to duty, honor, and the "sacredness" of the Southern cause.

The Spirit of the Confederate "Fighting Man": The Battle over the Soldiers and Sailors of the Confederacy Monument

The idea of a memorial at Gettysburg to the "passing of the Confederate army" was inspired by the Grand Army of the Republic memorial statue installed in Ziegler's Woods by the National Auxiliary of the Sons of Union Veterans in 1956, one month after the death of Albert Woolson, credited with being the last surviving Union veteran. Stirred by the 1959 death of Walter Williams, who claimed to be the last surviving Confederate veteran, the United Daughters of the Confederacy proposed what they saw as a complementary memorial marking passage of the Confederacy from memory to history. The UDC's efforts were spearheaded by Gertrude Kibler, who had previously chaired the committee that placed the Georgia monument in 1961.[24]

The UDC soon joined forces with its brother organization, the Sons of Confederate Veterans (which more than doubled its membership between 1953 and 1962), to finance the effort. The joint committee charged with selecting a design struggled mightily over what sort of tangible form would best represent all the soldiers and sailors of the Confederacy and the extent to which the connection to Williams should be stressed. An internal battle between two designs — one more traditional and restrained and the other more raw — tore the committee apart and resulted in significant infighting. Ultimately, the group chose the "energetic" design by sculptor Donald De Lue, which they prized for its depiction of a soldier in motion, made sweaty and disheveled by battle. Critics continued to argue that it was too similar to another of De Lue's pieces, on display at the time at the World's Fair, and resembled an athletic trophy more than a commemorative piece. The committee's chief SCV representative, however, claimed that De Lue "captured the ideals and fighting qualities of the Confederates that made them the most valorous and hard-fighting soldiers and sailors in history." He went on to predict that viewing the statue would impress on future generations the prowess of the Confederate fighting man and his valor in defending "the principles of Constitutional liberty and the sovereignty of his state." His colleague John May, who spoke at Gettysburg in 1963, implored leading southern politicians to endorse the project on the grounds that because the SUV had been allowed to erect a monument in honor of Union soldiers, "we, of the South, should have the same privilege."[25]

GNMP staff found the design problematic; Harry Pfanz argued in an internal memo that De Lue's figure was not true to the appearance of the average Confederate soldier. He worried that the inclusion of such a modernist design in the established commemorative landscape would disrupt the gravitas of the setting and serve as a stylistically jarring note in regards to the other memorials, "which have given the Park a character reminiscent of the era they commemorate." Pfanz also noted that the legitimacy of the Walter Williams story was questionable, concluding that a tribute to a man who may have never served the Confederacy would be an affront to the men who *did* fight and die at Gettysburg. Frederick Tilberg echoed some of Pfanz's critiques and also raised concerns about the proposed inscription, taking issue with the committee's language. "Southerners were hardly defenders of their *country*," he noted dryly. In reality, "they came rather near disrupting their *country*."[26]

Clearly feeling out of his depth, Wing, who was not a historian, asked the northeast regional office for advice on how to respond. "I am hesitant to take a stand in approval or disapproval," he wrote uncomfortably, "not feeling qualified to express a judgment either on the controversial points of history or on the aesthetics of the sculpture." His superiors accepted the design, but instructed Wing to encourage the committee to minimize the connection to the Williams story. The compromise language ultimately struck stated that "Walter Washington Williams was *recognized by the government of the United States* as the last surviving Confederate veteran." It did not say he actually *was* the last surviving veteran, nor that the figure depicted was intended to represent Williams. In a further effort to minimize the association, De Lue placed the text referencing Williams on the rear of the foundation pedestal, where only the most inquisitive visitors would encounter it.[27]

The memorial was dedicated in August 1965. Though representatives from the Sons of Union Veterans and its associated ladies' group, the National Auxiliary, briefly presented wreaths on behalf of their organizations at the dedication ceremony, it was otherwise a sectional affair. Taking a page out of the traditional Lost Cause manual, dedication speaker Sam Ervin, a senator from North Carolina, made an explicit point of arguing that the soldiers and sailors of the Confederacy were not fighting for slavery, insisting that few had a material stake in Confederate victory. Nor, he said, were they motivated by ambition, necessity, or a desire for fame, but "only simple obedience to duty as they understood it."[28]

The grandson of a Confederate veteran who blamed Reconstruction for the family's financial travails, Ervin was passionately interested in Civil War history and frequently used battlefield visits as an escape from Washington. One of the leading architects of the 1956 Southern Manifesto pledging resistance to *Brown v. Board of Education*, the senator was a strict constructionist who opposed all civil rights legislation. During the congressional battle over the Civil Rights Act of 1964, Ervin sparred with Attorney General Robert Kennedy for a solid month over every detail of the bill, until the Judiciary Committee chairman suspended the hearings. Ervin would later rocket to fame during the Watergate hearings for his fierce commitment to unraveling the coverup surrounding Nixon's actions. But in 1965, he arrived at Gettysburg fresh from his losing battle to block Congress from passing the Voting Rights Act, which undoubtedly influenced his thoughts on the "fighting men" of the Confederacy.[29]

The presence of state monuments along West Confederate Avenue was prominent enough by the summer of 1966 that Pennsylvania Klansmen put out a call to make the Mississippi monument a meeting place for members who wanted to stage a countermarch to Baltimore to protest the continuation of James Meredith's Mississippi March Against Fear by civil rights groups. Apparently unbeknownst to the Klansmen, Mississippi did not have a state monument at Gettysburg in 1966, and on the appointed day, the *Gettysburg Times* reported the presence of a small group of robed Klansmen wandering around the battlefield searching for the nonexistent monument. Ultimately, the group gave up on finding it, and marched south out of town brandishing a Confederate flag. Nonetheless, their desire to symbolically harness the power of a battlefield monument to legitimize and ground their cause remains significant. Commemorative symbols, after all, wield tremendous power, both in their interpretations of the past and in their malleability in serving contemporary needs.[30]

The timing of the postcentennial monument campaigns is important, for all were carried out in an era in which southern states were coming to terms with the changes wrought by the civil rights movement, while frequently continuing to fight ongoing campaigns for further transformation. All of these monument campaigns were acted out against a backdrop of shifting demographics in the South (between 1970 and 1973, more African Americans moved into the region than out of it), and increasing numbers of Black elected officials playing a role in government decisions. According to one statistical count, the number of Black elected officials in southern states jumped from 72 in 1965 to 1,555 ten years later.[31]

Both the promise and the limitations of the legislative victories of the mid-1960s were tried and tested in the following decade, which historian Stephen Tuck has deemed "the high-water mark of the Black liberation movement." Civil rights groups such as the NAACP played a key role in pushing for meaningful gains in employment, education, and political representation for Black Americans. *Brown v. Board of Education* may have ruled segregation in public education to be unconstitutional in 1954, but significant integration in American schools did not begin until after 1969, when courts began to order the use of busing to end racially identifiable schools. Civil rights lawyers led the way in ensuring that southern employers who discriminated in hiring and promotion were held accountable before the Equal Employment Opportunity Commission (EEOC). Black southerners also played key roles in fighting attempts to use at-large elections and legislative reapportionment to negate the effects of the Black vote and make it more difficult for newly enfranchised minority residents to elect candidates of color to public office. Despite this concrete progress, however, the 1970s was also a decade of retrenchment, urban crisis, and growing political conservatism. These were years of confusion and contradiction: was the old order vanquished, or was progress only an illusion? Though historians continue to debate the character of civil rights activity in this decade, what *is* clear is that for Arkansans, Louisianans, and Mississippians, the campaigns to place monuments at Gettysburg were part and parcel of this struggle to establish equilibrium in an altered world.[32]

Though Arkansas got a late start on its centennial activities, its commemoration of the Civil War was broad-based enough to win a centennial medallion from the CWCC in 1961, the only one ever bestowed upon an entire state's population. Focused largely on cemetery maintenance, erecting monuments and markers, and boosting tourism to the state, Arkansas's centennial observance "was as much New as Old South." Like most other southern states, it framed its Civil War history as a whites-only story and provided virtually no acknowledgement of Unionist activity in Arkansas. Yet while it embraced Lost Cause narratives of the war, it did not openly use the anniversary to fuel massive resistance to the civil rights movement. The Arkansas Gettysburg Memorial Commission chose a location north of the intersection of West Confederate Avenue and the Emmittsburg Road for its monument, near to the spot where the 3rd Arkansas, the only unit from the state to serve in Lee's army, began its assault on July 2. At the June 1966 dedication, commission chair Neill Bohlinger, an Arkansas State Supreme Court justice who had eagerly absorbed elderly veterans' stories of the battle as a child, floridly prophesied that were the Cold War battle for human freedom to come down to Americans, the defenders would bear in their souls "the memories of the valor at Gettysburg."[33]

As the monuments along West Confederate Ave. grew in number, Gettysburg Civil War Round Table leader Donald MacPhail reached out to contacts in Louisiana and Mississippi to encourage these states to undertake tributes to their troops. When MacPhail and Wallace Kingsbury initially visited the park to explore possible sites for the Louisiana monument, Kingsbury argued that the state should be allowed to disregard the "lines of battle" rule and place its memorial at the farthest site of Louisiana troops' penetration on July 2. His reasoning was that northerners and southerners both paid taxes to maintain the battlefield and thus were equally entitled to high-profile locations. Though this argument failed to sway NPS officials, by the following month, the Louisiana UDC had established a commission to erect a monument.[34]

Louisiana governor John J. McKeithen, a strong supporter of the project, flew a delegation to Gettysburg in his private plane in May 1967 to select a mutually agreeable location. The group selected a piece of ground on Seminary Ridge, located near the spot where the Washington Artillery fired the first shots of the July 3 cannonade. The group awarded the commission for the memorial to Donald De Lue, the creator of the Soldiers and Sailors of the Confederacy monument. De Lue's initial design depicted a female figure representing the spirit of memory blowing a trumpet over the lifeless form of a Washington Artillery cannoneer. Lying motionless under a Confederate battle flag, the figure of the cannoneer was intended to evoke a symbolic connection to "Knight Crusaders of other times" who also, presumably, died for sacred causes. De Lue's hope for the design was that it would not only honor the dead but also prove easy for present-day visitors to understand. The commission's chosen inscription focused heavily on the storied history of the Washington Artillery and the unit's role in firing the first shots of "the greatest artillery barrage that was ever laid down in America."[35]

GNMP's new chief historian, Thomas Harrison, pushed back on the centrality of the Washington Artillery in both the design and the text, pointing out that only a small percentage of the Louisiana troops that fought at Gettysburg served in artillery units. Harrison also argued that the claim that the artillery barrage preceding the charge was the largest in the nation's history was a subjective one that could not be substantiated. The northeast regional director seconded Harrison's revisions to the text, as well as his insistence that the most visible symbols of the Washington Artillery be removed, and both De Lue and the Louisiana Commission acceded. The monument was dedicated on June 11,

1971; like the ceremony for the Georgia monument ten years earlier, the program began with salutes to the U.S., Confederate, and state flags. The main speaker of the day, Governor McKeithen, lauded the Louisiana soldiers that fought at Gettysburg for their devotion to duty and honor. Grasping for a reconciliationist theme at a time when the nation's fighting force in Vietnam was increasingly fractured, McKeithen argued that those who warred at Gettysburg "were not fighting as enemies, but as brothers."[36]

"Our Brave Sires Fought for their Righteous Cause": Mississippi at Gettysburg

One could hardly argue that the group that banded together in the early 1970s to erect a monument to Mississippi soldiers at Gettysburg was motivated by the same purpose animating the Pennsylvania Klan members in 1966. But their efforts were also deeply rooted in contemporary politics, and the finished product showcased a state substantially transformed by the legacy of the civil rights movement, yet still profoundly marked by its past. The early 1970s were a period of great change in the state of Mississippi. In the 1950s and 1960s, Mississippi had been known as the most racially violent state in the nation: the place where fourteen-year-old Emmett Till was murdered in 1955 for allegedly whistling at a white woman, where NAACP leader Medgar Evers was assassinated in his driveway in 1963, and where civil rights activists Mickey Schwerner, James Chaney, and Andrew Goodman were abducted and murdered in 1964.

In 1955, in the wake of the murder of three Black men plus the young Emmett Till, the NAACP published a pamphlet entitled "M Is for Mississippi and Murder." White terrorism and less physical but equally effective forms of racial intimidation went virtually unchecked across the state, and Mississippi's political leaders' full-throated defiance of federal laws and court decisions supporting Black rights openly trampled upon residents' civil liberties. Tom P. Brady, a circuit court judge in the state's 14th Judicial District, played a key role in whipping up racial hysteria. One of the founders of the White Citizens' Council (WCC), Brady stumped around the state in the aftermath of *Brown v. Board of Education* terrifying white parents with dire predictions that school integration would be the ruination of the "white race." Brady's speeches, published in pamphlet form as "Black Monday" in 1955, served as a vital recruiting tool for the WCC. As avenues for resisting *Brown*, he called for the abolition of public schools, the eradication of the NAACP, and the creation of a separate state for Black Americans.[37]

Unlike in Arkansas, the state's observance of the Civil War Centennial was explicitly employed to mobilize white residents in resistance to perceived federal overreach. Programs sponsored by the Mississippi Commission on the War Between the States focused on collectively reinforcing narratives of Civil War heroics that they believed would protect the region from "a host of '-isms,'" including liberalism, Communism, socialism, and pacifism. By extension, commissioners believed that "in demonstrating the courage and high moral standards of Mississippi's past," they could convince whites outside the South to sympathize with their efforts to protect and defend white supremacy.[38]

Nonetheless, by the early 1970s, the plantation economy that had defined Mississippi for generations was collapsing. In 1940, 60 percent of Mississippi workers were involved in agriculture; by 1980, the number had fallen to 4 percent. This shift, however, and the rise in median income across the state did not necessarily spell increased prosperity for Blacks. The opening of the franchise, however, did dramatically transform the electoral landscape. In 1964, only 6 percent of Black Mississippians were registered to vote; by 1982, 75 percent were on the rolls. Their commitment to making use of this hard-won right made the state first in the nation in the number of Black elected officials. By the early 1970s, increasing numbers of Mississippi Blacks were exercising a level of electoral power that would have been unfathomable only ten years earlier. The state's public schools, furthermore, were no longer a bastion of legal segregation, thanks to the Supreme Court's 1969 decision in *Alexander v. Holmes County* that further delay in operating fully integrated school systems was not permissible.[39]

Yet how deeply did the changes penetrate? Many white Mississippians did not so much change their racial attitudes as find new avenues to express them. The state legislature passed a series of laws in 1966 aimed at diluting the impact of the Voting Rights Act through "colorblind" language, and white residents continued to resist school desegregation through withdrawing from the public schools. Mississippi senator John Stennis played a leading role in stoking the fires of opposition to busing on a national level, spearheading the charge to ban so-called "forced busing" and mandate uniform enforcement of desegregation in all parts of the county. Though Stennis was certainly correct that the long-cherished distinction between *de jure* and *de facto* segregation was nearly meaningless, his motivation was to obstruct desegregation in the South by scaring northern whites into championing inaction. In 1973, the year the new monument at Gettysburg was dedicated, the last of the seven men convicted of involvement in the 1964 murders of

Goodman, Schwerner, and Chaney were released from prison. Found guilty only on the charge of violating the three men's civil rights, they served less than ten years for a triple murder that gripped the nation, evidence of the continuing longevity of the old order.[40]

James W. Silver, the University of Mississippi historian who cemented the state's somewhat problematic reputation as an extremist outlier in an increasingly progressive nation, touched on white Mississippians' sense of history in the 1966 edition of his landmark book, *Mississippi: The Closed Society*. Silver wrote, "Like other Southerners, Mississippians are obsessed by their sense of the past, but this does not insure the accuracy of their historical picture; they see legend rather than history." The monument Mississippians erected at Gettysburg in 1973 was profoundly shaped by many of the myths and legends central to mid-twentieth-century conceptions of Confederate history. Established by the state legislature in 1968, representatives of the Mississippi Gettysburg Memorial Commission selected the spot where Barksdale's Mississippi Brigade launched its July 2 attack into the Peach Orchard for the monument's construction. The fact that their selection bordered the tract reserved for the Louisiana monument did not disturb the Mississippians, who quickly moved to engage De Lue as sculptor for their project as well.[41]

De Lue's design for the Mississippi monument gave visual form to the hard fighting the brigade experienced in the Peach Orchard (the assault cost Barksdale his life and resulted in desperate hand-to-hand fighting). In an initial letter to GNMP superintendent George Emery, De Lue explained that he hoped to depict a very specific scene: "The tide has turned against them, ammunition gone, the flag down, only the courage of desperation remains to the courageous young soldier who is a fine and vigorous specimen of manhood who gives his all for his Country." De Lue depicted this young soldier as a standing figure, swinging his musket to protect his fallen comrade, a color-bearer still clutching the flag. Generations of visitors, however, have read it differently, assuming that the standing figure is clubbing the prostrate one.[42]

As they had with De Lue's other designs, GNMP historians had mixed reactions to the proposal. While accepting that the design captured De Lue's theme, Thomas Harrison questioned its physical expression. Alice Allen deemed the sculpture a worthy piece of contemporary artwork but questioned whether such a stylistic design was appropriate for the Gettysburg battlefield. Bill Hubbard vigorously urged the NPS to reject the monument. Noting acidly that "though the figure has Greek god-like muscles bulging, his head, too small for the body, looks like he ran into a Mack truck instead of a few Yankees," Hubbard argued that the meaning of the statue would be indecipherable to visitors and its depiction of Civil War soldiers was inaccurate in the extreme.[43]

The flag De Lue placed in the color-bearer's hands was the Confederate battle flag, which had been deemed inappropriate for use on the Virginia monument in 1910. None of the park historians, however, questioned its inclusion, only the specifics of its rendering. Having received no pushback to his incorporation of the battle flag in the Louisiana monument two years earlier, De Lue made use of the symbol again, portraying the fallen soldier as loyal to the last to the flag. In its emphasis on themes of "Valor, Honor, and Devotion," the monument's design gave visual representation to the inscription's claim: "ON THIS GROUND, OUR BRAVE SIRES FOUGHT FOR THEIR RIGHTEOUS CAUSE, IN GLORY THEY SLEEP WHO GAVE TO IT THEIR LIVES, TO VALOR THEY GAVE NEW DIMENSIONS OF COURAGE, TO DUTY ITS NOBLEST FULFILLMENT, TO POSTERITY, THE SACRED HERITAGE OF HONOR." The theme of devotion to cause and comrades also found expression in the exposed toes of the standing soldier. Reminiscent of the "shoeless Confederates" trope, the figure's exposed foot highlighted the devotion of the Confederate soldier in the face of privation.[44]

Thomas Harrison opposed the use of the word "righteous" in the initial draft, suggesting that if it were not removed, "we will have to revise American History." Superintendent George Emery softened Harrison's critique in his feedback to the commission, diplomatically suggesting that the group consider a different word. The writers of the inscription—Tom P. Brady and Ed Sturdivant (the SCV officer who played a leading role in the creation of the Soldiers and Sailors of the Confederacy monument)—bristled at the suggestion. Despite the subjectivity of the sentiment, Brady nonetheless argued that the modifier "their" clearly established that "the righteous aspects of the cause related solely to the South's conception." Sturdivant went still further, responding to Emery that "it did not occur to any member of the commission that anyone would question our right to determine the appropriate word to modify the 'cause' for which our own flesh and blood fought and died." Noting disparagingly that Emery was an employee of the *present government of the United States*," he promised to take the issue to the other commissioners. The standoff dragged on for nearly a year before park officials withdrew their opposition to the inscription. The reasons for this reversal are difficult to identify; time does not seem to have been pressing, as it was in the case of the Georgia monument, and the park archives provide no hint of outside pressure. Perhaps Emery's successor, Jerry Schober, a native Mississippian, proved more sympathetic to the Mississippians' argument than Emery had been.[45]

In a state that was less than a decade removed from the violence of the early 1960s, one must question how universal the assertion that the Confederacy was a righteous cause would have been among Mississippians. Furthermore, what divergent interpretations might Black and white residents have given to a flag that was frequently utilized by the KKK during its reign of terror in the state? Byron de la Beckwith, who gunned down NAACP field secretary Medgar Evers in Jackson in 1963, frequently wrapped himself in the Confederate flag. To what extent did the sentiments in the monument's inscription refer as much to the Lost Cause upheld by Tom Brady's WCC as to the Civil War generation's? How did continuing devotion to Lost Cause beliefs shape the way that white Mississippians approached the last quarter of the twentieth century?[46]

The monument's presentation plaque lists the members of the Mississippi Gettysburg Memorial Commission and the governors who were in office during the years of the commission's work. The presence of William Waller's name near Brady's encapsulates the tension between clinging to and moving away from white supremacy that characterized life in Mississippi during the monument campaign. Waller, who held the governorship at the time the monument was dedicated, exemplified the new kind of Mississippi politician. The district attorney in Jackson at the time of Evers's murder, Waller could have easily mounted only a sham prosecution. In mid-twentieth-century Mississippi, white men were rarely convicted for killing African Americans. Waller, however, threw himself into proving Beckwith's guilt, his commitment to the case springing not from any admiration for the slain activist or his cause, but rather his own populist ideology and determination to show that Mississippians were not lawless. The trial ended in a hung jury, and Beckwith walked free for thirty years before being retried and convicted in 1994. But Waller's determined prosecution earned him the support of many African Americans, soon to be an important new voting bloc in the state. Waller's election to the governorship in 1972 was due in part to Black voters, and he subsequently appointed many African Americans to state positions.[47]

Tom Brady's role in shaping Mississippi's culture of racial violence has already been explored. Though he issued two rulings in the mid-1960s that upheld the rights of Black citizens, he made no secret of his disdain for the laws that mandated them. In August 1969, in response to a court of appeals ruling targeting recalcitrant Mississippi school districts, Brady spoke at a WCC rally in Jackson. Standing alongside fellow spokesmen for white resistance George Wallace and Lester Maddox, he vowed, "So long as we live, so long will we fight for segregation." Around the time of the monument dedication, Brady was serving as campaign chairman of the fundraising drive to build more WCC-sponsored segregation academies across Mississippi. Unlike Wallace and some other high-profile segregationists, he never (at least publicly) recanted his racist views, leaving little doubt about the way he meant for the monument's inscription to be interpreted.[48]

The monument's dedication ceremony took place on October 18, 1973, and featured Confederate music supplied by the U.S. Army Band and a keynote address by Senator James O. Eastland, who had represented Mississippi in the U.S. Senate since 1942. The deeply conservative Eastland—the longtime chair of the powerful Senate Judiciary Committee—was a staunch anticommunist and a stalwart foe of civil rights, which he perceived as a communist ploy to destroy the United States. By 1973, Eastland was serving as president *pro tempore* of the Senate, and the *Gettysburg Times* was quick to note that due to the recent resignation of Vice President Spiro Agnew, at the time of his visit to Gettysburg, the senator from Mississippi was second in line to the presidency. Eastland's pride in the actions of Mississippi soldiers was boundless; praising them as "the High Water Mark of the Confederacy," he expressed the hope that the monument would inspire future generations to uphold the tradition of "honoring God and country." Superintendent Schober followed Eastland at the podium. Speaking only two months after the withdrawal of American combat forces from Vietnam, he noted that the location offered a clear view of the Peace Light, which he sanguinely interpreted as a reassuring symbol that peace would prove lasting.[49]

THOUGH DEDICATED AFTER 1965, these monuments must be understood as part of the centennial-era transformation of the commemorative landscape along Seminary Ridge. As Confederate monumentation spread along West Confederate Avenue, the boundaries of what was considered appropriate symbolism and wording for a Gettysburg monument continued to expand, culminating in 1973 in Mississippi's visual paean to the Lost Cause. Throughout the centennial era, advocates for expanding the Confederate memorial presence at Gettysburg drew on Cold War language of unity and reconciliation to make the case that their soldiers must be remembered and their cause honored with the same kind of architectural permanence that characterized Union battle lines. Confederates, they argued, were not only courageous and dedicated soldiers, they were dutiful "Americans" and proto-anticommunists. Thus, despite the overall failure of the centennial to boost national unity, they employed Lost Cause rhetoric in the service of Cold War purpose, claiming that Confederate memory strengthened American patriotism. In approving these monuments, many of which would likely not have made it past the veterans who comprised the earliest battlefield commissions, NPS staff, perhaps influenced by this use of Cold War framing, significantly furthered the expansion of Lost Cause memory at Gettysburg National Military Park.[50]

Epilogue
War and Peace, Protest and Propaganda

The final years of the 1960s brought teach-ins, marches, and bitter divisions over an increasingly unpopular war in Southeast Asia to Gettysburg. The initially reconciliationist Eternal Peace Light Memorial emerged in this era as a prominent destination for large-scale demonstrations. Buddy Glover, a 1971 graduate of Gettysburg College, recollected, "We must have walked to that Peace Light I don't know how many times. It seemed to be when something came up, you had to have a march or a protest, and you'd go to that."[1] Unsurprisingly, the debates of this divisive era were intimately linked to the battlefield landscape and the constantly evolving memory of the Civil War. While racial justice remained a potent concern in the decade following the centennial, the twin foci of civil rights and the Cold War as the lens through which the battle's meaning and legacy were refracted was replaced by Vietnam.

With its roots in a long and bitter struggle for independence from European control, the Vietnam conflict both predated and postdated American involvement. When the Viet Minh's war with France ended in 1954 and the United Nations called for temporary partitioning of the nation, U.S. policymakers immediately set to work in support of establishing a pro-Western client state in the southern part of the country. By the late 1950s, U.S. funding accounted for 85 percent of South Vietnam's military budget, and U.S. military advisors filled Saigon. In the wake of Nikita Khrushchev's 1961 proclamation of support for "wars of national liberation," the Kennedy administration increased funding and the numbers of advisors still further, but refused to commit American troops to battle. U.S. airstrikes on North Vietnam began in the aftermath of alleged assaults on American ships in the Gulf of Tonkin in August 1964, and by March of the following year, the first American combat units entered South Vietnam. By the summer of 1965, 125,000 American troops were "in country"; two years later the total would reach half a million.[2]

As the Rolling Thunder bombing campaign accelerated, the Soldiers' National Cemetery experienced its first Vietnam burial in October 1965. The man interred, Ray Ellis, had previously worked for GNMP as a seasonal ranger, contributing to the upkeep, preservation, and interpretation of the

171

cemetery. The war was the primary focus of the annual Memorial Day activities in the cemetery the following year. The keynote speaker, retired air force general John Weikert, a World War II veteran and native of Adams County, offered a full-throated argument that honoring the nation's war dead meant eternal vigilance against new threats to peace and prosperity. Weikert's speech exemplified a line of reasoning popular among American military and political leaders in the 1960s, which interpreted the lasting lesson of World War II to be that the nation must always be willing to commit American troops to conflicts abroad in the name of national security.[3]

Framing the U.S. role in Vietnam as assisting a freedom-seeking people, Weikert railed against a so-called isolationist mindset that would prioritize American withdrawal over the safety and security of both South Vietnam and the world at large. Weikert insisted that U.S. withdrawal would only encourage the aggressors (unspecified but assumed to be a reference to the Soviet Union and/or the People's Republic of China) to provoke a broader war. In portraying the Vietnam conflict first and foremost as a proxy war, Weikert disregarded its nationalist thrust and the long history of the nation's struggle for independence. His remarks exemplify the argument that the World War II generation widely applied lenses and lessons from the previous conflict to Vietnam, with frequently disastrous results.[4]

An antiwar movement, made up mostly of college students and political leftists, began to take shape in the United States in the early months of 1965. As the ground war took on more and more of a "scorched earth" cast over the next two years, and images of the destruction wreaked by the bombing campaign spread around the world, public opinion in much of Europe, Japan, and the Third World—and to a certain extent, the United States itself—turned against American aggression in the region. By mid-1967, Americans were split nearly down the middle on the question of whether escalation or withdrawal was the better course in Vietnam, and the movement against the war had moved from the margins to the mainstream of American society. A hundred thousand people marched in protest in Washington, D.C., in October 1967. At Gettysburg the following month, in a formal dedication ceremony for the National Cemetery's Lincoln Speech Memorial, state senator George Wade seized the opportunity to brand antiwar protesters as unpatriotic and un-American. "We have suffered through sit-ins, walk-ins, shop-ins, teach-ins, draft card burning," he lamented. "But recent examples of mutilation and desecration of the American flag is one demonstration too many."[5]

In the wake of the Tet Offensive, the turn of his inner circle against the war, and the rise in public opposition to American involvement in Vietnam, a shaken Lyndon Johnson announced that he would not seek another term as president in 1968. Johnson's declaration cleared the way for a contentious Democratic primary season that further exposed many of the fault lines in American society, resulted in the assassination of one of the leading candidates, and boosted the appeal of Richard Nixon's "law and order" campaign. A majority of Adams Countians enthusiastically embraced their favorite leader's former running mate in 1968. Nixon handily carried the local Republican primary and crushed Hubert Humphrey in the general election by 5,310 votes. Third-party candidate George Wallace, running on a strategy of throwing the election into the House of Representatives and thus pressuring the federal government to end desegregation efforts, received 1,579 votes in the county. The borough of Gettysburg itself gave 1,746 votes to Nixon, 756 to Humphrey, and 147 to Wallace.[6]

Six months prior to the general election, Humphrey, then serving as Lyndon Johnson's vice president, accepted an invitation to speak at Gettysburg's Memorial Day ceremonies. As it had for Johnson himself in 1963, the invitation provided Humphrey the opportunity to utilize the "sacred ground" of the National Cemetery to speak to the most pressing social issue of the day in a way that subtly differentiated himself from the sitting president. Humphrey walked a difficult line; as Johnson's vice president, he could not criticize the administration's position on Vietnam too strongly, yet as a candidate, he could ignore neither the antiwar elements in his party nor the enthusiastic public response to Senator Robert Kennedy's increasingly outspoken criticism of the war.[7]

Torrential rain on the day of the ceremony canceled both the parade and the ceremonial strewing of flowers on soldiers' graves. When local organizers suggested moving the ceremonies into the junior high school auditorium, the vice president's staff overruled them on the grounds that the cemetery was the spot where "the thousands of veteran dead lie"—and the television cameras had already been set up. Though Humphrey himself protested his staff's decision, it was too late to switch the location again, and the ceremony proceeded with only about 300 spectators in attendance. The *Gettysburg Times* noted that many of the attendees were young, including a college student carrying a sign reading "Hope, Help, HHH."[8]

Humphrey obviously knew his audience, for the speech was a paean to "the spirit of youth." He openly acknowledged the validity of young people's opposition to the disproportionate burden the war in Vietnam placed upon them, and expressed sympathy with their frustration that war is "invoked by fathers when it must be fought by sons denied any part in the calling of it."

He expressed hope that peace would soon be achieved, and applauded young people's determination to find alternatives to armed conflict. Yet the vice president insisted that the war in Vietnam was necessary to defend the freedom and liberties of the South Vietnamese. "We act not in conquest or in hate," Humphrey insisted, "but for freedom and for peace." As befitting a man running for office, he lingered in the rain for thirty minutes after the close of the program, shaking hands and talking with spectators.[9]

The largest local protest march of the Vietnam era took place in October 1969, organized by college and seminary students in conjunction with the Moratorium to End the War in Vietnam actions taking place across the nation. The programming began with three evenings of teach-ins exploring "the historical, political, and moral implications of our past and present position in Vietnam," paving the way for a full day's worth of activities on October 15. The lineup included workshops, a chapel service, a film screening, facilitated opportunities for students to share their feelings about the war with their congressional representatives, and a chance for students to make the case for the antiwar position to local residents. Throughout the day, organizers also read the names of Americans killed in Vietnam from the steps of the college chapel.[10]

That evening, more than 500 students, faculty, staff, and local residents joined a silent march from Lincoln Square to the Peace Light, in the words of the Gettysburg College student newspaper, "amid the almost universal disinterest of the community." Though a few hecklers hassled the marchers in Lincoln Square, no other incidents took place. The event included a short service at the memorial featuring remarks from college chaplain John Vannorsdall and faculty members from the college and seminary alike. Noting that the service took place "between the symbolic crossfire of the three Civil War cannon and the Peace Light," the editors of the *Gettysburgian* ended their feature story on the "Gettysburg Peace Dedication" by reproducing the text of a marker tablet listing the casualties suffered by the Army of Northern Virginia at Gettysburg. "We hope fewer commemoration markers resembling the ones on Oak Ridge will appear on the hills of Vietnam," the editors concluded.[11]

The size and vibrancy of the following month's Veterans Day observance was likely in part a response to the protest, an opportunity for those who perceived opposition to the war as an attack on those who served to honor the nation's servicemen and women. The "largest and most impressive" commemoration of Veterans Day in many years included a memorial service at the VFW building, a parade, a ceremony at the National Cemetery, and a military ball. In his remarks at the memorial service, Rabbi Benjamin Samson noted sadly that while young men died in Vietnam, other young men engaged in violent battle at home over the perpetuation of the conflict. Despite this, however, Samson maintained that Veterans Day was not a time to argue about war aims or military policy.[12]

The Peace Light was again used as a destination point for antiwar marches in May 1970 in response to the Kent State shootings and May 1972 in protest against the Nixon administration's policy of mining and blockading North Vietnamese ports. Not all use of the memorial during these years was political, however; pre-Vietnam employment of the area by college students for romantic purpose continued as well. Indeed, the October 14, 1966, issue of the *Gettysburgian* contained a warning from GNMP's chief ranger that continued vandalism and littering would result in the closure of the entire park at night, as well as a "warning to young lovers" that "except at Oak Ridge and the Peace Light, two heads must be visible to patrolling park rangers."[13]

In the eyes of many Americans, including most famously Martin Luther King Jr., the war in Vietnam was deeply linked to racial inequality, and opposition to one stemmed from resistance to the other. Though most Black Americans supported the war effort in 1965, by the following year, they were more likely than whites to be opposed. Both the Student Nonviolent Coordinating Committee (SNCC) and the Congress of Racial Equality (CORE) officially came out against the war in 1966, and King and the Southern Christian Leadership Conference (SCLC) followed in 1967. This deep-seated opposition drew from many wells, including the disproportionate impact of the draft on impoverished Black communities, the shockingly high death rate for Black men in Vietnam, the internationalist vision of Black Power, and the diversion of needed funds from War on Poverty programs to pay for the war.[14]

In March 1972, civil rights activist C. T. Vivian came to Gettysburg for a demonstration coinciding with the ongoing trial of the Harrisburg Seven in the state's capital city. This group of religious antiwar activists, including well-known priest Philip Berrigan, faced charges of conspiring to raid federal offices, bomb government buildings, and kidnap national security advisor Henry Kissinger. Given the notoriety of the individuals involved and the element of espionage central to the prosecution's argument, the case was a *cause célèbre*, and received wide coverage across the nation. A group of approximately fifty marchers associated with the Harrisburg Defense Committee made Gettysburg a stop on a pilgrimage from Washington devoted to highlighting what they considered the injustices of the trial and the weaknesses of the case. Arriving in town, the marchers processed from the Peace

Light to the National Cemetery, where they held a short program. Later that evening, marchers mixed with local activists on the Gettysburg College campus for dinner and a peace liturgy. Speakers at the evening program included C. T. Vivian, women's liberation activist Susan Gregory, and the National Welfare Rights Organization's Jim Evans. A Freedom Rider and former member of the SCLC executive staff, Vivian served as an architect of demonstrations ranging from Birmingham and Selma to St. Augustine and Danville. Upon leaving SCLC in 1966 to continue community organizing in Chicago, he soon branched into antiwar activity.[15]

Vivian's speech to the marchers and their allies utilized the structure and framing of Lincoln's Gettysburg Address, as well as some of its key phrases, to situate the Harrisburg Seven in the context of the unfinished work to which Lincoln alluded. Vivian began the speech by flatly asserting that the Founding Fathers were not truly "dedicated to the proposition" of universal equality (at least not in practice). He went on to frame the contemporary upheaval in American society as a new Civil War, referring to both the Harrisburg Seven and all those committed to contemporary campaigns for peace, freedom, and gender equality as soldiers offering their lives in a nonviolent battle. Referencing the "sacred ground" on which he stood, Vivian argued that these radicals were "not unlike those that once gave their lives here, that this nation might live."[16]

Onlookers could never dedicate, consecrate, or hallow this new battlefield, Vivian continued; consecration could only be accomplished through the struggle itself. He singled out campus protesters, women's liberation activists, those beaten in Chicago in 1968, civil rights martyrs, and leaders of prison uprisings for particular commendation. Though bystanders could never hallow the new battlefield, Vivian maintained that the living could take inspiration from those gone before. He argued, "It is for we who live in the spirit of democracy, justice, and truth to dedicate ourselves to the unfinished work, so nobly done here, at this place dedicated to great tasks that remain before us — freedom for all peoples, a non-authoritarian world, non-violent resolution of human conflict, the end of law as an end in itself, the birth of so living through struggle we might define what it means to be human in the twentieth century, as they who died here so attempted in their century." Vivian called for a new birth of freedom around the globe and an increased commitment to human dignity and self-government by all peoples.[17]

THE CENTRAL NARRATIVE THRUST OF GNMP transformed significantly between the 100th and 150th anniversaries of the battle, shifting from the

"High Water Mark" to "A New Birth of Freedom." The NPS's Gettysburg Museum of the American Civil War, located in the visitor center opened in 2008, offers a rich and nuanced perspective on the Civil War era that places slavery, emancipation, and the struggle to define the future of the United States at the heart of the conflict. Contemporary park interpretive programming follows suit, providing visitors a wide array of access points into the social, political, and military aspects of the Gettysburg campaign, Lincoln's address, and the war more broadly. This orientation undergirded the park's approach to the sesquicentennial anniversary of the war, resulting in programming that, though rooted in the battlefield, significantly incorporated questions of causation and consequences and considered the anniversary through multiple lenses.

Looking back on the 100th anniversary from the vantage point of 2019, Jim Witt, the reluctant participant in the July 1963 vignettes, concluded that the sesquicentennial commemorations did a far better job of reflecting the historical significance of Gettysburg and situating the battle within the broader context of the Civil War. By contrast, the centennial anniversary could be best described as though "someone was writing a Golden Book about Gettysburg." Yet despite its many shortcomings, the concept of a usable past infused the Gettysburg centennial with contemporary meaning, transforming it into a vehicle to address racial injustice, foreign policy concerns, the proper relationship between state and federal authority, and the future of the United States.[18]

In their efforts to construct a usable past that helped make sense of the present, midcentury Americans acted on their visions of Gettysburg's meaning in diverse ways. Their constructions of Gettysburg contributed to forging narratives about the nation that were employed simultaneously to champion racial equality, legitimize antifederal sentiments and activities, and strengthen the U.S. position internationally. Both Abraham Lincoln's Gettysburg Address and the suffering and perceived devotion to duty and country of the men who fought at Gettysburg were broadcast widely as hallmarks of American national character that would save the globe from creeping totalitarianism. Though racial injustice complicated this narrative, the desire to claim the Gettysburg Address as the central philosophical underpinning of American foreign policy helped create space for mainstream civil rights leaders and their white allies to win public and governmental support for limited civil rights reform. Martin Luther King Jr. drew on the continued symbolic power of Gettysburg, and the Civil War writ large, in 1962 in an open letter to John F. Kennedy urging the president to issue a Second Emancipation Proclamation. "The struggle for freedom," King wrote, "of which the Civil War was but a bloody chapter, continues throughout our land today. The courage and heroism of Negro citizens at Montgomery, Little Rock, New Orleans, Prince Edward County, and Jackson, Mississippi, is only a further effort to affirm the democratic heritage so painfully won, in part, upon the grassy battlefields of Antietam, Lookout Mountain, and Gettysburg." For King, the line from Lincoln's new birth of freedom to the struggle for self-government for all Americans was both obvious and morally inescapable.[19]

Yet, as this book has revealed, Gettysburg has never been solely an image in the national and international imagination, handy for use in reinventing the United States on the global stage. Rather, it has been simultaneously an idea, a landscape, and a living community made up of people whose relationship with the Civil War has always been profoundly shaped by family history, economic need, and political worldview. In the mid-twentieth century, the relationship between residents and the legacy of the battle was also influenced by personal and collective perspectives on segregation, racial justice, and U.S. foreign policy. On a local level, the centennial anniversary dramatized the need for drastic action to preserve land threatened by commercial development and challenged GNMP's traditionally reconciliationist narrative, resulting in greater stature for *both* Lost Cause and emancipationist interpretations. The centennial years also profoundly altered the battlefield's commemorative landscape, giving rise to an assortment of Confederate monuments and a "functional memorial" (Neutra's Cyclorama Building) that would stand for decades as permanent testimony to the influence of civil rights and Cold War politics on the evolving narrative of Gettysburg.

The architecture and inscriptions of the new Confederate monuments further reinforced the centrality of the "High Water Mark" theme to park interpretation and accelerated GNMP's transformation from a Union memorial space to, in the words of superintendent John Latschar, "a reconciliationist space with 'a pervasive—although unintended—southern sympathy.'" In addition to legitimizing the Confederate cause, over the decades, the monuments have also played a key role in furthering the erasure of Black Americans from the narrative of the Civil War and symbolically constructing the battlefield as white space. These centennial-era state monuments stood for fifty years without any contextualization or counternarratives until committed GNMP staff members pushed for the installation of new interpretive waysides in 2021.[20]

Understanding the politics, passions, and divides of the era that birthed these Confederate monuments can be of assistance in helping to fashion contemporary responses to their claims. When seeking to understand the context from which these memorials sprang, though, it is important to remember that they never spoke with one voice. While certain significant elements of the narrative stretching from Georgia in 1961 to Mississippi in 1973 overlap (a factor which undoubtedly intensifies their interpretive impact), they should not all be read simply as attempts to weaponize Confederate history to battle the advancing forces of civil rights. Though this was certainly part of their purpose, they also provide a window into a world where fears of nuclear war were palpable, where international opinion could make or break national security, where honoring ancestors was a moral obligation, and perhaps most importantly, where history itself was a living force.

The shift from civil rights and the Cold War to Vietnam as the lens through which the battle's meaning and legacy were filtered has been repeated countless times between the late 1960s and the present. As the present changes, so do the usable pasts we construct to make meaning of the world that confronts us. In the years following the sesquicentennial, the rise of the Black Lives Matter movement, the escalating campaign against police violence, heightened concern over the future of Confederate symbols, and the resurgence of white supremacy emboldened by an openly racist president have again enlisted Gettysburg in the struggle to define the nation's future.

On July 1, 2017, armed self-described "patriots" converged on Gettysburg National Military Park in response to rumors that Antifa protesters planned to desecrate Confederate monuments. Though no Antifa protesters appeared, the "patriots'" open display of their arsenal angered and intimidated many residents and visitors alike, and gunshots rang out when one of the participants accidentally shot himself in the leg. An even larger action took place three years later, on July 4, 2020, when hundreds of armed bikers, skinheads, militia members, and supporters of white supremacist organizations flocked to Gettysburg in response to a social media hoax alleging an Antifa-sponsored flag-burning rally in support of abolishing police departments nationwide. Rumors that protesters planned to follow up their flag-burning by murdering white people and "burning down suburbs" also circulated.[21]

In the context of a tense summer roiled by a global pandemic exacerbating existing social and racial divides, economic constriction, widespread street protests against police violence, and increasingly confrontational clashes over the future of Confederate monuments, the fake threat tapped into deep-rooted fears among some white Americans that Gettysburg's "sacred space" would be defiled. Conflating Gettysburg with its Confederate symbols, heavily armed "defenders," many waving Confederate flags, positioned themselves around the battlefield, converging on the monuments along West Confederate Avenue and in and around the National Cemetery. While some were open to dialogue with counterprotesters, many were not, openly harassing a loose assortment of individuals holding contextual signs at monuments and a seminarian in a Black Lives Matter t-shirt visiting an ancestor's grave. The presence of this right-wing "army" deeply divided local residents, and the prevalence of assault rifles across the battlefield impeded GNMP's ability to maintain its educational, commemorative, and civic mission.[22]

As the association between Gettysburg and right-wing politics dominated the headlines, President Donald Trump, a persistent defender of Confederate symbols and monuments in the face of civil unrest, suggested that he might accept the Republican nomination for the presidency from the battlefield. Trump's announcement prompted significant pushback—and a Trumpian parody of the Gettysburg Address from a *Washington Post* columnist—and he ultimately chose the White House instead. However, his rival Joe Biden seized the Gettysburg stage, delivering a widely acclaimed speech in the waning days of the 2020 presidential campaign that warned that American democracy was in peril. Portraying the United States as "once again in a battle for the soul of the nation," Biden nonetheless laid out a Lincoln-esque vision of a more just future.[23] Trump and Biden's mutual desire to claim the mantle of Gettysburg at critical moments in an unprecedented election cycle and the town's role in the upheaval of the summer of 2020 are lasting reminders of the way that Gettysburg—simultaneously an idea, a landscape, and a living community—continues to serve as a stage for acting out national dramas. Who we *were*, who we *are*, and who we hope *to be* in the future continue to converge at Gettysburg, just like the roads that brought the armies in 1863.

Notes

Abbreviations for Archival Sources

AA   *Afro-American*

ACCWCC/ACHS
      Adams County Civil War Centennial Collection, Adams County Historical
      Society, Gettysburg, PA

ACHS   Adams County Historical Society, Gettysburg, PA

AF-NPS/NARA College Park
      Records of the National Park Service (RG 79), General Records,
      Administrative Files, 1949–1971, National Archives and Records
      Administration, College Park, MD

CWCC/NARA College Park
      U.S. Civil War Centennial Commission Records, Records of the National
      Park Service (RG 79), National Archives and Records Administration,
      College Park, MD

Gifford/ACHS
      Adams County Civil War Centennial 1961–1965 (Gifford Collection),
      Adams County Historical Society, Gettysburg, PA

GNMPA   Gettysburg National Military Park Archives, Gettysburg, PA

GNMPL   Gettysburg National Military Park Library and Research Center,
      Gettysburg, PA

GT   *Gettysburg Times*

IF-NPS/NARA College Park
      Records of the National Park Service (RG 79), General Records, Index Files,
      1949–1971, National Archives and Records Administration,
      College Park, MD

MG   Manuscript Group

NARA College Park
      General Records, Index Files, 1949–1971, National Archives and
      Records Administration, College Park, MD

NARA Philadelphia
      National Archives and Records Administration, Philadelphia, PA

NER-NPS/NARA Philadelphia
      Records of the National Park Service (RG 79), General Subject Files of
      Northeast Region, National Archives and Records Administration,
      Philadelphia, PA

NYT   *New York Times*

PCF/GNMPA   Park Central Files, 1954–1957, Gettysburg National Military Park
               Archives, Gettysburg, PA
PI   *Philadelphia Inquirer*
PPG   *Pittsburgh Post-Gazette*
PSA   Pennsylvania State Archives, Harrisburg, PA
PSP/PSA   Records of the Pennsylvania State Police (RG 30), Pennsylvania State
               Archives, Harrisburg, PA
RG   Record Group
SCCA/GC   Special Collections and College Archives, Musselman Library,
               Gettysburg College, Gettysburg, PA
VF/ACHS   Vertical Files, Adams County Historical Society, Gettysburg, PA
WP   *Washington Post*
WSP/PSA   William W. Scranton Papers, 1963–1967 (MG 208), Pennsylvania State
               Archives, Harrisburg, PA

Introduction

1. Weeks, *Gettysburg*, 155.

2. Blight, *Race and Reunion*, 4. For more on the interplay between commemoration of the war and contemporary events during the centennial years, see Cook, *Troubled Commemoration*; Wiener, "Civil War, Cold War, Civil Rights"; and Blight, *American Oracle*.

3. Nora, "Between Memory and History," 12.

4. Kammen, *Mystic Chords of Memory*, 3.

5. See Silber, *This War Ain't Over*.

6. Key works employing the Cold War civil rights framework include Dudziak, *Cold War Civil Rights*; Dudziak, *Exporting American Dreams*; Rosenberg, *How Far the Promised Land?*; Plummer, *Window on Freedom*; and Borstelmann, *The Cold War and the Color Line*.

7. Donald H. Becker, "Trends in Negro Segregation in Gettysburg from 1900 to 1953," MA thesis, University of Maryland, 1953, 19, 60–61, African Americans in Adams County Folder #1, VF/ACHS; Program, "Mr. Lincoln Goes to Gettysburg," October 18, 1952, Programs Folder, Gifford/ACHS.

8. "No Racial Issue Here," *GT*, June 14, 1963; "Similar Service to All Tourists in Gettysburg," *AA*, June 29, 1963.

9. See Isserman and Kazin, *America Divided*.

Chapter One

1. "Town Congested, but Order Holds Strict Upper Hand," *GT*, Ku Klux Klan Special Edition, September 19, 1925; "Ku Klux Klan Presents Gorgeous Display in Monster Procession This Afternoon," *GT*, September 19, 1925; "Town Turns Out by Thousands to Greet Klansmen," *GT*, September 19, 1925; "Klan Influx from Six States Begins; Expect Thousands over Sunday," *GT*, September 18, 1925.

2. I am indebted to Gary W. Gallagher for his identification of these four strands of Civil War memory. See Gallagher, *Causes Won, Lost, and Forgotten*, 2.

3. Examples include Sugrue, *Sweet Land of Liberty*; Countryman, *Up South*; Theoharis, Purnell, and Woodard, eds., *The Strange Careers*; Biondi, *To Stand and Fight*; and Spencer, *The Revolution Has Come*, among many others.

4. Creighton, *The Colors of Courage*, 4, 50–51; Paradis, *African Americans and the Gettysburg Campaign*, 2; Adams County Historical Society, "History of Adams County."

5. American Battlefield Trust, "Gettysburg Campaign"; Murray, *On a Great Battlefield*, 9–10; Creighton, *The Colors of Courage*, 49–50, 75–76.

6. Murray, *On a Great Battlefield*, 10–11.

7. For more about how veterans used the battlefield in the nineteenth and early twentieth centuries, see Janney, *Remembering the Civil War*, and Flagel, *War, Memory, and the 1913 Gettysburg Reunion*. Thomas Brown has convincingly argued that the growing ubiquity of Civil War monuments from the 1870s onward represents the soldier superseding the farmer "as the paradigmatic American citizen" for the Gilded Age. See Brown, *Civil War Monuments*, 2, 6.

8. Murray, *On a Great Battlefield*, 10–12; Weeks, *Gettysburg*, 71, 74–75; Becker, "Trends in Negro Segregation in Gettysburg," 19, 60–61, VF/ACHS.

9. Weeks, *Gettysburg*, 93–95; Weeks, "A Different View of Gettysburg," 177, 182; Becker, "Trends in Negro Segregation in Gettysburg," 44, VF/ACHS.

10. Craig, "There Is Hell Going on Up There," 324–25; Jenkins, *Hoods and Shirts*, 62–65, 70; Gordon, *The Second Coming of the KKK*, 2–3, 12.

11. Craig, "There Is Hell Going on Up There," 324–26; Jenkins, *Hoods and Shirts*, 62–67, 70.

12. James Rada Jr., "Looking Back: Klan Convenes in Gettysburg," *GT*, May 24, 2017; "Thanks Business People of Town," *GT*, September 21, 1925; "Klan Influx from Six States Begins"; Creighton, *The Colors of Courage*, 9, 15–16, 168–77.

13. "Klan Encampment Attracts Visitors," *GT*, September 19, 1925; "Ku Klux Klan Presents Gorgeous Display"; Pennsylvania Klan Reunion Program, September 19–20, 1925, Ku Klux Klan Folder, VF/ACHS. I am deeply grateful to John Rudy, whose astute analysis of the Klan photograph introduced me to this moment in Gettysburg history. For more, see Rudy, "Interpreting Beyond the Battles."

14. Craig, "There Is Hell Going on Up There," 327; "Town Turns Out by Thousands to Greet Klansmen"; "Klan Encampment Attracts Visitors"; "Thanks Business People of Town,"; "Klan Influx from Six States Begins"; "Ku Klux Klan Presents Gorgeous Display"; "Town Decorated for Klan Affair," *GT*, September 19, 1925; "Town Advertised by Klan Stickers," *GT*, September 19, 1925.

15. Craig, "There Is Hell Going on Up There," 330; Editorial, *The Blister* 5 (September 20, 1925), GettDigital: Historic Gettysburg College Publications, http://gettysburg.cdmhost.com/digital/collection/GBNP01/id/29226 (site discontinued), SCCA/GC. I am indebted to John Rudy for his discovery of this document.

16. "Colored Church Gets Klan Gift Sunday Evening," *Star and Sentinel*, October 24, 1925.

17. "Colored Church Gets Klan Gift Sunday Evening."

18. Jenkins, *Hoods and Shirts*, 66–67; Gordon, *The Second Coming of the KKK*, 40.

19. "Colored Citizens Propose to Force Their Children into Crowded Schools," *GT*, August 30, 1924; "Negroes Serve School Warning Saturday Night," *GT*, September 1, 1924.

20. "No Disturbance at Schools; Colored Pupils Are Missing," *GT*, September 2, 1924; "Retired Colored Minister Takes Stand Against Agitation; Praises School Board Here," *GT*, September 2, 1924.

21. Craig, "There Is Hell Going on Up There," 338–39; Gordon, *The Second Coming of the KKK*, 7; "Our Principles" advertisement, *GT*, May 27, 1927; "Klan Services Held at Grave," *GT*, July 16, 1927.

22. Murray, *On a Great Battlefield*, 18, 21, 25, 47–48. I am indebted to Jennifer Murray for her insightful framing of the influence of the "High Water Mark" theme on GNMP's interpretive and physical development.

23. Silber, *This War Ain't Over*, 46; Murray, *On a Great Battlefield*, 28–29, 31, 33, 38, 43.

24. Murray, *On a Great Battlefield*, 22–24; Rosiecki, "Fighting Today for a Better Tomorrow."

25. Hobbs, "A Southerner's Southerner," 18–20; Silber, *This War Ain't Over*, 2–7, 77–78; Murray, *On a Great Battlefield*, 23.

26. Harrison, "Louis Eugene King," 71–72, 76, 77, 78.

27. Hobbs, "A Southerner's Southerner," 19–20; Murray, *On a Great Battlefield*, 24; John Heiser, Historian and Librarian, Gettysburg National Military Park, email to author, September 13, 2018; Harrison, "Louis Eugene King," 78–79, 82; Transcript, Leon "Buddy" Glover '71 Interview with Devin McKinney, May 13, 2015, 29, SCCA/GC; Becker, "Trends in Negro Segregation," 29–30, VF/ACHS.

28. Murray, *On a Great Battlefield*, 23, Rosiecki, "Fighting Today for a Better Tomorrow."

29. Becker, "Trends in Negro Segregation in Gettysburg," 7, 35, 51–52, 55, 57, 65–66, 69, VF/ACHS; "Negroes Serve School Warning Saturday Night."

30. Rosiecki, "Fighting Today for a Better Tomorrow"; Silber, *This War Ain't Over*, 48; Oakes, "The Blue and Gray in Black and White"; Roosevelt, "Speech of the President, Gettysburg."

31. Marc Charisse, "Battlefield Perfect Place for Klan," *Evening Sun*, July 10, 2006.

32. Becker, "Trends in Negro Segregation in Gettysburg," 7, VF/ACHS; "Minstrel Tonight," *GT*, May 8, 1961. For examples of such coverage, see "Negro Driver Dies Suddenly at Car Wheel," *GT*, June 5, 1959; "4 Baltimore Negroes Sent to Jail Here," *GT*, April 11, 1961; "Hold Negro in Bank Robbery," *GT*, January 19, 1963, "Puerto Rican Indicted in Murder Case," *GT*, February 4, 1963; and "Jap Will Meet Eisenhower Here," *GT*, April 24, 1961.

33. Becker, "Trends in Negro Segregation in Gettysburg," 21–23, 30–31, 34, VF/ACHS. For examples of these attitudes across the North, see Theoharis, "I'd Rather Go to School in the South," 125–27; Sugrue and Goodman, "Plainfield Burning," 576; Theoharis, *A More Beautiful and Terrible History*, 34–40; Sokol, *All Eyes Are Upon Us*, 71–74; and Jones, *The Selma of the North*, 39–40.

34. Green interview; Becker, "Trends in Negro Segregation in Gettysburg," 65–66, VF/ACHS.

35. Becker, "Trends in Negro Segregation in Gettysburg," 43–47, 49, VF/ACHS; Green interview; Fox interview.

36. Becker, "Trends in Negro Segregation in Gettysburg," 45–46, VF/ACHS. Jason Sokol writes movingly about the mystique of northern exceptionalism and its simultaneous role in sustaining experiments in interracial democracy while also obscuring the existence of segregation and racism in *All Eyes Are Upon Us*. Some of Sokol's arguments about race and politics in northeastern cities are applicable to the small town environment of Gettysburg.

37. Becker, "Trends in Negro Segregation in Gettysburg," 51–53, VF/ACHS; Fox interview; Green interview.

38. Becker, "Patterns of Negro Segregation in Gettysburg," 55–57, VF/ACHS; "Surely, But Slowly," *AA*, June 11, 1960; Glatfelter, *A Salutary Influence*, 913; "The Legacy: The Presence of Blacks at Gettysburg College, 1837–2007," video recording; Glover interview transcript, 12–13; Glover, email to Devin McKinney, n.d., Glover Scrapbook, all in SCCA/GC.

39. Becker, "Trends in Negro Segregation in Gettysburg," 23, 35–36, 43, 47, 54, VF/ACHS; Green interview.

40. Becker, "Trends in Negro Segregation in Gettysburg," 72–73, 78, 92, VF/ACHS.

41. Becker, "Trends in Negro Segregation in Gettysburg," 80–90, VF/ACHS.

42. Decoration Day: Its Observance in Gettysburg," *Star and Sentinel*, June 4, 1873, clipping, Lincoln Cemetery Folder, VF/ACHS; Green interview; Neff, *Honoring the Civil War Dead*, 133.

43. Green interview; David W. Blight, "Forgetting Why We Remember," *NYT*, May 29, 2011; Milner Associates, Executive Summary, Lincoln Cemetery, 2; "Parade Will Be Feature," *Gettysburg Compiler*, May 27, 1933, both in Lincoln Cemetery Folder, VF/ACHS Archives.

44. Becker, "Patterns of Negro Segregation in Gettysburg," 60–61, VF/ACHS; Hammack, "Adele Gutman Nathan"; Program, "Mr. Lincoln Goes to Gettysburg," October 18, 1952, Gifford/ACHS; Muriel Dobbin, "Woman to Direct 'Battle' of Gettysburg," *Baltimore Sun*, March 3, 1963.

45. Becker, "Patterns of Negro Segregation in Gettysburg," 101–2, 107, VF/ACHS; Green interview; Fox interview; Elsie Morey, "Jack's Pool," *GT*, June 26, 2018.

46. Victoria Wolcott, "Here's the Disturbing History of Segregated Swimming Pools and Amusement Parks," *Huffington Post*, July 16, 2019, https://www.huffpost.com/entry/history-segregated-swimming-pools-parks-racism_b_5d289125e4b0f0348e32fdad; Niraj Chokshi, "Racism at American Pools Isn't New: A Look at a Long History," *NYT*, August 1, 2018; "Survey Ranks Pool High on 'Needs' List," *GT*, August 20, 1963; "Rec Board Is Considering Drive to Raise Fund for Pool," *GT*, April 4, 1963; Fox interview; Green interview.

Chapter Two

1. Eileen Marvin to John F. Kennedy, received March 29, 1961, Accession #079-66F-0048, Box 4, GNMP 1953–61 Folder, NER-NPS/NARA Philadelphia.

2. 1960 Census of Population, vol. 1, 40–22 and 40–248; 1960 Census of Population, Advance Report for Pennsylvania, March 29, 1961, 7; Fox interview; Green interview; Madison interview; Witt interview; "Equipment Lost by 'Field 'Ghost,'" *GT*, November 6, 1962.

3. "Fewer Adams Divorces than Across State," *GT*, September 21, 1961; "2nd Migrant Day Care Unit Is Launched," *GT*, July 6, 1961; "High Schools Crowded with 1,610 Pupils," *GT*, September 10, 1963; Bloom, "The Farmers Didn't Particularly Care for Us," 340.

4. Richey, *The Pennsylvania Manual*, 1961–1962, 95, 506, 513, 530; "Record County Vote Gives Nixon 4,866 Margin over Kennedy," *GT*, November 9, 1960; Eisenhower, *At Ease*, 361; "Ex-President Given First Medallion by NCWC Group," *GT*, September 4, 1961; Eisenhower, *Going Home to Glory*, 3–6, 10–12, 174–75; Stine, *The Pennsylvania Manual*, 1963–1964, 96, 558.

5. Birkner and Hegeman, *Eisenhower's Gettysburg Farm*, 78, 81, 83; "Republicans Lay Ground on Saturday for Victory," *GT*, July 2, 1962; "Ike and Mamie Gracious Hosts to Governors," *GT*, July 2, 1962; "Royal Couple Delighted with Visit on Saturday with the Eisenhowers," *GT*, September 9, 1963.

6. Fox interview.

7. "Need Flowers for Children Tomorrow," *GT*, May 29, 1963; "Children Honor Soldier Dead," *GT*, May 31, 1965; Program, 95th Annual Memorial Day Exercises, May 30, 1962, GETT 41160, Box 5, PCF/GNMPA; Fox interview; Madison interview; Program, 2nd Annual Civil War Conference, Gettysburg College, November 16–18, 1958, Accession #079-66F-0048, Box 4, GNMP 1953–61 Folder, NER-NPS/NARA Philadelphia.

8. Weeks, *Gettysburg*, 156, 158–59; Fox interview; "$300 Voted for Blue and Gray Skirmish," *GT*, November 15, 1961.

9. NCWWM advertisement, *GT*, Centennial Issue, June 28, 1963; National Museum Marks 25th Birthday; Over 5 Million See It," *GT*, June 24, 1964; Gettysburg National Museum advertisement, *GT*, June 24, 1964. "Arquette to Open Museum Here Sunday," *GT*, February 26, 1959, clipping, and brochure, Cliff Arquette's Soldiers Museum, c. 1959–1963; both in Arquette, Cliff Soldiers Museum File, VF/ACHS. Brochure, National Civil War Wax Museum, c. 1962, National Civil War Wax Museum File; and Brochure, Gettysburg National Museum, c. 1963, Gettysburg National Museum File, both in VF/ACHS.

10. Brochure, Hall of Presidents, c. 1960–63, Hall of Presidents File; Brochure, Lincoln Room Museum, c. 1960s, Folder 1, Wills House File; "Short History of the Wills House," Folder 2, Wills House File; Brochure, Jennie Wade House, c. 1960s, Jennie Wade House File, all in VF/ACHS.

11. Murray, *On a Great Battlefield*, 69, 90; 'Copter Tour of Gettysburg advertisement, 36; Gettysburg Battlefield Tours advertisement, 62; Horse 'N Buggy Museum advertisement, 37; Indian Village advertisement, 13; all in *GT* Visitors' Supplement, 1962, Tim Smith Collection, ACHS. "America the Beautiful: Heritage or Honky-Tonk?," *Changing Times: The Kiplinger Magazine*, November 1962, 3, clipping, Box 124, PA Gettysburg Commission Folder, CWCC/NARA College Park.

12. "Fantasyland Opens in July," *GT*, June 15, 1959; "'Fantasyland, Wonderland of Make Believe,' Will Open on Taneytown Rd. Saturday for Old and Young," *GT*, July 17, 1959. Brochure, "The Wonderful World of Fantasyland," c. 1960s, Fantasyland File; and Brochure, Fort Defiance, n.d., Fort Defiance File, both in VF/ACHS; Fort Defiance advertisement, 29, *GT* Visitors' Supplement, 1962, Tim Smith Collection, ACHS; Weeks, *Gettysburg*, 162–64.

13. A. Kenneth Dick, President, Fantasyland, Letters: "View on Gettysburg," *NYT*, June 14, 1959.

14. Weeks, *Gettysburg*, 136; Murray, *On a Great Battlefield*, 89, 108, 125; Mrs. S. Markle to Department of the Interior, August 20, 1960, Accession #079-66F-0048, Box 4, GNMP 1953–61 Folder, NER-NPS/NARA Philadelphia; "Form Group to Preserve Battlefield," *GT*, September 14, 1959; Jean White, "The 2nd Battle of Gettysburg," *WP*, April 8, 1959.

15. GBPA Fact Sheet, n.d., and GBPA, *Battleground* 2 (January 1963), both in Box 124, PA Gettysburg Commission Folder, CWCC/NARA College Park; White, "The 2nd Battle of Gettysburg"; Hans Knight, "Commercialism Launches the 2nd Battle of Gettysburg," *Patriot*, April 5, 1959; "County Home Auxiliary Big Factor in Attracting Interest in Institution," *GT*, May 6, 1961.

16. Ed Kiester, "The Fight Is On for Gettysburg," *Parade*, January 8, 1961, A 2 Subject File 1963–1967, Carton 29, Folder 2, WSP/PSA; "Many Protests Registered Against Commercialization of Gettysburg Battlefield," *GT*, October 15, 1959; Mrs. Joseph H. Bolling to Dwight Eisenhower, November 17, 1960, Accession #079-66F-0048, Box 4, GNMP 1953–61 Folder, NER-NPS/NARA Philadelphia; Platt, *This Is Holy Ground*, 52.

17. "Clark to Ask Hearings on Acquiring Battlefield Land," *GT*, March 24, 1959; "Cleveland Paper Wants to Preserve Civil War Shrines," *GT*, June 5, 1959; "Scott Urges More Funds to Save 'Field," *GT*, May 21, 1959; "Senate Votes $650,00 for Battlefields," *GT*, June 10, 1959; "Vote $450,000 for Two 'Fields," *GT*, June 16, 1959; "Gettysburg May Lose $450,00 to Purchase Land for Battlefield," *GT*, January 24, 1960; William R. Failor to Regional Director, April 27, 1961, RG 79, Division of Land Acquisition, Land Acquisition Files, 1933–1970, Box 29, GNMP 1961 Folder, NARA College Park.

18. GBPA Fact Sheet, n.d., and GBPA, *Battleground* 2 (January 1963), both in Box 124, PA Gettysburg Commission Folder, CWCC/NARA College Park; "Form Group to Preserve Battlefield," *GT*, September 14, 1959; "Cliff 'Charlie Weaver' Arquette Is Named Chairman," *GT*, December 4, 1959; "Distinguished Men Helping to Save Field," *GT*, January 11, 1960; "Arquette Is Honored by Civil War Unit," *GT*, October 31, 1960; Richard L. Graves, "The Fight to Preserve Gettysburg Battlefield," *Civil War Times* 2, no. 1 (April 1960): 10.

19. Joyce Schuller, "Kids vs. Commerce in a New Battle of Gettysburg," *Chicago Daily Defender*, March 1, 1962; "Pupils Send Pennies Here to Save Field," *GT*, May 31, 1962; "GBPA Acquires 8-Acre Plot on Battlefield," *GT*, November 19, 1962.

20. Frederick Tilberg, Annual Report of Information and Interpretive Services, February 1, 1961, 3–4, 6, DOI.NPS GNMP Interpretive Program Files, 1930-Present, GETT 43970, Box 25, Folder 8, GNMPA; Eric de Jonge to Frederick Tilberg, April 3, 1961, US.DOI.NPS GNMP Historian Files 1933–1676, GETT 41151, Box 2, Folder 11,

GNMPA; Minutes, GNMP Management Improvement Committee Meeting, May 3, 1961, Accession #079-68A-0275, Box 27, GETT Folder, NER-NPS/NARA Philadelphia; Unrau, *Administrative History*, 274, 277, 281.

21. Murray, *On a Great Battlefield*, 47–48; Carr, *Mission 66*, 3–7; Recommendations of the Mission 66 Advisory Committee, October 10–12, 1956, RG 79, EODC NAID 37489672, Container Codes HC1-80635646 to HC1-80635724, Box 14, A98 Mission 66 Folder, NARA Philadelphia.

22. Carr, *Mission 66*, 162, 19; Minutes of the 12th Meeting of the Executive Committee of the Civil War Centennial Commission, January 30, 1962, Box 60, January 30, 1962 Minutes Folder, CWCC/NARA College Park. Daniel Tobin to Conrad Wirth, September 25, 1956; and W. G. Carnes to Wirth, June 12, 1956, both in Accession #079-66F-0048, Box 11, GNMP Centennial Folder 3, NER-NPS/NARA Philadelphia.

23. Daniel J. Tobin, Memo to Director, January 17, 1957, Accession #079-64A-0046, Box 5, GNMP 1952–57 Folder; and Conrad Wirth to R. F. Lee and Herbert Kahler, May 18, 1956, Accession #079-66F-0048, Box 11, GNMP Centennial Folder 3, both in NER-NPS/NARA Philadelphia; Tobin, Memo to Chief, EODC, November 13, 1956, RG 79, EODC NAID 37489672, Container Codes HC1-80635646 to HC1-80635724, Box 44, GETT 1955–1960 Folder, NARA Philadelphia; Unrau, *Administrative History*, 258.

24. Tobin to Wirth, September 25, 1956, Accession #079-66F-0048, Box 11, GNMP Centennial Folder 3, NER-NPS/NARA Philadelphia.

25. Carnes to Wirth, June 12, 1956, Accession #079-66F-0048, Box 11, GNMP Centennial Folder 3; and George Palmer, Memo to Regional Director, December 26, 1956, Accession #079-64A-0046, Box 5, GNMP 1952–57 Folder, both in NER-NPS/NARA Philadelphia.

26. Ronald F. Lee, Memo to Director, January 7, 1957; and Edward S. Zimmer, Memo to Director, January 16, 1957, both in Accession #079-64A-0046, Box 5, GNMP 1952–57 Folder, NER-NPS/NARA Philadelphia.

27. Tobin to Wirth, January 18, 1957, RG 79, EODC NAID 37489672, Container Codes HC1-80635646 to HC1-80635724, Box 44, GETT 1955–1960 Folder, NARA Philadelphia.

28. John Littleton, Memo to Chief, EODC, June 14, 1957, Box 1, GETT #1 Folder; J. Carlisle Crouch to Chief, EODC, November 14, 1957, Box 44, GETT 1955–1960 Folder, both in RG 79, NAID 37489672, Container Codes HC1-80635646 to HC1-80635724, NARA Philadelphia.

29. National Park Service, Press Release, June 24, 1958, RG 79, NAID 37489672, Container Codes HC1-80635534 to HC1-80635538, Box 1, GETT #1 Folder, NARA Philadelphia; Harry W. Pfanz, Master Plan for the Preservation and Use of GNMP, Mission 66 Edition, August 1960, 1, Accession #079-70A-0370, Box 19, Mission 66 Gettysburg Folder, NER-NPS/NARA Philadelphia.

30. Pfanz, Mission 66 Master Plan, August 1960, 4, 6, Accession #079-70A-0370, Box 19, Mission 66 Gettysburg Folder, NER-NPS/NARA Philadelphia.

31. Cook, "Unfinished Business," 51; Cook, *Troubled Commemoration*, 15; Bodnar, *Remaking America*, 213. Jared Peatman has convincingly argued that in its commitment to fighting the Cold War through all avenues available, the Eisenhower admin-

istration was quick to recognize how carefully curated historical narratives could prove useful in efforts to present the United States as a beacon of freedom and democracy. Eisenhower and his advisors saw particular promise in the interpretive possibilities stemming from the interconnected anniversaries of the sesquicentennial of Abraham Lincoln's birth (1959) and the centennial of the American Civil War. For more, see Peatman, *The Long Shadow of Lincoln's Gettysburg Address*, 150–52.

32. Cook, *Troubled Commemoration*, 22, 31–33, 36–37; U.S. Civil War Centennial Commission, *Guide for the Observance of the Centennial of the Civil War* (Washington, DC: CWCC, 1959), 5, 14; Programs and Booklets Folder, ACCWCC/ACHS.

33. Cook, *Troubled Commemoration*, 41, 45–47; "Observance of Civil War Centennial Is Designed to Recapture Older and Nobler Concept of United States Citizenship," *GT*, May 21, 1959; Warren, *The Legacy of the Civil War*, 49. Written for the centennial anniversary, Warren's provocative meditation chided northerners and southerners alike for creating comforting myths about the wartime experiences and identities of their respective regions that distorted the complexity and contradictions of Civil War history and absolved them of responsibility for contemporary problems. Warren's framing of the "Great Alibi" and the "Treasury of Virtue" will be discussed in further detail in later chapters.

34. "Public Asked to Participate in Centennial of Civil War," *GT*, December 14, 1960.

35. Franklin, "A Century of Civil War Observance," 104–5; Wakefield, "Civil War Centennial," 95, 97; Angle, "The Tragic Years," 379–82, 389; Jesse Lemisch, *Nation*, April 8, 1961, 300–301.

36. "See Little Glory in Rebellion," *AA*, March 4, 1961; Editorial, "War Between the You Know What," *AA*, January 16, 1960; Cook, "Red Termites and Rebel Yells," 157.

37. Cook, "From Shiloh to Selma," 137; "South Carolina Retorts," *NYT*, March 15, 1961; Cook, *Troubled Commemoration*, 89–90, 95, 98, 101, 103, 107; Brown, *Civil War Canon*, 192. Telegram, Roy Wilkins to Karl S. Betts, March 16, 1961; and Memo, Roy Wilkins to Presidents of Branches and State Conferences, March 17, 1961, both in Civil War Centennial Folder, Group III: Box A76, NAACP Papers, Library of Congress.

38. "General Grant No Chip Off the Old Block," *AA*, April 1, 1961; Cook, *Troubled Commemoration*, 136–42.

39. Cook, *Troubled Commemoration*, 171–75; Allan Nevins to Arthur Schlesinger, September 5, 1962, Box 80, Emancipation Proclamation Folder, CWCC/NARA College Park.

40. "State Will Provide Some Funds for Observance of Battle Anniversary in '63," *GT*, March 30, 1961; S. K. Stevens to Karl Betts, June 26, 1958, Box 123, PA State Commission Folder, CWCC/NARA College Park; Louis Simon, ed., *Gettysburg 1963: An Account of the Centennial Commemoration—Report of the Commission to the General Assembly* (Harrisburg, PA: Commission, 1964), ix, 1–3, copy in 11-63-A, Park History File, Vertical Files, GNMPL; Malcolm Hay to David S. Baldwin, November 20, 1961, GETT 41160, Box 7, Folder 3, PCF/GNMPA.

41. W. Clayton Jester to Karl Betts, June 14, 1961, Box 124, PA Gettysburg Commission Folder, CWC/NARA College Park; "Schools Note Beginnings of Centennial," *GT*,

January 11, 1961; "34-Star Flag to Fly for CW Centennial," *GT*, December 14, 1960; "Weaner Named Chairman of Civil War Unit," *GT*, July 16, 1959; W. Clayton Jester to Dwight D. Eisenhower, January 13, 1961, Miscellaneous Correspondence and Bills Folder, ACCWCC/ACHS.

42. "34-Star Flag to Fly for CW Centennial"; Meeting Minutes, January 10, 1961, Minutes Folder, ACCWCC/ACHS; "OK Script for Centennial Event Apr. 22," *GT*, March 29, 1961; "150 Boys in Blue Coming Here Apr. 22," *GT*, January 28, 1961; "300 Rehearse for Pageant Here April 22," *GT*, April 11, 1961; "90-Minute Pageant," *GT*, April 24, 1961; Program, "Mr. Lincoln Goes to Gettysburg," October 18, 1952, Gifford/ACHS.

43. "Casting for Pageant of Century Ago Here April 22," *GT*, March 31, 1961; "'63 Costumes Will Be Made by Area Clubs," *GT*, February 15, 1961; Meeting Minutes, February 14, 1961, Minutes Folder, ACCWCC/ACHS.

44. "Porter Guard Pageant Cut Short by Snow," *GT*, February 2, 1961. Script, "Porter Guards at Gettysburg," February 1, 1962, 3–4, Miscellaneous Correspondence and Bills Folder; Meeting Minutes, January 23, 1962, Minutes Folder, both in ACCWCC/ACHS.

45. Program, Centennial Reenactment Pageant of the Cashtown-Fairfield Raid, October 14, 1962, and Script, Program at Cashtown, October 14, 1962, both in Cashtown-Fairfield Raid Reenactment Folder, ACCWCC/ACHS. Meeting Minutes, May 22, 1962; Meeting Minutes, January 9, 1962; Meeting Minutes, September 9, 1962; Meeting Minutes, October 9, 1962, all in Minutes Folder, ACCWCC/ACHS. James B. Myers to Ronald Lee, November 5, 1962, Accession #079-66F-0048, Box 12, GNMP Folder, NER-NPS/NARA Philadelphia; "Countians to Take Part in War Pageants," *GT*, August 29, 1962.

46. "Campaign Gettysburg Dinner Will Preview Civil War Era for Gettysburg's Buildings," *GT*, September 20, 1961; "Jaycees Push New Look for Town's Center," *GT*, November 17, 1961; "End 'Campaign Gettysburg' in June; 64 Ready," *GT*, February 7, 1963.

47. "Big Memorial Day Parade Is Planned Here," *GT*, May 26, 1961; "5-Day Series of Memorial Services Opens on Friday; Governor Here on Tuesday," *GT*, May 27, 1961; "Large Crowd Witnesses May 30 Parade, Exercises at National Cemetery Here," *GT*, May 31, 1961; "3 Russians Impressed by Services Here," *GT*, May 31, 1961.

48. "American People Are Ready to Pay Whatever Price Is Necessary to Preserve Freedom," *GT*, May 30, 1961.

49. "American People Are Ready to Pay."

50. "American People Are Ready to Pay"; Bryant, *The Bystander*, 361.

51. "Remembrance Day Program on Saturday," *GT*, November 16, 1961; "Dedication Day Events Are Listed," *GT*, November 17, 1961; "Text of Senator Dirksen's Address Here on Sunday," *GT*, November 20, 1961.

52. "Announcing Gettysburg College's Sixth Annual Civil War Lectures," 1962, Box 124, PA Gettysburg Commission Folder, CWCC/NARA College Park; Cook, "Bruce Catton, Middlebrow Culture, and the Liberal Search for Purpose," 109.

53. Cook, "Bruce Catton, Middlebrow Culture," 110, 114, 123–24; "Bruce Catton Says Lincoln Believed Once Slaves Were Freed," *GT*, November 19, 1962.

54. "Bruce Catton Says Lincoln Believed Once Slaves Were Freed"; "Catton Urges Real Faith in Emancipation," *GT*, November 20, 1962.

55. Bruce Catton, "The Irrepressible Centennial," November 19, 1962, 1, GETT 41160, Box 7, Folder 3, PCF/GNMPA; Blight, *American Oracle*, 103–4, 117.

56. Catton, "The Irrepressible Centennial," 2, 6, PCF/GNMPA; Blight, *American Oracle*, 110.

57. Harry Pfanz, Mission 66 Master Plan, August 1960, 6, Accession #079-70A-0370, Box 19, Mission 66 Gettysburg Folder, NER-NPS/NARA Philadelphia; "To Dedicate Monument to Georgia Dead," *GT*, September 6, 1961; "Memorial to 3,100 Georgia Dead Unveiled This Morning," *GT*, September 21, 1961. James B. Myers to Mrs. Forrest Kibler, July 14, 1961; Regional Director to Director, August 15, 1961; and Mary Givens Bryan, Director, Georgia Department of Archives and History, to Ronald F. Lee, August 16, 1961, all in GETT 41160, Box 34, Folder 1, PCF/GNMPA.

58. "Many Georgia Officials on 'Field Today," *GT*, September 21, 1961; "Memorial to 3,100 Georgia Dead Unveiled"; Order of Ceremonies, n.d., GETT 41160, Box 34, Folder 1, NER-PCF/GNMPA.

59. Memorial to 3,100 Georgia Dead Unveiled"; Henderson, "Ernest Vandiver Jr. (1918–2005)"; Hatfield, "Desegregation of Higher Education"; Ronald F. Lee, "Acceptance of the Georgia State Memorial, GNMP," September 21, 1961, GETT 41160, Box 34, Folder 1, PCF/GNMP Archives. For more on the impact of the Albany campaign, which profoundly affected the future of both SNCC and the SCLC, see Lewis, *King*, 140–70, and Hogan, *Many Minds, One Heart*, 66–77.

Chapter Three

1. Carr, *Mission 66*, 3, 10–12, 19, 162–63, 193; Cook, *Troubled Commemoration*, 264; Murray, *On a Great Battlefield*, 70.

2. Carr, *Mission 66*, 13, 127; Murray, *On a Great Battlefield*, 49.

3. Tobin to Director, January 21, 1957; Crouch to Director, February 8, 1957, both in RG 79, EODC NAID 37489672, Container Codes HC1-80635646 to HC1-80635724, Box 44, GETT 1955–1960 Folder, NARA Philadelphia.

4. J. Walter Coleman, Memo to Regional Director, January 4, 1956; Coleman, Memo to Regional Director, July 29, 1957; George Palmer to Regional Director, December 26, 1956; all in Accession #079-64A-0046, Box 5, GNMP 1952–57 Folder, NER-NPS/NARA Philadelphia. Ronald F. Lee, Memo to Chief, EODC, May 5, 19[??], RG 79, EODC NAID 37489672, Container Codes HC1-80635646 to HC1-80635724, Box 44, GETT 1955–1960 Folder, NARA Philadelphia; Draft news release, "Gettysburg National Military Park Visitor Center to Be Dedicated," November 16, 1962, GETT 41160, Box 5, Folder 5, PCF/GNMPA.

5. Carr, *Mission 66*, 162–63; Neutra, *Life and Shape*, 303–4; J. Walter Stauffer to Conrad Wirth, April 29, 1958; Wirth to Stauffer, May 8, 1958, both in RG 79, EODC NAID 37489672, Container Codes HC1-80635534 to HC1-80635538, Box 1, GETT #1 Folder, NARA Philadelphia; "Builders Get Briefing on New Building," *GT*, December 18, 1959; Draft Order of Ceremonies, "Dedication, Visitor Center Cyclorama," c.1962, GETT 41160, Box 5, Folder 5, PCF/GNMPA.

6. Weeks, *Gettysburg*, 124–26, 303–4; John S. Patterson, "Whose Hallowed Ground?," 1, 11-27-A, Park History, Vertical Files Collection, GNMPL; "New Home at Gettysburg," *PI*, July 1, 1962, 12; Richard J. Neutra and Robert E. Alexander, "Gettysburg Visitor Center, GNMP, Outline Specifications Basis for Design Control Estimate," November 7, 1958, 2, Container Codes HC1-80635260 to HC1-80635306, Box 11, GNMP 1955–1958 Folder; DOI press release, "National Park Service to Open Bids for Gettysburg Visitor Center," September 3, 1959, Container Codes HC1-80635308 to HC1-80635438, Box 39, Gettysburg 1959–1964 Folder, both in RG 79, EODC NAID 37489672, NARA Philadelphia.

7. NPS, press release, November 18, 1962, RG 79, EODC NAID 37489672, Container Codes HC1-80635534 to HC1-80635538, Box 1, GETT #1 Folder, NARA Philadelphia.

8. Neutra, *Life and Shape*, 312–13; Patterson, "Whose Hallowed Ground?," 2, GNMPL; Neutra and Alexander, "Outline Specifications Basis for Design Control Estimate," 1, NARA Philadelphia.

9. Neutra and Alexander, "Outline Specifications Basis," 1, NARA Philadelphia; Esenwein, "Modern Architecture and Preserving the Historical Milieu;" Allaback, *Mission 66 Visitor Centers*, chap. 3.

10. King, Address to the NYS Civil War Centennial Commission, 7–8.

11. DOI press release, "National Park Service to Open Bids for Gettysburg Visitor Center," September 3, 1959; DOI press release, "Contracts Awarded for Visitor Center in GNMP, Pennsylvania," October 30, 1959, both in RG 79, EODC NAID 37489672, Container Codes HC1-80635308 to HC1-80635438, Box 39, Gettysburg 1959–1964 Folder, NARA Philadelphia. Program, "Dedication of Visitor Center-Cyclorama," November 19, 1962, GETT 41160, Box 5, Folder 5, PCF/GNMP Archives; Brickley S. Orndorff to James B. Myers, June 12, 1961, Archival Box Collection, Box 80-A, NPS Gettysburg Visitor Center Plans, 1954–1962, Folder 2, GNMPL; Myers to Orndorff, March 14, 1961; Myers to Orndorff, May 11, 1961; Myers to Orndorff, August 8, 1961; Myers to Orndorff, June 3, 1960; David O. Smith, Gettysburg Visitor Center & Cyclorama, July 14, 1960; Smith, Gettysburg Visitor Center & Cyclorama, July 29, 1960; Orndorff to Myers, November 2, 1961; Orndorff to Myers, December 11, 1961, all in GETT 41160, Box 5, Folder 4, GNMPL. Allaback, *Mission 66 Visitor Centers*, chap. 3.

12. Lee, Memo to Chief, EODC, April 17, 1959, Container Codes HC1-80635646 to HC1-80635724, Box 44, GETT 1955–1960 Folder; Walter Nitkiewicz to Chief, Division of Interpretation, December 1, 1958, Container Codes HC1-80635260 to HC1-80635306, Box 11, GNMP, 1955–1958 Folder, both in RG 79, NAID 37489672, NARA Philadelphia; Minutes, GNMP Management Improvement Committee Meeting, March 29, 1962, Accession # 079-68A-0275, Box 27, GETT Folder, NER-NPS/NARA Philadelphia, "New Home at Gettysburg," 11–12; Ralph Lewis, Memo to Regional Director, May 18, 1962; [??] to J. Walter Coleman, April 15, 1956, both in GETT 41160, Box 29, Folder 13, PCF/GNMP Archives; Brenneman and Boardman, *The Gettysburg Cyclorama*, 35, 40.

13. Ronald F. Lee, Memo to Chief, EODC, May 5, 19[??]; Prospectus for the Exhibition and Interpretation of the Gettysburg Cyclorama, n.d., both in Container Codes

HC1-80635646 to HC1-80635724, Box 44, GETT 1955–1960 Folder; Lee, Memo to NPS Director, February 19, 1960, Container Codes HC1-80635534 to HC1-80635538, Box 1, GETT #1 Folder, all in EODC NAID 37489672, NARA Philadelphia; Murray, *On a Great Battlefield*, 96.

14. Script, "The Gettysburg Cyclorama," Record Copy for Gettysburg, October 1961, US.DOI.NPS GNMP Historian Files 1933–1676, GETT 41151, Box 5, Folder 11, GNMPA; Draft Order of Ceremonies, "Dedication, Visitor Center Cyclorama," c. 1962, GETT 41160, Box 5, Folder 5, PCF/GNMPA; Wilbur L. Savage to Gettysburg Superintendent, June 8, 1962, RG 79, Office of Design & Construction, General Files of the Philadelphia Planning and Service Center, 1954–1968, Box 49, GETT Sound and Light Folder, NARA College Park; Donald J. Erskine to Superintendent, GNMP, February 19, 1964, Box 12, Areas G Part II Folder, IF-NPS/NARA College Park; Murray, *On a Great Battlefield*, 96.

15. Murray, *On a Great Battlefield*, 95; "New Center Is Dedicated Here Monday," *GT*, November 20, 1962. James Myers to Ronald Lee, March 20, 1962, Box 7, Folder 4; Sons of Union Veterans, "An Invitation to Spend a Weekend in Gettysburg, Pennsylvania," c. 1962, Box 5, Folder 5; Draft Order of Ceremonies, "Dedication, Visitor Center Cyclorama," c. 1962, Box 5, Folder 5, all in GETT 41160, PCF/GNMPA. Daniel Beard to Superintendent, Gettysburg, May 8, 1962, Box 12, Areas G Part II Folder, IF-NPS/NARA College Park; Minutes, GNMP Management Improvement Committee Meeting, October, 25, 1961; Minutes, GNMP Management Improvement Committee Meeting, January 29, 1962; Minutes, GNMP Management Improvement Committee Meeting, July 30, 1962; Minutes, GNMP Management Improvement Committee Meeting, June 12, 1962; all in Accession #079-68A-0275, Box 27, GETT Folder, NER-NPS/NARA Philadelphia.

16. Alice Hickman to National Park Service, July 18, 1961; and Daniel Beard to Hickman, July 27, 1961, both in Accession #079-66F-0048, Box 4, GNMP, 1953–61 Folder, NER-NPS/NARA Philadelphia. Murray, *On a Great Battlefield*, 95; Pfanz to Charles Lowell Barlow, March 10, 1960, US.DOI.NPS GNMP Historian Files 1933–1676, GETT 41151, Box 2, Folder 10, GNMPA.

17. "New Home at Gettysburg," 12. Neutra to John Cabot, July 7, 1958; and Inter Office Memo, Neutra to REA, CHM, DN, August 6, 1958, both in RG 79, EODC NAID 37489672, Container Codes HC1-80635260 to HC1-80635306, Box 11, GNMP, 1955–1958 Folder, NARA Philadelphia.

18. Neutra to Cabot, July 7, 1958; and Inter Office Memo, Neutra to REA, CHM, DN, August 6, 1958, both in RG 79, EODC NAID 37489672, Container Codes HC1-80635260 to HC1-80635306, Box 11, GNMP, 1955–1958 Folder, NARA Philadelphia. Murray, *On a Great Battlefield*, 96; Script, "The Exhibition and Interpretation of the Gettysburg Cyclorama," May 10, 1963, Sue Boardman Collection; Allaback, *Mission 66 Visitor Centers*, chap. 3.

19. Pfanz to Barlow, March 10, 1960; Barlow to Pfanz, March 21, 1960, both in US.DOI.NPS GNMP Historian Files 1933–1676, GETT 41151, Box 2, Folder 10, GNMPA. Lee to Director, April 26, 1960, Accession #079-71A-0379, Box 14, GNMP VC Exhibit Plan Folder, NER-NPS/NARA Philadelphia.

20. Russell Baker, "Observer," *NYT*, October 8, 1962.

21. Lebow and Stein, *We All Lost the Cold War*, 20, 29, 33, 40–50, 103, 118.

22. Fox interview; Lebow and Stein, *We All Lost the Cold War*, 120, 122–24.

23. "New Center Is Dedicated Here Monday," *GT*, November 20, 1962; Draft Order of Ceremonies, "Dedication, Visitor Center Cyclorama," c. 1962, Park Central Files 1954–1987, GETT 41160, Box 5, Folder 5, GNMPA.

24. Draft news release, "Gettysburg National Military Park Visitor Center to Be Dedicated," November 16, 1962; James B. Myers, Memo to Park Staff, November 16, 1962; Program, "Dedication of Visitor Center-Cyclorama," November 19, 1962; John J. Bachensky to Wirth, August 2, 1962; Remarks by Conrad L. Wirth, Director, National Park Service, Dedicating the Visitor Center, Gettysburg National Military Park, Gettysburg, Pennsylvania, November 19, 1962, 2, 3, 6, all in GETT 41160, Box 5, Folder 5, GNMPA. Carr, *Mission 66*, 162–63; "New Center Is Dedicated Here Monday," *GT*, November 20, 1962.

25. Ralph H. Lewis to Superintendent, Gettysburg, March 28, 1963, Box 12, Areas G Part II Folder, IF-NPS/NARA College Park; Wolf Von Eckardt, "The Park Service Dares to Build Well," *WP*, March 29, 1964, clipping, RG 79, EODC NAID 37489672, Container Codes HC1-80635308 to HC1-80635438, Box 39, Gettysburg 1959–1964 Folder, NARA Philadelphia; Minutes, GNMP Management Improvement Committee Meeting, March 29, 1962, Accession #079-68A-0275, Box 27, GETT Folder, NER-NPS/NARA Philadelphia; Fox interview; Witt interview.

26. Ronald F. Lee to Director, January 29, 1962, RG 79, Office of Design & Construction, General Files of the Philadelphia Planning and Service Center, 1954–1968, Box 49, GETT Sound and Light Folder, NARA College Park; Donald J. Erskine to Superintendent, GNMP, February 26, 1963, Box 12, Areas G Part II Folder, IF-NPS/NARA College Park; Kittridge Wing, Superintendent's Monthly Report—November 1963, December 13, 1963, Box 192, 1963 Folder, AF-NPS/NARA College Park; Donald S. Nutt to Superintendent, Gettysburg, April 26, 1962, RG 79, EODC NAID 37489672, Container Codes HC1-80635308 to HC1-80635438, Box 39, Gettysburg 1959–1964 Folder, NARA Philadelphia.

27. Wing to Regional Director, July 30, 1965; J. Carlisle Crouch to Superintendent, Gettysburg, February 3, 1964; Edward P. Crouch and John B. Lukens to Assistant Regional Director, Operations, June 30, 1965; Nathan B. Golub to Crawford Door Sales Company, May 17, 1965, all in Accession #079-71A-0379, Box 12, Gettysburg PA 1952–65 Folder, NER-NPS/NARA; Allaback, *Mission 66 Visitor Centers*, chap. 3.

28. Carlos Whiting, Memo to GNMP Superintendent, October 7, 1963; C. Gordon Fredine, Memo to GNMP Superintendent, July 15, 1965; Byron Sutton, Memo to GNMP Superintendent, July 20, 1965; all in Box 12, Areas G Part II Folder, IF-NPS/NARA College Park. Wing, Superintendent's Report—April 1963, May 17, 1963, Box 192, Superintendent's Reports 1963 Folder, AF-NPS/NARA College Park.

29. James B. Myers, Superintendent's Monthly Report, December 1962, Accession #079-67-0018, Box 3, Gettysburg December 1958—December 1964 Folder 1, NER-NPS/NARA Philadelphia.

Chapter Four

1. Johnson, "Memorial Day Remarks at Gettysburg."

2. In the wake of a 1961 reenactment of the First Battle of Manassas that drew a firestorm of criticism for trivializing war, damaging historic resources, and legitimizing massive resistance (and resulted in a $75,000 lawsuit against the federal government), the National Park Service banned reenactments on NPS land. Under the leadership of Allen Nevins and James Robertson, the CWCC also strongly opposed reenactments as a desecration of hallowed ground. See James Robertson to Adam G. Adams, October 2, 1963, Box 111, Florida Civil War Centennial Commission 1961 Folder, CWCC/NARA College Park. See also Murray, *On a Great Battlefield*, 99.

3. "Resents 'Carnival' Aspects of Civil War Observance," *Chicago Daily Defender*, December 10, 1962.

4. Malcolm Hay to David S. Baldwin, November 20, 1961; Richard C. D. Hunt, Minutes of the December 12, 1961 PA Gettysburg Commission Meeting; Ronald Lee to Wirth, April 30, 1962, all in GETT 41160, Box 7, Folder 3, PCF/GNMPA. Hunt to Robertson, March 2, 1962, Box 124, PA Gettysburg Commission Folder, CWCC/NARA College Park.

5. "Pastors Laud Commission's Plans for '63," *GT*, December 17, 1962; "3 Speak on Race Issues," *GT*, May 15, 1963.

6. Hunt, Minutes of the December 12, 1961, PA Gettysburg Commission Meeting, GETT 41160, Box 7, Folder 3, PCF/GNMPA. Hunt to Robertson, March 2, 1962; Malcolm Hay to John F. Kennedy, January 29, 1962, both in Box 124, PA Gettysburg Commission Folder, CWCC/NARA College Park.

7. Jordan, "We Stand on the Same Battlefield," 488; Adele Gutman Nathan to Betty Gifford, July 10, 1963; Nathan to Gifford, October 28, 1962, both in Programs Folder, Gifford/ACHS; Muriel Dobbin, "Woman to Direct 'Battle' of Gettysburg," *Baltimore Sun*, March 3, 1963.

8. Gettysburg National Museum brochure, n.d., Gettysburg National Museum File, VF/ACHS; "200 Guests at Preview of Museum," *GT*, May 4, 1963; Fox interview.

9. "Employment in Local Areas Up 900 Since April; Expect New Upsurge During Fall," *GT*, September 21, 1963; "3 Speak on Race Issues"; "Church Women Told to Widen Race Opinions," *GT*, May 4, 1963; "Says Racial Prejudice Has Many Causes," *GT*, February 19, 1963; Green interview.

10. Green interview; "3 Speak on Race Issues"; "Church Women Told to Widen Race Opinions"; "Says Racial Prejudice Has Many Causes."

11. Green interview; "Says Racial Prejudice Has Many Causes"; Becker, "Trends in Negro Segregation in Gettysburg," 43, VF/ACHS; "Race and Civil Rights in the Early 1960s and Gettysburg College—A Reflection by Edward Southworth '64," November 10, 2018, 3, GCVFM-521, SCCA/GC; Madison interview; Fox interview.

12. Glatfelter, *A Salutary Influence*, 911–13; Becker, "Trends in Negro Segregation in Gettysburg," 97, VF/ACHS; Green interview.

13. "1,854 Register at Gettysburg," *GT*, October 9, 1963. "The Legacy: The Presence of Blacks at Gettysburg College, 1837–2007," video recording; Southworth, "Race and Civil Rights," 3–4, both in SCCA/GC.

14. "To Observe Race Relations Sunday," *GT*, February 9, 1963; "Rev. Haggler Challenges Congregation," *GT*, August 12, 1963; "Asks Pastors to Fight for Human Rights," *GT*, October 9, 1963; Bloom, "The Farmers Didn't Particularly Care for Us," 333, 337, 340–42, 345; "Says Racial Prejudice Has Many Causes"; "3 Speak on Race Issues"; "Church Women Told to Widen Race Opinions"; "Civil Rights Discussed by Churchwomen," *GT*, June 25, 1963.

15. Virginia W. Parry, Letter to the Editor, *GT*, April 14, 1961; "Says Racial Prejudice Has Many Causes"; "3 Speak on Race Issues; "Church Women Told to Widen Race Opinions."

16. "Says Racial Prejudice Has Many Causes"; "3 Speak on Race Issues"; "Church Women Told to Widen Race Opinions."

17. Southworth, "Race and Civil Rights," 3, SCCA. "Gettysburg Tourists Protected Against Racial Discrimination," *Human Relations Report: Quarterly Newsletter of the Pennsylvania Human Relations Commission*, June 1963, Carton 2; Elliott M. Shirk, Memo to Regional Supervisors, December 21, 1962, Carton 25, both in RG 10.105 Office of the Governor, Records of the Pennsylvania Human Relations Commission, 1956–2000, PSA. "No Racial Issue Here," *GT*, June 14, 1963; "Similar Service to All Tourists in Gettysburg," *AA*, June 29, 1963.

18. Mayor's Welcome, *GT*, June 27, 1963; "Negro Pastor Tells Rotary of Race Issue," *GT*, June 11, 1963. For more on the rising tide of demonstrations against segregation and discrimination in recreational activities and how "recreation riots" fit into the broader landscape of protest in 1963, see Wolcott, *Race, Riots, and Roller Coasters*, 158–93.

19. Mayor's Welcome; Green interview.

20. Countryman, *Up South*, 122–23, 147; Trotter and Day, *Race and Renaissance*, 91–93; "Demand Jobs for Negroes," *GT*, July 25, 1963; "Major Jeered from Stand at Racial Rally," *GT*, July 4, 1963; "NAACP Plans Integration Drive in North," *GT*, July 3, 1963; "NAACP Eyes Rose Parade Changes," *GT*, July 2, 1963; Neil Gilbride, "Acts to Avoid Segregation in Business," *GT*, July 2, 1963.

21. Levy, *The Great Uprising*, 230–31, 235–37; Kalish, *The Story of Civil Rights*, 31, 35–36, 39, 45–46; Douglas, *Jim Crow Moves North*, 261. It is a little-known fact that *Brown v. Board of Education* directly impacted the practices of some northern schools.

22. Kalish, *The Story of Civil Rights*, 32, 51; Levy, *The Great Uprising*, 240. For an extensive discussion of police-community relations in northern communities, see Sugrue, *Sweet Land of Liberty*.

23. Levy, *The Great Uprising*, 238–39, 248–49; Kalish, *The Story of Civil Rights*, 51–53; "York Negroes Meet in Police Protest," *GT*, July 22, 1963; "Negroes to March in York Tonight," *GT*, July 24, 1963; "York Negroes Make Wednesday March," *GT*, July 26, 1963.

24. Henry M. Scharf to James I. Robertson, February 7, 1962; Scharf to Robertson, December 26, 1962; Pennsylvania Gettysburg Commission, news release, n.d., all in Box 124, PA Gettysburg Commission Folder, CWCC/NARA College Park. Louis Simon to Clayton Jester, December 12, 1963, Minutes Folder, ACCWCC/ACHS; "Members of State Centennial Group Are Guests of Honor at Testimonial Dinner at Hotel Gettysburg Tuesday," *GT*, November 21, 1962; "Testimonial Dinner Briefs," *GT*, November 21, 1962.

25. "Centennial Group Is Reappointed," *GT*, January 31, 1963; "James Myers Is Promoted to Hatteras," *GT*, February 18, 1963; "Successor to James Myers Is Announced," *GT*, March 6, 1963; Betty Gifford to Kittridge Wing, July 11, 1963, Vignettes Folder, Gifford/ACHS; Ronald F. Lee to Kittridge Wing, August 2, 1963, Accession #079-66F-0048, Box 11, GNMP Centennial Folder 1, NER-NPS/NARA Philadelphia.

26. Dobbin, "Woman to Direct 'Battle' of Gettysburg"; "Some Changes to Be Made in Centennial Program Here," *GT*, March 12, 1963; "JFK Declines Local Invitation," *GT*, May 11, 1963; "President and Family Visit Field Sunday," *GT*, April 1, 1963; Jordan, "We Stand on the Same Battlefield," 490; J. Walter Coleman to Herbert Kahler, January 10, 1963, GETT 41160, Box 8, Folder 1, PCF/GNMPA; Official Program, "A Nation United on the 100th Anniversary of the Battle of Gettysburg, July 1–3, 1963," 3–5, Mullen Collection, Series 10: Gettysburg and Other Civil War Anniversaries, Box 8, Gettysburg Centennial Program Folder, ACHS; William Scranton to Stewart L. Udall, May 6, 1963, A 2 Subject File 1963–1967, Carton 29, Folder 4, WSP/PSA.

27. "76 County Units Invited to Aid in Centennial," *GT*, March 14, 1963; "55 County Organizations Volunteer Services for Centennial Programs Here," *GT*, March 20, 1963; "A. W. Larson Named to Head Travel Group," *GT*, May 8, 1963; Minutes of Meeting with Community Organizations, March 19, 1963, Minutes Folder, ACCWCC/ACHS.

28. "Seek Extra Water Supply for Summer," *GT*, April 5, 1963; "Expect 1,000 Casualties a Day in July 1–4 Period Here," *GT*, April 11, 1963; "Countians Are Eager to Serve in Any Capacity to Aid Centennial Program," *GT*, May 2, 1963; "Free Parking Here July 1–4," *GT*, May 4, 1963; "State Takes Health Steps on Centennial," *GT*, May 7, 1963; "Says County Should Make Name Change," *GT*, April 4, 1963. Jack MacMillan to Kittridge Wing, June 14, 1963, GETT 41160, Box 8, Folder 3; Gettysburg Centennial Commemoration news release, May 1, 1963, GETT 41160, Box 8, Folder 2, both in PCF/GNMP Archives. E. Wilson Purdy to Louis Simon, February 11, 1963, Series 30.12 Gettysburg 100th Anniversary, Folder 2, PSP/PA State Archives.

29. "Bemused Tourists Create Tangled Traffic Problems," *GT*, July 24, 1963; James B. Myers, Memo to Regional Director, January 22, 1960, RG 79, EODC NAID 37489672, Container Codes HC1-80635534 to HC1-80635538, Box 1, GETT #1 Folder, NARA Philadelphia; "$8 Million Expended on Adams Roads in 3 Years," *GT*, June 26, 1962; "5 Interchanges Off New Rt. 15 Bypass to Lead to Town," *GT*, June 23, 1962.

30. Branch, *Pillar of Fire*, 90–92; David M. Shribman, "LBJ's Gettysburg Address," *NYT*, May 24, 2013.

31. "19-Gun Salute Given Vice President on Arrival Here Today," *GT*, May 30, 1963; "LBJ to Fly to Gettysburg on May 30; Will Delay Parade," *GT*, May 11, 1963; "Vice President Pleads for End of Hate Among Men," *GT*, May 31, 1963; Program, 96th Annual Memorial Day Exercises, May 30, 1963, Memorial Day 1950s–1980s File, VF/ACHS.

32. Program, 96th Annual Memorial Day Exercises; "Vice President Pleads for End of Hate Among Men"; Johnson, "Memorial Day Remarks at Gettysburg."

33. King, "Letter from Birmingham City Jail," 153–58; Shribman, "LBJ's Gettysburg Address"; Risen, *The Bill of the Century*, 54.

34. Johnson, "Memorial Day Remarks at Gettysburg"; Countryman, *Up South*, 141–42.

35. Shribman, "LBJ's Gettysburg Address"; Risen, *The Bill of the Century*, 54; Drew Pearson, "LBJ Carries the Ball on Rights," *WP*, June 9, 1963.

36. Branch, *Pillar of Fire*, 93; Pauley, *LBJ's American Promise*, 94; "Four Divisions Will Make Up Annual Memorial Day Parade," *GT*, May 29, 1963; Buser, ed., *The Pennsylvania Manual*, 97, 626.

37. "Johnson Challenge Pleads for Justice," *AA*, June 8, 1963; Editorial, "Moment of Challenge," *PI*, June 3, 1963; Editorial, "A Voice from the South," *WP*, June 1, 1963; Hall, "Fantasizing Robert E. Lee as a Civil Rights Pioneer."

38. Pearson, "LBJ Carries the Ball on Rights"; Warren, *The Legacy of the Civil War*, 59, 64.

39. "Centennial Offices in P.O.," *GT*, April 25, 1963; "Urge Congress to Establish Centennial Commission," *GT*, May 23, 1963; "House Passes Deficit Bill for July Fete," *GT*, June 25, 1963; "Senate Okays $28,000 Bill for Fete Here," *GT*, June 27, 1963.

40. "Stamp Orders Are Flooding Post Office," *GT*, June 2, 1963; "Steady Demand for Gettysburg Stamp," *GT*, August 29, 1963; "GBPA Reports Big Demand for 'Covers,'" *GT*, April 22, 1963. GBPA, *Battleground* 2 (February 1963); Rocky Aithens to John F. Kennedy, June 3, 1963, both in Box 124, PA Gettysburg Commission Folder, CWCC/NARA College Park. In his letter to Kennedy, thirteen-year-old Aithens noted bitterly that after seeing the extent of commercialization at Gettysburg, "it is the first time I'm not proud to be an American."

41. Ronald F. Lee, Memo to Superintendent, GNMP, December 21, 1962; Lee, Memo to Chief, EODC, December 20, 1962, both in RG 79, EODC NAID 37489672, Container Codes HC1-80635534 to HC1-80635538, Box 1, GETT #1 Folder, NARA Philadelphia. "Campfire Site Will Be Ready for July 1st," *GT*, June 26, 1963; "2,000 Initiate Amphitheater Here for NPS," *GT*, July 2, 1963; "Campfire Movie Seen by 13,000," *GT*, September 2, 1963; Wing, Superintendent's Report—July 1963, August 14, 1963, Box 192, 1963 Folder, AF-NPS/NARA College Park.

42. "Rebel Money Will Be Used June 15 to 22," *GT*, April 24, 1963; "Offer Prizes in 'Campaign Gettysburg,'" *GT*, May 25, 1963; "Civil War Is Unfinished Business, 4000 Told at Gettysburg Battlefield," *PI*, June 30, 1963; "Civil War Drummer Boys to Compete Here on Saturday," *GT*, June 11, 1963; "Drummer Boy Winners Are Chosen Here," *GT*, June 17, 1963.

43. "$1,400,000 Spent Here to Restore Image of '63," *GT*, June 14, 1963; "Weaver Reads Proclamation for Jaycees," *GT*, June 17, 1963; "Choir to Lead 'Sing-Along' of War Songs," *GT*, June 18, 1963; "Old Ballads Are Sung Here on Wednesday," *GT*, June 20, 1963; "Campaign Gettysburg Will Go On," *GT*, November 12, 1963.

44. "Wednesday's High Reading Here 95," *GT*, June 27, 1963; "Early Takes Gettysburg After Sharp Fighting in Town Square on Thursday," *GT*, June 28, 1963; Meeting Minutes, June 11, 1963, Minutes Folder, ACCWCC/ACHS.

45. "Dixie Rises! Grits at Gettysburg," *Los Angeles Times*, July 1, 1963; "Leaders Will Have Kin Here at Centennial," *GT*, June 26, 1963; Daniel Langan, "Scranton Tribute Will Open Gettysburg Fete," *PI*, June 30, 1963; Jean White, "Eisenhower Preaches

Self-Reliance in Speech at Gettysburg Battlefield," *WP*, July 1, 1963; "Paternal View Rapped," *Baltimore Sun*, July 1, 1963.

46. Civil War Is Unfinished Business"; John M. Cummings, "Gettysburg Then, Now," *PI*, June 30, 1963; John M. Cummings, "Gettysburg: Blue and Gray," *PI*, July 2, 1963; "Gettysburg Hears Plea to Fight Discord," *Chicago Tribune*, July 2, 1963; Betty Gifford to Michael West, May 6, 1963, Vignettes Folder, Gifford/ACHS. E. Wilson Purdy to Martin H. Brackbill, May 20, 1963, Series 30.12 Gettysburg 100th Anniversary, Folder 3; Pennsylvania State Police Operational Plan, Gettysburg Anniversary, 5, 1963, Folder 1, both in PSP/PSA. "Get 'Copter to Guide Traffic," *GT*, June 26, 1963; Wing to Unspecified, June 5, 1963, GETT 41160, Box 8, Folder 3, PCF/GNMPA.

Chapter Five

1. Uncle Dudley, "A Meeting Engagement," *Boston Globe*, July 1, 1963; Ralph McGill, "A Negro Tells Why He Hates," *Boston Globe*, July 1, 1963.

2. Ted Lippman, "One Last Charge Up at Gettysburg," *Atlanta Constitution*, July 3, 1963; James Free, "Roberts Asks Why O'Dell Paid by Negro Race Group," *Atlanta Constitution*, July 3, 1963.

3. Bryant, *The Bystander*, 371, 375–76; Risen, *The Bill of the Century*, 8, 42–43, 47–49; Burns, *To the Mountaintop*, 205.

4. "Relive History," Centennial Edition Advertisement, *GT*, March 28, 1963; "Did Any of Your Relatives Serve in the Civil War?," *GT*, April 30, 1963; "Our Centennial Edition," *GT* Centennial Edition, June 28, 1963; "Thank You," *GT*, July 12, 1963; Kolk, *Taking Possession*, 113.

5. Bix-Sway Men & Boy's Shop advertisement; Martin Optical Company advertisement; Fissel's Grocery advertisement; Bear's Department Store advertisement; Peoples Drug Store advertisement; Wentz's advertisement; Teeter Stone, Inc. advertisement, all in *GT* Centennial Edition, June 28, 1963.

6. Dengler Bros. Grocery advertisement; Columbia Gas of Pennsylvania advertisement; Forman's Motel advertisement; Carol Ann Shoppe advertisement; Five Star Restaurant advertisement; Gettysburg Shoe Company advertisement; Gettysburg Glass Company advertisement; Baker's Battery Service advertisement; Gettysburg National Museum advertisement, all in *GT* Centennial Edition, June 28, 1963.

7. Richardson, *To Make Men Free*, 249–52, 258–62; Bryant, *The Bystander*, 371–76.

8. Scranton proclamation; Hoff proclamation; Faubus proclamation; Romney proclamation, all from *GT* Centennial Edition, June 28, 1963.

9. Chafee proclamation; Russell proclamation; Barnett proclamation, all from *GT* Centennial Edition, June 28, 1963.

10. Reed proclamation; Harold Hughes proclamation; Dempsey proclamation; Rolvaag proclamation, all from *GT* Centennial Edition, June 28, 1963.

11. "Symbolic Re-Enactments, Pageantry, Parade to Be Features of July Events," *GT*, April 25, 1963; "Eisenhowers Will Join Catholic Dignitaries at Field Mass Here June 29," *GT*, May 30, 1963; "Plans Are Near Completion for Mass June 29," *GT*, June 5, 1963; "At Least Eight Bishops in Pontifical Robes to Attend Field Mass Here," *GT*, June 15, 1963; "Priest Calls for Negro Freedom," *WP*, June 30, 1963; "Gettysburg

Mass Will Honor Dead," *WP*, June 22, 1963; "Field Mass Attracts 5,000, Rev. Fr. Hesburgh Calls for Americans to Be Emancipators," *GT*, July 1, 1963; Joseph P. Kealy to Kittridge Wing, July 5, 1963, GETT 41160, Box 8, Folder 6; Kittridge Wing to Thomas J. O'Donnell, April 18, 1963, Box 36, Folder 4, both in PCF/GNMPA.

12. "President of University of Notre Dame Will Speak at Field Mass on June 29," *GT*, June 21, 1963; "Fr. Hesburgh Holds Posts in Many Areas," *GT*, June 28, 1963; Hesburgh, "Gettysburg: Yesterday and Today"; "17 L.A. Stores Hit by Student Unity Pickets," *Los Angeles Tribune*, April 1, 1960.

13. Levy, *Civil War on Race Street*, 82–86; King, "Letter from Birmingham City Jail," 156–57; Mabel Booth quoted in Levy, *Civil War on Race Street*, 77.

14. Ike to Talk on Lincoln," *GT*, February 1, 1963; "Ike to Speak at Firemen's Memorial on Sunday Night," *GT*, June 29, 1963; "Civil War Is Unfinished Business, 4000 Told at Gettysburg Battlefield," *PI*, June 30, 1963; Jean White, "Eisenhower Preaches Self-Reliance in Speech at Gettysburg Battlefield," *WP*, July 1, 1963; "Paternal View Rapped," *Baltimore Sun*, July 1, 1963; "Eisenhower Tells Audience of 6,000 That Lincoln Gave True Meaning of Battle Here," *GT*, July 1, 1963; "Gettysburg: The Task Remaining," *Newsweek*, July 15, 1963.

15. "Eisenhower," *Chicago Daily Defender*, July 11, 1963; Edward T. Folliard, "Black Man's Burden," *WP*, June 9, 1963.

16. James Brann, "Civil War Left Major 'Unfinished Business,'" *Patriot*, July 2, 1963; Jean White, "Pledge of Equality Is Unfulfilled, Gettysburg Fete Visitors Told," *WP*, July 2, 1963; "28 Governors Invited to Attend Local Centennial," *GT*, February 28, 1963; Dave Leherr, "Nation Eyes Gettysburg as Centennial Re-creation of Battle Draws Near," *GT*, June 26, 1963; "Scranton Opens Gettysburg Fete," *PPG*, July 2, 1963; Official Centennial Program, 3, Mullen Collection, ACHS.

17. Simon report, 81–83, GNMPL; Burns, *To the Mountaintop*, 18; Green interview; "Large Crowd Witnesses May 30 Parade, Exercises at National Cemetery Here," *GT*, May 31, 1961; "Sunrise Rite on Oak Ridge," *GT*, March 12, 1963.

18. Simon report, 81–83, GNMPL; "Gettysburg Commemorative Stamp Is Dedicated; 20 Acres of Battle Land Given to U.S.; Scranton Talks Monday," *GT*, July 2, 1963; Cook, *Troubled Commemoration*, 197–98; "Will Lay Wreaths, Dedicate Gettysburg Commemorative Stamp at Peace Light July 1," *GT*, June 14, 1963.

19. C. R. Owens, "Take Up Negro Rights Cause; Says Peabody at Gettysburg," *Boston Globe*, July 1, 1963; "Mother of Massachusetts Governor Jailed in Florida," *NYT*, April 1, 1964; Brann, "Civil War Left Major 'Unfinished Business'"; Robert D. McFadden, "William W. Scranton, 96, G.O.P. Prodigy Who Led Pennsylvania, Is Dead," *NYT*, July 29, 2013. Endicott Peabody's 72-year-old mother, Mary, would be jailed for her participation in a sit-in in St. Augustine, Florida, the following spring.

20. Owens, "Take Up Negro Rights Cause"; Dempsey proclamation, *GT* Centennial Edition, June 28, 1963.

21. Warren, *The Legacy of the Civil War*, 59–76. For an example of the assertion that direct confrontation on racial issues was inappropriate in a region supposedly aware "that its soldiers freed the slaves," see "Right Way, Wrong Way" editorial, *Newsday*, January 3, 1963.

22. Bryant, *The Bystander*, 379–80; Niven, *The Politics of Injustice*, 6, quoted in Arsenault, *Freedom Riders*, 506.

23. "William W. Scranton, 96, G.O.P. Prodigy Is Dead"; White, "Pledge of Equality Is Unfulfilled"; Daniel Langan, "Scranton Urges Speed in Extension of Rights to All U.S. Citizens," *PI*, July 2, 1963; Commonwealth of Pennsylvania, Governor's Office Press Release, "Address by Gov. William Scranton at Opening Ceremonies of the Battle of Gettysburg," July 1, 1963, A 2 Subject File 1963–1967, Carton 29, Folder 2, WSP/PSA.

24. "William W. Scranton, 96, G.O.P. Prodigy Is Dead"; Bette Grill Aversa to Mr. and Mrs. Scranton, June 29, 1963; Commonwealth of Pennsylvania, Governor's Office Press Release, February 28, 1963; Draft letter, Scranton to George C. Wallace, February 25, 1963; Fred Schwengel to Scranton, July 9, 1963, all in A 2 Subject File 1963–1967, Carton 29, Folder 4, WSP/PSA; "Scranton Would Modify Bill for Public Accommodations," *GT*, July 17, 1963; John M. Cummings, "Gov. Scranton Eyed for '64," *PI*, July 3, 1963.

25. "Gettysburg Commemorative Stamp Is Dedicated"; Brann, "Civil War Left Major 'Unfinished Business'"; Bill Rasco, "Wallace Popular at Gettysburg," *Montgomery Advertiser*, July 2, 1963; Conrad Wirth to Frank Masland Jr., July 29, 1963, Accession #079-66F-0048, Box 11, GNMP Centennial Folder 1, NER-NPS/NARA Philadelphia; Pennsylvania State Police Operational Plan, 22–23, Series 30.12 Gettysburg 100th Anniversary, Folder 1, PSP/PSA.

26. Rasco, "Wallace Popular at Gettysburg"; "260 Persons Attend Scranton's Luncheon," *GT*, July 2, 1963; Cook, "Red Termites and Rebel Yells," 161; "Wallace Says He's Safer Than at Home," *Birmingham News*, July 3, 1963; James Brann, "Pennsylvanians Good Yankees," *Patriot*, July 3, 1963.

27. Rex Thomas, "Wallace Stands Teller in Eyes of Many Since His Showdown on Racial Issue," *Birmingham News*, July 3, 1963; "Wallace Honors Gettysburg Dead," *Birmingham News*, July 1, 1963; Edith Evans Asbury, "Hughes Charges Moral Failure to Aid Negroes Since Civil War," *NYT*, July 2, 1963; Cook, "(Un)Furl That Banner," 908–9; Jordan, "We Stand on the Same Battlefield," 500–502; "Wallace Plugs for Southerner in White House," *Florence Morning News*, July 2, 1963; "Nation Needs Southerner in White House, Says Wallace," *GT*, July 1, 1963. Emphasis mine.

28. "Wallace Says He's Safer Than at Home"; Bill Rasco, "Gettysburg Poet Praises Gov. Wallace," *Montgomery Advertiser*, July 3, 1963; "Belle of the Ball at Gettysburg," *Montgomery Advertiser*, July 2, 1963; Official Centennial Program, 8–16, Mullen Collection, ACHS.

29. Brann, "Pennsylvanians Good Yankees"; "Nation Needs Southerner in White House."

30. Branch, *Pillar of Fire*, 100; Risen, *The Bill of the Century*, 58; "JFK Gives Urgent Go Sign on Rights," *Chicago Daily Defender*, June 5, 1963; Drew Pearson, "LBJ Carries the Ball on Rights," *WP*, June 9, 1963.

31. Branch, *Pillar of Fire*, 101, 106–7; Bryant, *The Bystander*, 419–21.

32. Pauley, *The Modern Presidency and Civil Rights*, 111, 120–21, 125; Arsenault, *Freedom Riders*, 279.

33. Pauley, *The Modern Presidency and Civil Rights*, 157; "Kennedy's Bid for Civil Rights Parallels Lincoln's Freedom Call," *AA*, December 7, 1963; "Kennedy Address Draws Enthusiastic Praise," *AA*, June 22, 1963.

34. "So. Carolina Memorial on Field Planned," *GT*, March 30, 1961; James Myers to Payne Williams, January 16, 1963; Myers to Williams, February 15, 1963; Kittridge Wing to Regional Director, March 11, 1963; Williams to Wing, April 3, 1963; Olin D. Johnston to Secretary of the Interior, April 5, 1963, all in GETT 41160, Box 34, Folder 2, PCF/GNMPA.

35. Lee to NPS Director, April 11, 1963; John A. Carver Jr. to Johnston, April 18, 1963, both in GETT 41160, Box 34, Folder 2, PCF/GNMPA. Paul Danahy to Sam M. Gibbons, June 7, 1963, Vertical Files Collection, Drawer 17, Folder 43, GNMPL.

36. Pauley, *The Modern Presidency and Civil Rights*, 121–2; Anderson, "Bleached Souls and Red Negroes," 93–94; Silber, *This War Ain't Over*, 141.

37. Cook, "Red Termites and Rebel Yells," 149, 161–62; Brann, "Pennsylvanians Good Yankees"; "Gettysburg Poet Praises Gov. Wallace"; Bryant, *The Bystander*, 424; "S.C. Memorial Dedicated by Gov. Russell," *GT*, July 3, 1963.

38. "S.C. Memorial Dedicated by Gov. Russell"; Risen, *The Bill of the Century*, 69; Betty Dorsey Myers, "Segregation in Death: Gettysburg's Lincoln Cemetery," Lincoln Cemetery File, VF/ ACHS. I am indebted to Andrew Dalton, executive director of the Adams County Historical Society, for sharing the results of the deed and census research he has conducted that confirms the Watts's family's ownership of this land.

39. Moore, "Running Up the Flag"; Frederickson, "Corporate Culture," 361–62, 366; John A. May to Olin D. Johnston, July 15, 1964, GETT 41160, Box 33, Folder 9, PCF/ GNMPA; Connelly, "In Dixie's Land I'll Take My Stand," 53–54.

40. Frederickson, "The 'Slowest State' and 'Most Backwards Community,'" 177–78, 200, 210–12.

41. See "History: Civil Rights Timeline" from Columbia SC 63's website.

42. Cook, "Red Termites and Rebel Yells," 144; Woodward, "Reflections on a Centennial," 107; Warren, *The Legacy of the Civil War*, 57.

43. "S.C. Monument Dedicated by Gov. Russell"; "Wallace Says He's Safer Than at Home"; White, "Pledge of Equality Is Unfulfilled"; Brann, "Pennsylvanians Good Yankees."

44. Buser, ed., *The Pennsylvania Manual, 1965-1966*, 97, 624; Daniel Langan, "Scranton Tribute Will Open Gettysburg Fete"; Green interview; "Wallace Says He's Safer Than at Home"; "Gov. Wallace Back Home; Plans Rest," *Montgomery Advertiser*, July 4, 1963; Pennsylvania State Police Operational Plan, 3–4, Series 30.12 Gettysburg 100th Anniversary, Folder 1, PSP/PSA; Jack MacMillan to George C. Wallace, May 28, 1963, A 2 Subject File 1963-1967, Carton 29, Folder 4, WSP/PSA.

45. Lees and Gaske, *Recalling Deeds Immortal*, 249–53.

46. "Rep. Gibbons Dedicates Fla. Shaft," *GT*, July 4, 1963. The absence of Confederate iconography was striking, perhaps not fully intentional. The master of ceremonies noted that a troop of infantrymen had been scheduled to give a rifle demonstration, but plans had fallen through. See Transcript, Florida Gettysburg Memorial Commission Monument Dedication Ceremonies, July 3, 1963, Vertical Files Collection, Drawer 17, Folder 43, GNMPL.

47. Dempsey proclamation; Hughes proclamation, both in *GT* Centennial Edition, June 28, 1963. The international fallout from the Birmingham crisis included a strong condemnation of the United States by the Organization of African Unity, an association of African heads of state, which warned that continuing racial abuses would "seriously deteriorate" U.S.-African relations. See Dudziak, "Birmingham, Addis Ababa, and the Image of America," 188.

48. Mormino, "Sunbelt Dreams and Altered States," 5, 12; Colburn, *From Yellow Dog Democrats to Red State Republicans*, 2–3.

49. Colburn, *From Yellow Dog Democrats to Red State Republicans*, 20–22, 24–25; Dillon, "Civil Rights and School Desegregation in Sanford," 318; Faherty, *Florida's Space Coast*, 15, 18, 53–58; Rose, *The Struggle for Black Freedom in Miami*, 180–87; Hartley, "A Long Hot Summer," 23, 25–26.

50. Lees and Gaske, *Recalling Deeds Immortal*, 187, 260–70.

51. "Young Lawyer Battled for Perry Marker," *GT*, June 27, 1963; Paul Danahy to Louis Simon, April 11, 1963; Danahy to Harry Pfanz, July 23, 1963; Wing to Regional Director, June 10, 1963; Lee to Wirth, June 13, 1963; Telegram, Hillory Tolson to Superintendent, GNMP, June 14, 1963, all in GETT 41160, Box 34, Folder 6, PCF/GNMPA.

52. Danahy to Simon, April 11, 1963, GETT 41160, Box 34, Folder 6, PCF/GNMPA; Danahy to Gibbons, June 27, 1963, Vertical Files Collection, Drawer 17, Folder 43, GNMPL.

53. Douglas Martin, "Sam Gibbons, Democrat of Florida, Dies at 92," *NYT*, October 10, 2012; Florida Monument Dedication Ceremonies transcript, GNMPL; Dudziak, "Birmingham, Addis Ababa, and the Image of America," 188; Andrew Meacham, "Sam Gibbons, Congressman and 'True American Hero,' Dies at Age 92," *Tampa Bay Times*, October 11, 2012.

54. Dudziak, "Birmingham, Addis Ababa, and the Image of America," 181–82, 189–92; Borstelmann, *The Cold War and the Color Line*, 115.

55. Lebow and Stein, *We All Lost the Cold War*, 20, 29, 33, 120, 122–24; Mike Clary, "Cuban Missile Crisis: I Hoped I Would Not Be the First to Fire," *Sun Sentinel* (South Florida), October 14, 2012; "Cuban Missile Crisis"; Fox interview.

56. Florida Monument Dedication Ceremonies transcript, GNMPL.

57. "Rep. Gibbons Dedicates Fla. Shaft"; Martin, "Sam Gibbons Dies at 92"; "House Vote #87 in 1965 to Pass H.R. 6400"; Florida Monument Dedication Ceremonies transcript, GNMPL; "House Vote #182 in 1964 H.R. 7152"; Draft speech for Congressman Gibbons, July 24, 1964, Box 1: 1966–1, Folder 1; Sam Gibbons, "Comments on Executive Order 11114," June-August, 1963, Box 5: 1966–5, Folder 13; Sam M. Gibbons to Edwin S. Howard, November 7, 1963, Box 5: 1966–5, Folder 12, all in Sam Gibbons Collection, 1940–2000, Special Collections, University of South Florida Libraries.

58. Krenn, "The Unwelcome Mat," 171; Pauley, *The Modern Presidency and Civil Rights*, 118, 122–24.

59. New Jersey Monument Rededication Invitation, n.d.; "North Carolina at Gettysburg," July 1, 1963, both in Box 124, PA Gettysburg Commission Folder, CWCC/NARA College Park; Brann, "Civil War Left Major 'Unfinished Business'"; "Rebel Rally Features N.C. Field Rites," *GT*, July 2, 1963; "N. Carolina Reception Is Held Monday," *GT*, July 2, 1963.

60. Wefing, *The Life and Times of Richard J. Hughes*, 98–106; Asbury, "Hughes Charges Moral Failure to Aid Negroes Since Civil War"; Brann, "Civil War Left Major 'Unfinished Business'"; White, "Pledge of Equality Is Unfulfilled."

61. Lemisch, "Who Won the Civil War, Anyway?," 302; Brann, "Civil War Left Major 'Unfinished Business'"; White, "Pledge of Equality Is Unfulfilled."

62. "July 2 Parade to Be Pageant of War Events," *GT*, February 23, 1963; Gettysburg Centennial Commission, news release, May 29, 1963, GETT 41160, Box 8, Folder 2, PCF/GNMPA; "6,500 Marchers Will Parade," *GT*, June 29, 1963; Jean M. White, "Small-Town Festivities Highlight Day's Celebration in Gettysburg," *WP*, July 3, 1963; "Crowd of More Than 35,000 View Centennial Parade on Tuesday," *GT*, July 3, 1963; "Old, New Seen in Big Parade at Gettysburg," *Chicago Tribune*, July 3, 1963.

63. "Club Is Told of Vignettes of Centennial," *GT*, April 11, 1963; "Further Plans for July Fete," *GT*, February 20, 1963; Witt interview.

64. Vignettes of History flier, July 1963, Vignettes of History Folder, ACCWCC/ACHS; Michael West to Betty Gifford, April 30, 1963, Programs Folder, Gifford/ACHS; "Some Changes to Be Made in Centennial Program Here," *GT*, March 12, 1963; Witt interview; "Human Interest Stories of Battle of Gettysburg Will Be Re-enacted Here," *GT*, April 20, 1963; "80 Local Citizens Offer 7 Historical Vignettes During Centennial Days," *GT*, June 18, 1963; "Claim 50,000 Saw Vignettes in Four Days," *GT*, July 11, 1963; "Leaves Hospital," *GT*, July 4, 1963.

65. J. Walter Coleman to Herbert Kahler, January 10, 1963, RG 79, Accession #079-66F-0048, Box 11, GNMP Centennial Folder 2, NER-NPS/NARA Philadelphia; "Human Interest Stories of Battle of Gettysburg Will Be Re-enacted Here"; Vignettes of History scripts, July 1963, Vignettes of History Folder, ACCWCC/ACHS.

66. Witt interview.

67. "Claim 50,000 Saw Vignettes in Four Days"; Witt interview; Invoice, Van Horn & Son, Inc., July 1963, Untitled Folder, Gifford/ACHS.

68. Witt interview; Pennsylvania Centennial Commission, July Battle Anniversary Commemoration Recap, n.d., Box 124, PA Gettysburg Commission Folder; George Kaufmann, Circular, July 20, 1963, Box 40, Gettysburg Civil War Roundtable Folder, both in CWCC/NARA College Park; Muriel Dobbin, "Woman to Direct 'Battle' of Gettysburg," *Baltimore Sun*, March 3, 1963; "Claim 50,000 Saw Vignettes in Four Days"; Betty Gifford to Joe [Codori?], May 23, 1963, Vignettes Folder, Gifford/ACHS; Kittridge A. Wing, Superintendent's Report—July 1963, August 14, 1963, Box 192, 1963 Folder, AF-NPS/NARA College Park.

69. Pfanz to Myers, May 17, 1962, GETT 41160, Box 7, Folder 3, PCF/GNMPA; "Symbolic Re-Enactments, Pageantry, Parade to Be Features of July Events," *GT*, April 25, 1963; "Paternal View Rapped."

70. "Symbolic Re-Enactments, Pageantry, Parade to Be Features of July Events"; "21 States to Send Units to July 3 Event," *GT*, May 25, 1963; "Skirmishers Will Camp on County Land," *GT*, June 5, 1963; White, "Pledge of Equality Is Unfulfilled"; Wing—Superintendent's Report—July 1963, August 14, 1963, RG 79, Box 192, 1963 Folder, AF-NPS/NARA College Park; MacMillan to Wing, June 14, 1963, GETT 41160, Box 8, Folder 3; Chester Shriver to Sons of Veterans Reserve Units, Re-Activated Civil War Units, and North-South Skirmish Units, April 10, 1963, Box 8, Folder 6, both PCF/GNMPA.

71. "Gettysburg Poet Praises Gov. Wallace"; Witt interview.

72. "Swope Tells Civic Council Battle Plans," *GT*, January 22, 1963; "Sons of Veterans Will Present Symbolic Attack"; "Smoke Pots to Create Effect of Big Battle," *GT*, May 24, 1963; "21 States to Send Units"; Edith Evans Asbury, "Battle of Gettysburg Relieved at Centennial," *NYT*, July 4, 1963; "Troopers from 24 States Staged Lively Spectacle in Full-Dress Re-creation," *GT*, July 4, 1963; Richard Bernstein, Pickett's Charge script, June 1963, GETT 41160, Box 8, Folder 5, PCF/GNMPA.

73. "40,000 See Reb Charge Reenacted," *Patriot*, July 4, 1963; PCC, July Commemoration recap, Box 124, PA Gettysburg Commission Folder, CWCC/NARA College Park; Myers to Lee, October 9, 1962, GETT 41160, Box 7, Folder 3; Confederate High Command Press Release, n.d., Park Central Files 1954–1987, GETT 41160, Box 8, Folder 3; Wing to Donald Ramsay, June 11, 1963; Wing to Ramsay, July 21, 1964, Box 8, Folder 4, all in PCF/GNMPA; "Sons of Veterans Will Present Symbolic Attack"; "Smoke Pots to Create Effect of Big Battle"; "Pickett's Disastrous Charge Reenacted," *Los Angeles Times*, July 4, 1963; "Unity Keynote at Gettysburg Battle Finish," *Chicago Tribune*, July 4, 1963; "Troopers from 24 States"; Gordon C. Fredine to Conrad Wirth, May 13, 1963, Accession #079-66F-0048, Box 11, GNMP Centennial Folder 2, NER-NPS/NARA Philadelphia; "Charge Halts Press Battle with People," *GT*, July 4, 1963; Dorothy Elderdice to Betty Gifford, July 8, 1963, Programs Folder, Gifford/ACHS.

74. Fox interview; PCC, July Commemoration recap, Box 124, PA Gettysburg Commission Folder, CWCC/NARA College Park; Jean White, "40,000 Watch Pickett Charge Again at Gettysburg," *WP*, July 4, 1963; "Troopers from 24 States"; "Pickett's Charge," *GT*, July 4, 1963; Daniel Langan, "Pickett's Charge Is Re-Enacted at Gettysburg Site," *PI*, July 4, 1963; "Battle Hero's Son Here for Re-Enactment," *GT*, July 4, 1963.

75. Fox interview; PCC, July Commemoration recap, Box 124, PA Gettysburg Commission Folder, CWCC/NARA College Park; Frank Masland Jr. to Conrad Wirth, July 11, 1963, Accession #079-66F-0048, Box 11, GNMP Centennial Folder 1, NER-NPS/NARA Philadelphia.

76. "40,000 See Reb Charge Reenacted."

77. "County Civil War Program Is Moved to July Fourth," *GT*, June 24, 1963; Program, "Memorial Service for Civil War Soldiers of Adams County," July 4, 1963, Minutes Folder, ACCWCC/ACHS; "40 Persons Hold Vigil on Thursday," *GT*, July 4, 1963. Back issues of the *Gettysburg Times* reveal that the group held a similar demonstration the previous year.

78. "Cannon Pound in Impromptu Troop Battle," *GT*, July 4, 1963.

79. "Centennial Medical Work Is Reported," *GT*, July 24, 1963; "40,000 See Reb Charge Reenacted"; "Park Visitors Set New High for 6 Months," *GT*, July 13, 1963; Wing, Superintendent's Report—July 1963, August 14, 1963, Box 192, Superintendent's Reports 1963 Folder, AF-NPS/NARA College Park.

80. Robertson to Simon, July 10, 1963, Box 124, PA Gettysburg Commission Folder, CWCC/NARA College Park; "Letters Laud Centennial's Battle Memorial Program for 'Purposeful Dignity,'" *GT*, July 15, 1963; Frank Skidmore to Betty Gifford, July 9, 1963; Henry Scharf to Gifford, July 5, 1963; Simon to Gifford, July 11, 1963; Wing to Gifford, July 9, 1963; Nathan to Gifford, July 10, 1963; Nathan to Gifford, July 16,

1963, all in Programs Folder, Gifford/ACHS; Wing, Superintendent's Report—July 1963, August 14, 1963, Box 192, 1963 Folder, AC-NER/NARA College Park.

81. Wing, Superintendent's Report—July 1963, August 14, 1963, Box 192, 1963 Folder, AF-NPS/NARA College Park; Wing to Detailed Rangers, July 9, 1963, GETT 41160, Box 8, Folder 6, PCF/GNMPA; Frederick Tilberg to Tom Warfield, July 19, 1963, US.DOI.NPS GNMP Historian Files 1933–1676, GETT 41151, Box 3, GNMPA; Wirth to Masland, July 29, 1963, Accession #079-66F-0048, Box 11, GNMP Centennial Folder 1, NER-NPS/NARA Philadelphia.

82. Max Freedman, "Men at Gettysburg Held Hinge of Destiny and Gave It New Pattern," *Los Angeles Times*, July 4, 1963; "100 Years Since Gettysburg," *WP*, July 4, 1963.

83. John McClave, "For the Next One Hundred Years," *PI*, July 5, 1963; Elizabeth A. Woodman, "Editorial," *PI*, July 10, 1963.

84. Don Robertson, "Vulgar Show at Gettysburg," *Plain Dealer*, July 14, 1963; "Gettysburg: The Task Remaining," *Newsweek*, July 15, 1963.

85. Nelson Murdock to Wing, July 19, 1963, GETT 41160, Box 8, Folder 6, PCF/GNMPA; Cook, *Troubled Commemoration*, 191; King, "I Have a Dream."

Chapter Six

1. Peatman, *The Long Shadow*, 169–70; Simon report, 42–43, GNMPL; E. J. Stackpole to William W. Scranton, December 12, 1963, A 2 Subject File 1963–1967, Carton 29, Folder 3, WSP/PSA; "Note Lincoln Speech 100th Anniversary," *GT*, November 6, 1963; Jean White, "40,000 Watch Pickett Charge Again at Gettysburg," *WP*, July 4, 1963.

2. For more on the use of Lincoln's image and the ideals of the Gettysburg Address during World War II, see Silber, *This War Ain't Over*, chap. 6, and Peatman, *The Long Shadow*, chap. 4.

3. It is somewhat surprising that none of these individuals was military personnel, given how extensively both mainstream civil rights leaders and government officials linked the desegregation of the U.S. military, the Cold War, and Black advancement and sought to portray the expanded roles played by Black soldiers in the Korean War and the early days of the Vietnam conflict as emblematic of American racial progress. For more on this, see Phillips, "Did the Battlefield Kill Jim Crow?," 208–29.

4. Peatman, *The Long Shadow*, 138; Murray, *On a Great Battlefield*, 65; Fried, *The Russians Are Coming*, 29–30.

5. Fried, *The Russians Are Coming*, 32–38, 43; "Daily Programs, Parades Rededicate Community to American Heritage," *Maroon & White*, November 3, 1948, clipping; "1863 Cemetery Platform Scene to Be Recreated at Freedom Train Site Friday," *GT*, November 18, 1948, clipping, both in Freedom Train File, VF/ACHS; Recording, Gettysburg Freedom Train, 85th Anniversary of Lincoln's Address Rededication Ceremony, November 19, 1948, m008_0001-0074_0091_GettysburgFreedom_19481119, MG-8.1, Miscellaneous Pennsylvania Manuscripts, 1626–1998, PSA.

6. Freedom Train recording, PSA; Silber, *This War Ain't Over*, 159.

7. Sugrue, "Hillburn, Hattiesburg, and Hitler," 88–91; Hart, "Making Democracy Safe for the World," 56, 71–74, 81.

8. Phillips, *War!*, 89; Borstelmann, *The Cold War and the Color Line*, 56; Silber, *This War Ain't Over*, 160, 171.

9. Phillips, *War!*, 89; Borstelmann, *The Cold War and the Color Line*, 57.

10. Fried, *The Russians Are Coming*, 101; Harry Ferguson, "Lincoln Stands Tall in Eyes of Most Europeans," *Chicago Daily Defender*, April 9, 1962.

11. "Carl Sandburg, World Famous Authority on Lincoln, Will Speak," *GT*, November 12, 1959; "Rep. Schwengel's Address Text," *GT*, November 19, 1959; Peatman, *The Long Shadow*, 152–54.

12. Betty J. Canno, "All Created Equal," *AA*, October 12, 1963; Cook, *Civil War Memories*, 171–72; "Goldberg to Speak at 'Equal Opportunity' Event," *Chicago Daily Defender*, November 8, 1961; "Urban League to Back Lincoln Credo Stamp," *Chicago Daily Defender*, November 5, 1960; Hall, "The Response of the Moderate Wing of the Civil Rights Movement," 681; "JFK Tells Urban League Hope for Equality Grows Each Year," *AA*, November 25, 1961.

13. Peatman, *The Long Shadow*, 168–71, 185; "A Symposium on Abraham Lincoln's Gettysburg Address," January 13, 1964, Box 77, Gettysburg Symposium & Dinner Folder, CWCC/NARA College Park; "Good Taste, Restraint Urged for Centennial Observance," *GT*, January 10, 1963; "Observance of Centennial of Lincoln's Address to Climax Anniversary Fetes," *GT*, July 27, 1963.

14. Peatman, *The Long Shadow*, 176; Scranton to Brooks Hays, May 18, 1963, A 2 Subject File 1963–1967, Carton 29, Folder 2, WSP/PSA; Simon to Gifford, December 17, 1964, Vignettes Folder, Gifford/ACHS.

15. "Urge Congress to Establish Centennial Commission," *GT*, May 23, 1963; Scranton to Hays, May 18, 1963, A 2 Subject File 1963–1967, Carton 29, Folder 2, WSP/PSA; "House Passes Deficit Bill for July Fete," *GT*, June 25, 1963; "Observance of Centennial of Lincoln's Address."

16. Simon to John E. Carland, September 26, 1963, Box 124, PA Gettysburg Commission Folder, CWCC/NARA College Park; Peatman, *The Long Shadow*, 176; Simon report, 46, GNMPL. Scranton to U Thant, September 30, 1963; U Thant to Scranton, October 5, 1963, both in A 2 Subject File 1963–1967, Carton 29, Folder 6, WSP/PSA.

17. Wing, Superintendent's Monthly Report—September 1963, October 8, 1963, Box 192, 1963 Folder, AF-NPS/NARA College Park; "Catch 4 Students with Stolen Signs," *GT*, September 16, 1963; "Body on Tower Is Football Stunt," *GT*, September 12, 1963; "Approximately 10,000 View 'A Day in the Life of a Civil War Soldier,'" *GT*, September 23, 1963.

18. Acting Superintendent, Superintendent's Monthly Report—August 1963, September 13, 1963, Box 192, 1963 Folder, AF-NPS/NARA College Park; "Travel Council Urges Fee Study," *GT*, September 11, 1963; "Seeking $25,000 Here for Tourist Promotion," *GT*, September 26, 1963; "Travel Group Seeks $3000 for Road Signs," *GT*, December 11, 1963; "Commanders Plan 'Battle' Here Sept. 22," *GT*, September 9, 1963; "450 Men in Uniforms of Civil War," *GT*, September 20, 1963; "Approximately 10,000 View 'A Day in the Life of a Civil War Soldier.'"

19. "450 Men in Uniforms of Civil War"; "Approximately 10,000 View 'A Day in the Life of a Civil War Soldier'"; Carmichael, *The War for the Common Soldier*, 190–97.

20. Unrau, *Administrative History*, 277, 282; Wing, Superintendent's Monthly Report—October 1963, November 15, 1963, Box 192, 1963 Folder; Wing, Superintendent's Monthly Report—November 1963, December 13, 1963; Wing, Superintendent's Monthly Report—December 1963, January 14, 1964, all in AF-NPS/NARA College Park; "Will Clear 130 Acres of Land in Park Here," *GT*, October 8, 1963; "Battlefield Clearance Is Half Finished," *GT*, December 4, 1963; "Battlefield Is Presented in 100-Year-Ago-Appearance" *GT*, February 12, 1964; Minutes of the GNMP Management Improvement Committee, May 3, 1961, Accession #079-68A-0275, Box 27, GETT Folder, NER-NPS/NARA Philadelphia.

21. "Mayor Given Irish Flag," *GT*, November 11, 1963; "Irish Brigade Presented to Mayor Monday," *GT*, November 12, 1963.

22. "Special Lincoln Edition Will Be Published," *GT*, October 31, 1963; *GT* Lincoln Centennial Edition, November 19, 1963.

23. "WGET Aired Centennial Events, Serviced Other Networks without Charge," *GT*, November 20, 1963; "Plan Annual Remembrance Day Program," *GT*, September 7, 1963; "State Adjutant General Will Speak Here," *GT*, September 14, 1963; "GAR Units to Hold Pageant at Monument," *GT*, November 15, 1963; "Says Lincoln Linked Gospel with Freedom," *GT*, November 18, 1963.

24. Official Program of the 100th Anniversary of Lincoln's Address, November 17–19, 1963, Programs and Booklets Folder, ACCWCC/ACHS; "Highlights of Four-Day Centennial Observance," *GT*, November 16, 1963; "Three Countries Will Be Represented," *GT*, November 8, 1963; Lee to Wirth, April 30, 1962, GETT 41160, Box 7, Folder 3, PCF/GNMPA; "Secretary of State Dean Rusk Will Officially Open Lincoln Program," *GT*, October 17, 1963.

25. "Declares Secretary of State," *GT*, November 18, 1963.

26. "Remarks by the Honorable Dean Rusk," Simon report, 96–99, GNMPL.

27. Romano, "No Diplomatic Immunity," 550; Borstelmann, *The Cold War and the Color Line*, 111–12, 116–17, 128–29.

28. Romano, "No Diplomatic Immunity," 547–52, 559, 575–77.

29. "Remarks by the Honorable Dean Rusk," Simon report, 99, GNMPL; Romano, "No Diplomatic Immunity," 547, 575–77.

30. "Remarks by the Honorable Dean Rusk," Simon report, 99–100, GNMPL.

31. "Address Delivered by H.E.M. Herve Alphand," Simon report, 100–101, GNMPL.

32. Fenoaltea address, 101–3; "Remarks by J. E. Chadwick," 103–5, both in Simon report, GNMPL; "Finest Human Expression," *GT*, November 26, 1963.

33. "Will Deliver Fortenbaugh Lecture Here," *GT*, October 23, 1963; "War Justified in 'Address' Here," *GT*, November 18, 1963.

34. "If A. Lincoln Were Speaking Here Today," *GT* Lincoln Commemorative Edition, November 19, 1963; GCC Press Release, November 13, 1963, Adams County Civil War Centennial Committee 1963 File, VF/ACHS.

35. "If A. Lincoln Were Speaking Here Today"; "Three Countries Will Be Represented"; Temple University Libraries, "Alexander, Raymond Pace."

36. Lincoln Was Tired, Beset with Anxieties," *GT*, November 19, 1963; "Mayor Weaver Is President of Lincoln Fellowship," *GT*, November 20, 1963; "Park Service Is

Presented Tract of Land," *GT*, November 20, 1963; "GBPA Elects John Cobaugh," *GT*, November 20, 1963.

37. GBPA Fact Sheet, n.d., Box 124, PA Gettysburg Commission Folder, CWCC/NARA College Park; "Mayor Weaver Is President"; Murray, *On a Great Battlefield*, 124–25.

38. "Lincoln Was Tired, Beset with Anxieties"; "General Eisenhower and Governor Scranton Will Speak Here," *GT*, October 8, 1963; "Procession to Cemetery Was Similar to '63 Event," *GT*, November 20, 1963; "Some Schools Will Close," *GT*, November 14, 1963; "10,000 Are Thrilled and Emotionally Moved," *GT*, November 20, 1963; "Marian Anderson Joins in Gettysburg Ceremony," *AA*, November 30, 1963; Wing to Regional Director, November 20, 1963, Accession #079-66F-0048, Box 11, GNMP Centennial Folder 1, NER-NPS/NARA Philadelphia.

39. Scranton to Hays, May 18, 1963, A 2 Subject File 1963–1967, Carton 29, Folder 2, WSP/PSA; "10,000 Are Thrilled and Emotionally Moved"; "Lincoln's Gettysburg Ideals Echoed at Talk's Centennial," *Evening Star*, November 20, 1963; "Marian Anderson Joins in Gettysburg Ceremony"; Edith Evans Asbury, "Negroes Join Eisenhower to Rededicate Gettysburg," *NYT*, November 20, 1963.

40. Nichols, *A Matter of Justice*, 66–67; 99; "Too Late, Ike," *Chicago Daily Defender*, October 15, 1963.

41. "Too Late, Ike"; Nichols, *A Matter of Justice*, 2, 67, 99.

42. "Remarks by General Dwight D. Eisenhower," Simon report, 119–20, GNMPL.

43. "Address by Governor William W. Scranton," Simon report, 117–19, GNMPL; Asbury, "Negroes Join Eisenhower to Rededicate Gettysburg."

44. "Scranton Is Under Fire on Civil Rights," *GT*, November 20, 1963.

45. Speech by E. Washington Rhodes, Simon report, 115–17, GNMPL; Asbury, "Negroes Join Eisenhower to Rededicate Gettysburg"; "E. Washington Rhodes, 1895–1970," *Philadelphia Tribune*, August 22, 2011.

46. "Marian Anderson Joins in Gettysburg Ceremony"; John M. Cummings, "Speech Long Remembered," *PI*, n.d., clipping, Gettysburg Address Anniversaries Vertical File, Folder 1, VF/ACHS; Silber, *This War Ain't Over*, 115. For more on Lincoln's emerging identity as a symbol of racial justice, see Silber, *This War Ain't Over*, chap. 4.

47. "Kennedy Is Assassinated," *GT*, November 22, 1963; "Eisenhower Is Shocked," *GT*, November 22, 1963; "Gettysburg Stunned by Tragic News from Dallas," *GT*, November 23, 1963.

48. "Gettysburg Stunned by Tragic News from Dallas"; "Two Masses Offered for Late Leader," *GT*, November 25, 1963; "Hold Services for Kennedy This Morning," *GT*, November 25, 1963; "Gettysburg, County Join in Mourning," *GT*, November 25, 1963; Wing to Milton G. Baker, November 29, 1963, GETT 41160, Box 8, Folder 6, PCF/GNMPA; "Finest Human Expression," *GT*, November 26, 1963.

49. "Johnson Voices Plea for Equality," *AA*, November 30, 1963; "President Lyndon B. Johnson," *AA*, December 7, 1963.

50. "2 Events Here This Year Had Wide Publicity," *GT*, December 5, 1963; "Simon Thanks Community for Co-operation," *GT*, December 11, 1963.

51. Wing, Superintendent's Monthly Report—December 1963, January 14, 1964; Wing, Superintendent's Monthly Report—November 1963, December 13, 1963, both in Box 192, 1963 Folder, AF-NPS/NARA College Park.

52. Wing to Regional Director, November 20, 1963, Accession #079-66F-0048, Box 11, GNMP Centennial Folder 1, NER-NPS/NARA Philadelphia; "2 Events Here This Year Had Wide Publicity"; "Simon Thanks Community for Co-operation."

Chapter Seven

1. "2 Events Here This Year Had Wide Publicity," GT, December 5, 1963; "Simon Thanks Community for Co-operation," GT, December 11, 1963. W. Clayton Jester to Dwight D. Eisenhower, January 13, 1961, Miscellaneous Correspondence and Bills Folder; Helen McCauslin, Supplement to the Minutes of the Adams County Centennial Commission of Gettysburg, Pennsylvania, October 1964, Minutes Folder, both in ACCWCC/ACHS. "34-Star Flag to Fly for CW Centennial," GT, December 14, 1960; Thomas J. Harrison, Interpretive Prospectus for Gettysburg NMP, February 1968, viii, RG 79, Office of Design & Construction, General Correspondence of the Assistant Director for Design & Construction, 1965–1968, Box 112, GETT 67–68 Folder, AF-NPS/NARA College Park; Murray, *On a Great Battlefield*, 116, 128.

2. Cook, *Troubled Commemoration*, 193–94.

3. Cook, *Troubled Commemoration*, 206–7, 224.

4. "Large Crowd Sees 101st Anniversary Parade Here," GT, July 3, 1963; Alfred Runte to Stewart Udall, December 1, 1964, Division of Land Acquisition, Land Acquisition Files, 1933–1970, Box 29, GNMP 1963–67 Folder, NARA College Park; John M. Virden to Harry Pfanz, December 2, 1965, GETT 41160, Box 34, Folder 8, PCF/GNMPA.

5. "Week Long Observance of 101st Battle Anniversary," GT, June 27, 1963; "Conway Talks at N.C. Marker," GT, July 4, 1964; Woods, *Prisoners of Hope*, 99.

6. Wing, Superintendent's Monthly Report—November 1964, December 14, 1964, Box 192, Folder 2, AF-NPS/NARA College Park; "Lincoln's Famous Gettysburg Address Is 'Like a Prayer to Tragedy of Human Condition," GT, November 19, 1964.

7. Wing, Superintendent's Monthly Report—December 1964, January 14, 1965; Wing, Superintendent's Monthly Report—June 1964, July 14, 1964; Wing, Superintendent's Monthly Report—July 1964, August 14, 1964; Wing, Superintendent's Monthly Report—July 1965, August 13, 1965; Wing, Superintendent's Monthly Report—September 1965, October 15, 1965, all in Box 192, Folder 2, AF-NPS/NARA College Park. Acting Regional Director to Director, December 14, 1964, Accession #079-71A-0379, Box 21, Gettysburg 1964–67 Folder, NER-NPS/NARA Philadelphia; "Tourist Volume Here Tops Mark Set by Centennial Year for First Six Months," GT, July 7, 1964; "Provide Tape Message for Tourist Tour," GT, May 21, 1964; Murray, *On a Great Battlefield*, 116, 128.

8. Harrison, Interpretive Prospectus for Gettysburg NMP, AF-NPS/NARA College Park; George F. Emery to Regional Director, April 29, 1966, RG 79, Division of Land Acquisition, Land Acquisition Files, 1933–1970, Box 29, GNMP 1963–67 Folder, NARA College Park; Murray, *On a Great Battlefield*, 120–21, 128.

9. "Will Deliver Lecture Here," GT, February 18, 1964; Madison interview; Tom Heston, President, Human Relations Forum to Fellow Students, Spring 1965, MS-194: Richard Hutch '67 Papers, Box 1, Folder 1, SCCA/GC; "King Calls for Wider Vote Drive," WP, April 2, 1965; Yale University, "John Vannorsdall."

10. Yale University, "John Vannorsdall"; "Knoxville, Gettysburg Colleges Swap Students," *AA*, December 4, 1965. "Knoxville Students to Arrive Here Sunday," *Gettysburgian* 68 (November 12, 1965); "The Legacy: The Presence of Blacks at Gettysburg College, 1837–2007," video recording; Buddy Glover '71, email to Devin McKinney, n.d., Buddy Glover Scrapbook, all in SCCA/GC.

11. Madison interview. Southworth, "Race and Civil Rights," 2–4; Glover interview transcript, 17, both in SCCA/GC.

12. Glover interview transcript, 35–37; "Peace Week to Flower, Sat. April 20," *Gettysburgian*, April 19, 1968, both in SCCA/GC.

13. Green interview.

14. Kalish, *The Story of Civil Rights*, 55–56; Stevens, *Radical L.A.*, 307, 314–15.

15. Garrow, "The Voting Rights Act in Historical Perspective," 391–92; "A New U.S. Chapter," *Chicago Daily Defender*, August 10, 1965; Lauri Lebo, "York City's Summer of Rage," *York Dispatch*, July 16, 2019.

16. Levy, *The Great Uprising*, 261, 274; Green interview; "Eagle Soars into Orbit on Trip Home," *GT*, July 21, 1969; "At Least 7 Wounded in York Strife," *GT*, July 22, 1969; "Disturbances in York Like Guerilla War," *GT*, July 23, 1969.

17. "Dr. Franklin to Speak Here November 19," *GT*, November 13, 1965; Andrew L. Yarrow, "John Hope Franklin, Scholar of African-American History, Is Dead at 94," *NYT*, March 25, 2009; Franklin, "The Dilemma of the American Negro Scholar," 70–76.

18. Franklin, "The Dilemma of the American Negro Scholar," 74; Cook, *Troubled Commemoration*, 181–83.

19. "Says Racists Tried to Twist Lincoln's Views," *GT*, November 20, 1965.

20. Gettysburg College Bulletin, Catalogue Number 1963–1965 (April 1963), Internet Archive, 132–35, https://archive.org/details/gettysbu196365196971gett/page /n139/mode/2up; "Lecturer Franklin to Talk on Lincoln, Reconstruction," *Gettysburgian* 68 (November 12, 1965), both in SCCA/GC. Madison interview.

21. Program, Dedication Day, November 19, 1957, Gettysburg Address Anniversaries File, VF/ACHS; "Lecturer Franklin to Talk on Lincoln, Reconstruction," *Gettysburgian* 68 (November 12, 1965), SCCA/GC. Photograph, "Participants in the Conference— 1st Civil War Conference," November 1957; and photograph, "Speakers at 5th Annual Civil War Conference," November 1961, both in MS-122: Civil War Institute, Box 9, Folder 5, SCCA/GC. Franklin, "The Dilemma of the American Negro Scholar," 75–76.

22. Cook, *Troubled Commemoration*, 262–64; "What Ailed the Civil War Centennial," *WP*, April 14, 1965; Virden to Pfanz, December 2, 1965, GETT 41160, Box 34, Folder 8, PCF/GNMPA.

23. Philip Smith, "Civil War Centennial Ends," *NYT*, February 28, 1965; Cook, *Troubled Commemoration*, 212–15, 264.

24. Program, Grand Army of the Republic Memorial Statue dedication, September 12, 1956, GETT 41160, Box 33, Folder 2; Gertrude Kibler to James B. Myers, August 10, 1962, Box 33, Folder 7; Myers to Kibler, August 14, 1962, Box 33, Folder 7, all in PCF/GNMPA.

25. Gertrude Kibler to Committee Members, March 5, 1963; Kibler to Maybelle Smith and Ed Sturdivant, November 20, 1963; Sturdivant to Kibler, November 27,

1963; Smith to Kibler, December 2, 1963; Kibler to Wing, December 30, 1963; Wing to NPS Regional Director, January 9, 1964; Wing to Kibler, February 3, 1964, all in GETT 41160, Box 33, Folder 7, PCF/GNMPA. Smith to Wing, May 1, 1964; William M. Beard to Wing, July 17, 1964; Ronald F. Lee to NPS Director, June 23, 1964; Beard to Mrs. Jasper Smith, October 19, 1964; John A. May to Olin D. Johnston, July 13, 1963; Kibler, "Report to UDC Committee on Monument at Gettysburg," March 9, 1964, all in GETT 41160, Box 33, Folder 9, PCF/GNMPA. Warrick, "Mississippi's Greatest Hour," 106; "Sculptor of Confederates' Memorial Did 'The Rocket Thrower' at New York Fair," *GT*, August 25, 1965.

26. Harry W. Pfanz, "Comments on Proposed Memorial by De Lue," June 3, 1964; Frederick Tilberg, "Comments on the Proposed Confederate States Memorial," June 3, 1964, both in GETT 41160, Box 33, Folder 9, PCF/GNMPA. Emphasis mine.

27. "Successor to James Myers Is Announced," *GT*, March 6, 1963. Wing to Regional Director, June 4, 1964; Ben H. Thompson to Regional Director, July 9, 1964; Wing to Smith, July 30, 1964; Wing to Donald De Lue, August 11, 1964, all in GETT 41160, Box 33, Folder 9, PCF/GNMPA. Emphasis mine.

28. Wing to Clark Stratton, August 27, 1964; Beard to Stratton, September 30, 1965, both in GETT 41160, Box 33, Folder 9, PCF/GNMPA. "500 Witness Dedication of Confederate Memorial on Battlefield Wednesday," *GT*, August 26, 1965; "Ervin Lauds Rebel Spirit at Unveiling," *GT*, August 26, 1965.

29. Campbell, *Senator Sam Ervin*, 24–27, 105–6, 141–44, 148.

30. "Handful of KKK Marching," *GT*, June 11, 1966.

31. Minchin, "Making Best Use of the New Laws," 695–96.

32. Tuck, "'We Are Taking Up Where the Movement of the 1960s Left Off,'" 641; Minchin, "Making Best Use of the New Laws," 670–74, 678, 688–94; Minchin and Salmond, *After the Dream*, 20–24, 76–77; Sokol, *There Goes My Everything*, 8. For more on this historiographical debate, see Lassiter, *The Silent Majority*; MacLean, *Freedom Is Not Enough*; Crosby, *A Little Taste of Freedom*; and Hall, "The Long Civil Rights Movement," 1233–63.

33. "Arkansas Monument Dedicated," *GT*, June 20, 1966; Granade, "Arkansas Commemorates the Civil War Centennial," 434–37. Pfanz to "File," February 15, 1966; Virden to Pfanz, November 17, 1965; J. B. Hill to Wing, September 29, 1965; George F. Emery to Regional Director, February 9, 1966; Lemuel Garrison to Emery, March 8, 1966; Program, Dedication of Arkansas Monument at Gettysburg, June 18, 1966, all in GETT 41160, Box 34, Folder 8, PCF/GNMPA.

34. Pie Dufour, "Gettysburg Battle Monument Is Eyed," *Times-Picayune*, April 17, 1966, clipping; J. Wallace Kingsbury to Emery, November 15, 1966; Katherine Letteer to Emery, December 30, 1966, all in GETT 41160, Box 34, Folder 10, PCF/GNMPA.

35. "Governor of Louisiana Is Speaker for Dedication," *GT*, June 12, 1971; Angela Gregory to Emery, April 18, 1967; "LA Committee Visits Field," *GT*, May 25, 1967, clipping; Emery to Regional Director, June 2, 1967; Gregory to Emery, May 16, 1968; Gregory to Commission Members, Seidenberg, Rice, and De Lue, August 6, 1968; De Lue to Emery, October 31, 1968; Thomas Harrison to Emery, November 26, 1968, all in GETT 41160 Box 34, Folder 10, PCF/GNMPA.

36. Harrison to Emery, November 26, 1968; Emery to Regional Director, November 26, 1968; Regional Director to Emery, December 11, 1968; Emery to Letteer, December 19, 1968; Letteer to Emery, January 2, 1969; Letteer to John J. McKeithen, December 8, 1970; Letteer to Karl Smith, January 21, 1971; Dedication Program, June 11, 1971, all in GETT 41160 Box 34, Folder 10, PCF/GNMPA; "Governor of Louisiana Is Speaker for Dedication."

37. Crespino, *In Search of Another Country*, 20, 25; Hustwit, "Thomas P. Brady"; Brady, "Segregation and the South," 6–9, 13.

38. Warrick, "Mississippi's Greatest Hour," 96–98.

39. Crespino, *In Search of Another Country*, 7, 141–43, 173; Asch, *The Senator and the Sharecropper*, 254–58.

40. Crespino, *In Search of Another Country*, 7, 9, 13; Sokol, *There Goes My Everything*, 327.

41. Silver, *Mississippi: The Closed Society*, 5. Gray Evans to GNMP, October 6, 1966; "Mississippi House Votes for Memorial," *GT*, May 9, 1968, clipping; George F. Emery to Regional Director, June 13, 1969, all in GETT 41160, Box 34, Folder 5, PCF/GNMPA.

42. Emery to Regional Director, June 13, 1969; Donald De Lue to Emery, September 24, 1970, both in GETT 41160, Box 34, Folder 5, PCF/GNMPA; "State of Mississippi Monument."

43. Harrison to Superintendent, October 2, 1970; Allen comments, October 2, 1970; Hubbard comments, October 2, 1970, all in GETT 41160, Box 34, Folder 5, PCF/GNMPA.

44. Harrison to Superintendent, October 2, 1970, GETT 41160, Box 34, Folder 5, PCF/GNMPA.

45. Harrison to Superintendent, October 2, 1970; Emery to Ed Sturdivant, October 7, 1970; Tom P. Brady to Sturdivant, October 21, 1970; Sturdivant to Jerry Schober, July 14, 1971; Sturdivant to Emery, December 12, 1970; Schober to Brady, September 20, 1971; Schober to M. Ney Williams Jr., November 4, 1971, all in GETT 41160, Box 34, Folder 5, PCF/GNMPA. Emphasis mine.

46. Ronald Smothers, "Town Distances Itself from Suspect in Evers Case," *NYT*, December 21, 1990; "Byron De La Beckwith: White Supremacist Served Life for '63 Killing of Medgar Evers," *Los Angeles Times*, January 24, 2001.

47. "Jury Ponders Murder Case," *GT*, July 2, 1963; "Arraign Man in Evers Case," *GT*, July 3, 1963; Amy McCullough, "Former Gov. Bill Waller Dies at 85," *Mississippi Business Journal* 33, no. 49 (December 5, 2011); Nossiter, *Of Long Memory*, 148–56; Lehman, "Civil Rights in Twilight," 416–17.

48. Crespino, *In Search of Another Country*, 117, 183, 234.

49. Program, Mississippi Gettysburg Memorial Monument Dedication Ceremony, October 19, 1973, GETT 41160, Box 34, Folder 5, PCF/GNMPA; "Senator Eastland Dedicates Monument to Mississippi Men Who Fought Here in '63," *GT*, October 19, 1973. For more about Eastland, see Asch, *The Senator and the Sharecropper*.

50. Weir, "The Graying of Gettysburg National Military Park," 61.

Epilogue

1. Glover interview transcript, 13, SCCA/GC.

2. Hunt and Levine, *Arc of Empire*, 185–87, 192, 197, 199–203, 210.

3. Wing, Superintendent's Monthly Report—October 1965, November 15, 1965, Box 192, Folder 2, AF-NPS/NARA College Park; "Lessons of History Are Cited," *GT*, May 31, 1966; Stoler, "The Second World War in U.S. History and Memory," 384, 389.

4. "Lessons of History Are Cited"; Stoler, "The Second World War," 389.

5. Hunt and Levine, *Arc of Empire*, 216–19, 223; "Lincoln Speech Memorial Dedicated Sunday," *GT*, November 20, 1967.

6. Hunt and Levine, *Arc of Empire*, 225–26; Brittingham, *The Pennsylvania Manual*, 99, 664–68, 687.

7. "Vice Pres. Humphrey to Be Speaker," *GT*, May 11, 1968; Hunt and Levine, *Arc of Empire*, 227.

8. "Vice Pres. Humphrey to Be Speaker"; "Humphrey Speaks to Hardy Crowd," *GT*, May 31, 1968.

9. "Vice President to Speak," *GT*, May 30, 1968; "Humphrey Speaks to Hardy Crowd."

10. Small, *Antiwarriors*, 107–8. "Dissenters Organize Oct. 15 Moratorium," *Gettysburgian*, October 10, 1969; "March Climaxes War Dedication; Peace Light Rally Attracts 500," *Gettysburgian*, October 17, 1969, both in SCCA/GC.

11. "Dissenters Organize Oct. 15 Moratorium"; "March Climaxes War Dedication"; "No Such Thing as . . . ," *Gettysburgian*, October 17, 1969; "A Little Bit of War," *Gettysburgian*, October 17, 1969, all in SSCA/GC.

12. "Largest Veterans' Day Parade in Years," *GT*, November 10, 1969.

13. "Strike," *Gettysburgian*, May 8, 1970; "Nixon's Speech on War Strategy Prompts Anti-War March, Vigil," *Gettysburgian*, May 12, 1972; "Renewed Damage Promises to Curb Battlefield Lovers," *Gettysburgian*, October 14, 1966, all in SCCA/GC.

14. Lucks, *Selma to Saigon*, 6–7, 114, 117–18, 124, 134–36, 195–96.

15. Herbert Mitgang, "Harrisburg Seven: Inevitably, The War Itself Will Be on Trial," *NYT*, January 30, 1972; Homer Bigart, "It Is Not a Funny Trial," *NYT*, February 27, 1972; Bigart, "Antiwar Protests Begun by Backers of the Harrisburg 7," *NYT*, March 27, 1972; Bigart, "Berrigan Case: A Strategy that Backfired," *NYT*, April 9, 1972; "50 Marchers Hold Program at Cemetery," *GT*, March 25, 1972; Fairclough, *To Redeem the Soul of America*, 78, 161–68, 187, 237, 323, 330.

16. C. T. Vivian, "The Second Gettysburg Address," March 24, 1972, MS-036 Radical Pamphlets Collection, Series II, Box 24, Folder 3, SCCA/GC.

17. Vivian, "The Second Gettysburg Address."

18. Witt interview.

19. King, "Appeal to the Honorable John F. Kennedy," quoted in Blight, *American Oracle*, 17.

20. Latschar, "Coming to Terms with the Civil War"; Bill Broun, "Why Confederate Monuments Should Be Removed from Gettysburg," *Morning Call*, August 20, 2017. For more on this theme, see Scott Hancock, "In Gettysburg, the Confederacy Won," *CityLab*, August 24, 2017, https://www.bloomberg.com/news/articles/2017-08-24/taking-aim-at-the-confederate-monuments-of-gettysburg.

21. Christine Vendel, "Armed 'Patriot' Accidentally Shoots Self in Leg at Gettysburg Battlefield," *Penn Live*, July 1, 2017; Shawn Boburg and Dalton Bennett, "Militias Flocked to Gettysburg," *WP*, July 4, 2020.

22. Boburg and Bennett, "Militias Flocked to Gettysburg"; Hancock, "Fear of a Black Planet (Part 1)"; Carmichael, "Gettysburg National Military Park and July 4, 2020."

23. Lauren Gambino, "Trump Says He May Accept Presidential Nomination at Gettysburg Battlefield," *Guardian*, August 10, 2020; David Von Drehle, "Trump's (Tremendous) Gettysburg Address," *WP*, August 11, 2020; Darragh Roche, "Joe Biden's Gettysburg Speech Was 25 Minutes Long, Didn't Mention Trump Once," *Newsweek*, October 7, 2020; John Avlon, "Joe Biden's Gettysburg Address Is the Best of His Campaign," *CNN*, October 6, 2020.

Bibliography

Archival Sources

Adams County Historical Society
    Adams County Civil War Centennial Collection
    Adams County Civil War Centennial 1961–1965 (Gifford Collection)
    Mullen Collection
    Tim Smith Collection
    Vertical Files Collection
Gettysburg National Military Park (GNMP) Archives
    GNMP Historian Files, 1933–1676 (41151)
    GNMP Interpretive Files, 1939–Present (43973)
    GNMP Park Central Files, 1954–1987 (41160)
    GNMP Planning Files, 1936–Present (43973)
Gettysburg National Military Park Library and Research Center
    Archival Box Collection
    Vertical Files Collection
Library of Congress
    Papers of the NAACP
National Archives and Records Administration, College Park, MD
    Records of the National Park Service, Branch of Forestry, Correspondence
        and Subject Files, 1922–1959
    Records of the National Park Service, Correspondence and Subject Files,
        1922–1959
    Records of the National Park Service, Division of Land Acquisition, Land
        Acquisition Files, 1933–1970
    Records of the National Park Service, General Records, Administrative Files,
        1949–1971
    Records of the National Park Service, General Records, Index Files, 1949–1971
    Records of the National Park Service, Office of Design and Construction,
        General Correspondence of the Assistant Director for Design and Construction,
        1965–1968
    Records of the National Park Service, Office of Design and Construction,
        General Files of the Philadelphia Planning and Service Center, 1954–1968
    Records of the National Park Service, U.S. Civil War Centennial Commission
        Records
National Archives and Records Administration, Philadelphia, PA
    Records of the National Park Service, Eastern Office of Design and Construction,
        NAID 37489672
    Records of the National Park Service, General Subject Files of Northeast Region

Pennsylvania State Archives
  Office of the Governor, Records of the Pennsylvania Human Relations
    Commission, 1956–2000 (RG 10)
  Pennsylvania Collection (MG 8)
  Records of the Pennsylvania State Police (RG 30)
  Records of Special Commissions (RG 25)
  William W. Scranton Papers, 1963–1967 (MG 208)
Special Collections and Archives, Musselman Library, Gettysburg College
  The Blister
  Buddy Glover, interview with Devin McKinney, May 13, 2015, transcript
  Buddy Glover Scrapbook
  Class of 1963 Collection
  Edward Southworth Reflection
  Gettysburgian
  Radical Pamphlets Collection
  The Legacy
Special Collections, University of South Florida Libraries
  Sam Gibbons Collection, 1940–2000

Newspapers and Magazines

Afro-American (Baltimore)
Atlanta Constitution
Baltimore Sun
Birmingham News
Boston Globe
Chicago Defender
Chicago Tribune
CityLab
Civil War Times
Evening Star
  (Washington, DC)
Evening Sun (Hanover)

Florence Morning News
Gettysburg Compiler
Gettysburg Times
Guardian
Huffington Post
Los Angeles Times
Los Angeles Tribune
Montgomery Advertiser
Morning Call (Allentown)
Newsweek
New York Times
Patriot (Harrisburg)

Philadelphia Inquirer
Philadelphia Tribune
Pittsburgh Post-Gazette
Plain Dealer
Reader's Scope
Star and Sentinel
  (Gettysburg)
Sun Sentinel (South Florida)
Tampa Bay Times
Times-Picayune
Washington Post
York Dispatch

Interviews by Author

Fox, Terry. Interview by author, March 7, 2019.
Green, Jean. Interview by author, July 4, 2019.
Madison, James H. Interview by author, December 17, 2018.
Witt, Jim. Interview by author, April 2, 2019.

Articles and Books

Allaback, Sarah. *Mission 66 Visitor Centers: The History of a Building Type.*
  Washington, DC: U.S. Department of the Interior, 2000. https://www.nps.gov
  /parkhistory/online_books/allaback/.

Adams County Historical Society. "History of Adams County." Accessed July 7, 2019. https://www.achs-pa.org/about-us/history-of-adams-county. Site discontinued.

American Battlefield Trust. "Gettysburg Campaign." Accessed March 20, 2021. https://www.battlefields.org/learn/civil-war/gettysburg-campaign.

Anderson, Carol. "Bleached Souls and Red Negroes: The NAACP and Black Communists in the Early Cold War, 1948–1952." In *Window on Freedom: Race, Civil Rights, and Foreign Affairs, 1945-1988*, edited by Brenda Gayle Plummer, 93–113. Chapel Hill: University of North Carolina Press, 2003.

Angle, Paul M. "The Tragic Years: The Civil War and Its Commemoration." *South Atlantic Quarterly* 63 (Autumn 1961): 375–89.

Arsenault, Raymond. *Freedom Riders: 1961 and the Struggle for Racial Justice*. Pivotal Moments in American History. New York: Oxford University Press, 2006.

Asch, Chris Myers. *The Senator and the Sharecropper: The Freedom Struggles of James O. Eastland and Fannie Lou Hamer*. New York: New Press, 2008.

Bartley, Abel A. "The 1960 and 1964 Jacksonville Riots: How Struggle Led to Progress." *Florida Historical Quarterly* 78, no. 1 (1999): 46–73.

Biondi, Martha. *To Stand and Fight: The Struggle for Civil Rights in Postwar New York City*. Cambridge, MA: Harvard University Press, 2003.

Birkner, Michael J., and Carol Hegeman. *Eisenhower's Gettysburg Farm*. Images of America. Charleston, SC: Arcadia, 2017.

Blight, David W. *American Oracle: The Civil War in the Civil Rights Era*. Cambridge, MA: Belknap Press / Harvard University Press, 2011.

———. *Race and Reunion: The Civil War in American Memory*. Cambridge, MA: Belknap Press / Harvard University Press, 2001.

Bloom, John. "'The Farmers Didn't Particularly Care for Us': Oral Narrative and the Grass Roots Recovery of African American Migrant Farm Labor History in Central Pennsylvania." *Pennsylvania History* 78, no. 4 (Autumn 2011): 323–54.

Bodnar, John. *Remaking America: Public Memory, Commemoration, and Patriotism in the Twentieth Century*. Princeton, NJ: Princeton University Press, 1992.

Borstelmann, Thomas. *The Cold War and the Color Line: American Race Relations in the Global Arena*. Cambridge, MA: Harvard University Press, 2001.

Brady, Tom P. "Segregation and the South," October 4, 1957. https://dc.lib.odu.edu/digital/collection/npsdp/id/1151/.

Branch, Taylor. *Pillar of Fire: America in the King Years, 1963–65*. New York: Simon & Schuster, 1998.

Brenneman, Chris, and Sue Boardman, *The Gettysburg Cyclorama: The Turning Point of the Civil War on Canvas*. El Dorado Hills, CA: Savas Beatie, 2015.

Brittingham, George, R., Jr., ed. *The Pennsylvania Manual, 1968–1969*. Harrisburg, PA: Commonwealth of Pennsylvania Department of Property and Supplies, 1969.

Brown, Thomas J. *Civil War Canon: Sites of Confederate Memory in South Carolina*. Civil War America. Chapel Hill: University of North Carolina Press, 2015.

———. *Civil War Monuments and the Militarization of America*. Civil War America. Chapel Hill: University of North Carolina Press, 2019.

Bryant, Nick. *The Bystander: John F. Kennedy and the Struggle for Black Equality*. New York: Basic Books, 2006.

Burk, Robert Fredrick. *The Eisenhower Administration and Black Civil Rights*. Knoxville: University of Tennessee Press, 1984.

Burns, Stewart. *To the Mountaintop: Martin Luther King, Jr.'s Sacred Mission to Save America, 1955–1968*. New York: HarperCollins, 2004.

Buser, Daniel S., Jr., ed. *The Pennsylvania Manual, 1965–1966*. Harrisburg, PA: Commonwealth of Pennsylvania Department of Property and Supplies, 1966.

Campbell, Karl E. *Senator Sam Ervin, Last of the Founding Fathers*. Chapel Hill: University of North Carolina Press, 2007.

Carmichael, Peter S. "Gettysburg National Military Park and July 4, 2020: Personal Reflections." *Muster* (blog). July 20, 2020. https://www.journalofthecivilwarera .org/2020/07/gettysburg-national-military-park-and-july-4-2020-personal -reflections/.

———. *The War for the Common Soldier: How Men Thought, Fought, and Survived in Civil War Armies*. Littlefield History of the Civil War Era. Chapel Hill: University of North Carolina Press, 2018.

Carr, Ethan. *Mission 66: Modernism and the National Park Dilemma*. Amherst: University of Massachusetts Press, 2007.

Carson, Clayborne, ed. *The Eyes on the Prize Civil Rights Reader: Documents, Speeches, and Firsthand Accounts from the Black Freedom Struggle, 1954–1990*. New York: Penguin Books, 1991.

Colburn, David R. *From Yellow Dog Democrats to Red State Republicans: Florida and Its Politics since 1940*. Gainesville: University Press of Florida, 2007.

Cook, Robert J. "Bruce Catton, Middlebrow Culture, and the Liberal Search for Purpose in Cold War America." *Journal of American Studies* 47 (February 2013): 109–26.

———. *Civil War Memories*. Baltimore: Johns Hopkins University Press, 2017.

———. "'From Shiloh to Selma:' The Impact of the Civil War Centennial on the Black Freedom Struggle in the United States, 1961–1965." In *The Making of Martin Luther King and the Civil Rights Movement*, edited by Brian Ward and Tony Badger, 131–46. New York: New York University Press, 1996.

———. "Red Termites and Rebel Yells: The Civil War Centennial in Strife-Torn Alabama, 1961–1965." *Alabama Review* 64 (April 2011): 143–67.

———. *Troubled Commemoration: The American Civil War Centennial, 1961–1965*. Making the Modern South. Baton Rouge: Louisiana State University Press, 2007.

———. "Unfinished Business: African Americans and the Civil War Centennial." In *Legacy of Disunion: The Enduring Significance of the American Civil War Era*, edited by Susan-Mary Grant and Peter J. Parish, 48–64. Baton Rouge: Louisiana State University Press, 2003.

———. "(Un)Furl That Banner: The Response of White Southerners to the Civil War Centennial of 1961–1965." *Journal of Southern History* 68, no. 4 (2002): 879–912.

Coski, John M. *The Confederate Battle Flag: America's Most Embattled Emblem*. Cambridge, MA: Harvard University Press, 2005.

Countryman, Matthew. *Up South: Civil Rights and Black Power in Philadelphia*. Politics and Culture in Modern America. Philadelphia: University of Pennsylvania Press, 2006.

Cox, Karen L. *Dixie's Daughters: The United Daughters of the Confederacy and the Preservation of Confederate Culture*. New Perspectives on the History of the South. Gainesville: University Press of Florida, 2003.

Craig, John M. "'There Is Hell Going on Up There': The Carnegie Klan Riot of 1923." *Pennsylvania History: A Journal of Mid-Atlantic Studies* 72, no. 3 (2005): 322–46.

Creighton, Margaret S. *The Colors of Courage: Gettysburg's Forgotten History: Immigrants, Women, and African Americans in the Civil War's Defining Battle*. New York: Basic Books, 2005.

Crespino, Joseph. *In Search of Another Country: Mississippi and the Conservative Counterrevolution*. Politics and Society in Twentieth-Century America. Princeton, NJ: Princeton University Press, 2007.

Crosby, Emilye. *A Little Taste of Freedom: The Black Struggle in Claiborne County, Mississippi*. Chapel Hill: University of North Carolina Press, 2005.

"Cuban Missile Crisis." Key West Historic Marker Tour. Accessed March 21, 2021. http://keywesthistoricmarkertour.org/marker/453.

Delmont, Matthew F. *Why Busing Failed: Race, Media, and the National Resistance to School Desegregation*. Oakland: University of California Press, 2016.

Desjardin, Thomas A. *These Honored Dead: How the Story of Gettysburg Shaped American Memory*. Cambridge, MA: Da Capo, 2003.

Dillon, Patricia. "Civil Rights and School Desegregation in Sanford." *Florida Historical Quarterly* 76, no. 3 (1998): 310–25.

Douglas, Davison M. *Jim Crow Moves North: The Battle over Northern School Segregation, 1865–1954*. Cambridge Historical Studies in American Law and Society. New York: Cambridge University Press, 2005.

Dudziak, Mary L. "Birmingham, Addis Ababa, and the Image of America: International Influence on U.S. Civil Rights Politics in the Kennedy Administration." In *Window on Freedom: Race, Civil Rights, and Foreign Affairs, 1945–1988*, edited by Brenda Gayle Plummer, 181–99. Chapel Hill: University of North Carolina Press, 2003.

———. *Cold War Civil Rights: Race and the Image of American Democracy*. Politics and Society in Twentieth-Century America. Princeton, NJ: Princeton University Press, 2000.

———. *Exporting American Dreams: Thurgood Marshall's African Journey*. Oxford: Oxford University Press, 2008.

Eisenhower, David, with Julie Nixon Eisenhower. *Going Home to Glory: A Memoir of Life with Dwight D. Eisenhower, 1961–1969*. New York: Simon & Schuster, 2010.

Eisenhower, Dwight D. *At Ease: Stories I Tell to Friends*. Garden City, NY: Doubleday, 1967.

Faherty, William Barnaby. *Florida's Space Coast: The Impact of NASA on the Sunshine State*. Florida History and Culture. Gainesville: University Press of Florida, 2002.

Fairclough, Adam. *To Redeem the Soul of America: The Southern Christian Leadership Conference and Martin Luther King, Jr*. Athens: University of Georgia Press, 1987.

Flagel, Thomas R. *War, Memory, and the 1913 Gettysburg Reunion*. Kent, OH: Kent State University Press, 2019.

Franklin, John Hope. "A Century of Civil War Observance." *Journal of Negro History* 47, no. 2 (1962): 97–107.

———. "The Dilemma of the American Negro Scholar." In *Soon, One Morning: New Writing by American Negroes, 1940–1962*, edited by Herbert Hill, 62–76. New York: Knopf, 1969.

Frederickson, Kari. "Corporate Culture, the Cold War, and the American South in the 1950s and 1960s." In *Liberty and Justice for All?*, edited by Kathleen G. Donohue, 361–82. Rethinking Politics in Cold War America. Amherst: University of Massachusetts Press, 2012.

———. "The 'Slowest State' and 'Most Backwards Community': Racial Violence in South Carolina and Federal Civil-Rights Legislation, 1946–1948." *South Carolina Historical Magazine* 98, no. 2 (April 1997): 177–202.

Fried, Richard M. *The Russians Are Coming! The Russians Are Coming: Pageantry and Patriotism in Cold-War America*. New York: Oxford University Press, 1998.

Gallagher, Gary W. *Causes Won, Lost, and Forgotten: How Hollywood and Popular Art Shape What We Know About the Civil War*. Chapel Hill: University of North Carolina Press, 2008.

Garrow, David J. "The Voting Rights Act in Historical Perspective." *Georgia Historical Quarterly* 74, no. 3 (Fall 1990): 377–98.

Glatfelter, Charles H. *A Salutary Influence: Gettysburg College, 1832–1985*, vol. 2. Gettysburg, PA: Gettysburg College, 1987.

Gordon, Linda. *The Second Coming of the KKK: The Ku Klux Klan of the 1920s and the American Political Tradition*. New York: Liveright, 2017.

Granade, S. Ray. "Arkansas Commemorates the Civil War Centennial: An Exercise in Pragmatism." *Arkansas Historical Quarterly* 73, no. 4 (2014): 414–37.

Hall, Andy. "Fantasizing Robert E. Lee as a Civil Rights Pioneer." *Civil War Monitor* (blog). July 3, 2012. https://www.civilwarmonitor.com/blog/fantasizing-lee-as-a-civil-rights-pioneer.

Hall, Jacqueline Dowd. "The Long Civil Rights Movement and the Political Uses of the Past." *Journal of American History* 91, no. 4 (2005): 1233–63.

Hall, Simon. "The Response of the Moderate Wing of the Civil Rights Movement to the War in Vietnam." *Historical Journal* 46, no. 3 (September 2003): 669–701.

Hammack, Loraine. "Adele Gutman Nathan." In *Jewish Women: A Comprehensive Historical Encyclopedia*. Jewish Women's Archive. Last modified March 20, 2009. https://jwa.org/encyclopedia/article/nathan-adele-gutman.

Hancock, Scott. "Fear of a Black Planet (Part 1)." *Muster* (blog). July 20, 2020. https://www.journalofthecivilwarera.org/2020/07/fear-of-a-black-planet-part-i/.

Harrison, Ira E. "Louis Eugene King: The Anthropologist Who Never Was." In *African-American Pioneers in Anthropology*, edited by Ira E. Harrison and Fay Venetia Harrison, 70–84. Urbana: University of Illinois Press, 1999.

Harrison, Kathleen Georg. "'Patriotic and Enduring Efforts': An Introduction to the Gettysburg Battlefield Commission." In *Gettysburg 1895–1995: The Shaping of an*

American Shrine. Gettysburg Seminar Papers. Accessed March 21, 2021. http://
npshistory.com/series/symposia/gettysburg_seminars/4/essay3.htm.

Hart, Justin. "Making Democracy Safe for the World: Race, Propaganda, and the
Transformation of U.S. Foreign Policy During World War II." *Pacific Historical
Review* 73, no. 1 (February 2004): 49–84.

Hartley, Robert. "A Long Hot Summer: The St. Augustine Racial Disorders of 1964."
In *St. Augustine, Florida, 1963–1964: Mass Protest and Racial Violence*, edited by
David J. Garrow, 3–92. Brooklyn, NY: Carlson, 1989.

Hatfield, Edward A. "Desegregation of Higher Education." In *New Georgia
Encyclopedia*. Last modified February 25, 2021. https://www.georgiaencyclopedia
.org/articles/history-archaeology/desegregation-higher-education.

Henderson, Harold Paulk. "Ernest Vandiver Jr." In *New Georgia Encyclopedia*. Last
modified July 23, 2018. https://www.georgiaencyclopedia.org/articles
/government-politics/ernest-vandiver-jr-1918-2005.

Hesburgh, Theodore. "Gettysburg: Yesterday and Today." Speech transcript in 109
Cong. Rec., A4254-55, July 9, 1963.

"History: Civil Rights Timeline." Columbia SC 63. Accessed May 3, 2021. https://
www.columbiasc63.com/history/.

Hobbs, Malcolm. "A Southerner's Southerner." *Reader's Scope*, May 1946, 8–21.

Hogan, Wesley C. *Many Minds, One Heart: SNCC's Dream for a New America*.
Chapel Hill: University of North Carolina Press, 2007.

"House Vote #87 in 1965 to Pass H.R. 6400, the 1965 Voting Rights Act." GovTrack.
Accessed March 21, 2021. https://www.govtrack.us/congress/votes/89-1965/h87.

"House Vote #182 in 1964 H.R. 7152, Civil Rights Act of 1964." GovTrack. Accessed
March 21, 2021. https://www.govtrack.us/congress/votes/88-1964/h182.

Hunt, Michael H. *Arc of Empire: America's Wars in Asia from the Philippines to Vietnam*.
H. Eugene and Lillian Youngs Lehman Series. Chapel Hill: University of North
Carolina Press, 2012.

Hustwit, William. "Thomas P. Brady." In *Mississippi Encyclopedia*. Accessed
March 20, 2021. https://mississippiencyclopedia.org/entries/thomas-p-brady/.

Isserman, Maurice, and Michael Kazin, *America Divided: The Civil War of the 1960s*.
Oxford: Oxford University Press, 1999.

Janney, Caroline E. *Remembering the Civil War: Reunion and the Limits of
Reconciliation*. Littlefield History of the Civil War Era. Chapel Hill: University of
North Carolina Press, 2013.

Jenkins, Philip. *Hoods and Shirts: The Extreme Right in Pennsylvania, 1925–1950*.
Chapel Hill: University of North Carolina Press, 1997.

Johnson, Larry, Deirdre Cobb-Roberts, and Barbara Shircliffe. "African Americans
and the Struggle for Opportunity in Florida Public Higher Education, 1947–1977."
History of Education Quarterly 47, no. 3 (2007): 328–58.

Johnson, Lyndon B. "Memorial Day Remarks at Gettysburg." May 30, 1963. Lyndon
Baines Johnson Presidential Library. http://www.lbjlibrary.net/collections
/selected-speeches/.

Johnson, S. Marianne, and Ian Isherwood. "Gettysburg and the Great War." *War and
Society* 36, no. 3 (August 2017): 217–34.

Jones, Patrick D. *The Selma of the North: Civil Rights Insurgency in Milwaukee*. Cambridge, MA: Harvard University Press, 2009.

Jordan, Brian Matthew. "'We Stand on the Same Battlefield': The Gettysburg Centenary and the Shadow of Race." *Pennsylvania Magazine of History and Biography* 135, no. 4 (2011): 481–511.

Kalish, Jim. *The Story of Civil Rights in York, Pennsylvania: A 250 Year Interpretive History*. York, PA: York County Audit of Human Rights, 2000.

Kammen, Michael. *Mystic Chords of Memory: The Transformation of Tradition in American Culture*. New York: Vintage Books, 1993.

Kelland, Lara Leigh. *Clio's Foot Soldiers: Twentieth-Century U.S. Social Movements and Collective Memory*. Amherst: University of Massachusetts Press, 2018.

King, Martin Luther, Jr. "Address to the New York State Civil War Centennial Commission," September 12, 1962. http://exhibitions.nysm.nysed.gov/mlk/images/MLK-Transcription.pdf.

———. "I Have a Dream." Address Delivered at the March on Washington for Jobs and Freedom, August 28, 1963. Martin Luther King Jr. Research and Education Institute, Stanford University. https://kinginstitute.stanford.edu/king-papers/documents/i-have-dream-address-delivered-march-washington-jobs-and-freedom.

———. "Letter from Birmingham City Jail." In *The Eyes on the Prize Civil Rights Reader*, edited by Clayborne Carson, David J. Garrow, Gerald Gill, Vincent Harding, and Darlene Clark Hine, 153–58. New York: Penguin Books, 1991.

Kolk, Heidi Aronson. *Taking Possession: The Politics of Memory in a St. Louis Town House*. Amherst: University of Massachusetts Press, 2019.

Krenn, Michael. "The Unwelcome Mat: African Diplomats in Washington, D.C., during the Kennedy Years." In *Window on Freedom: Race, Civil Rights, and Foreign Affairs, 1945–1988*, edited by Brenda Gayle Plummer, 163–80. Chapel Hill: University of North Carolina Press, 2003.

Kytle, Ethan J., and Blain Roberts. *Denmark Vesey's Garden: Slavery and Memory in the Cradle of the Confederacy*. New York: New Press, 2018.

Lassiter, Matthew. *The Silent Majority: Suburban Politics in the Sunbelt South*. Princeton, NJ: Princeton University Press, 2006.

Lau, Peter F. *Democracy Rising: South Carolina and the Fight for Black Equality since 1865*. Civil Rights and the Struggle for Black Equality in the Twentieth Century. Lexington: University Press of Kentucky, 2006.

Latschar, John. "Coming to Terms with the Civil War at Gettysburg National Military Park." *CRM: The Journal of Heritage Stewardship* 4, no. 2 (Summer 2007). https://www.nps.gov/CRMjournal/Summer2007/view1.html.

Layton, Azza Salama. *International Politics and Civil Rights Policies in the United States, 1941–1960*. Cambridge: Cambridge University Press, 2000.

Lebow, Richard Ned, and Janice Gross Stein. *We All Lost the Cold War*. Princeton Studies in International History and Politics. Princeton, NJ: Princeton University Press, 1994.

Lee, Ronald F., and National Park Service. *The Origin and Evolution of the National Military Park Idea*. Washington, DC: U.S. National Park Service, Office of Park Historic Preservation, 1973.

Lees, William B., and Frederick P. Gaske. *Recalling Deeds Immortal: Florida Monuments to the Civil War*. Gainesville: University Press of Florida, 2014.

Lehman, Christopher Paul. "Civil Rights in Twilight: The End of the Civil Rights Movement Era in 1973." *Journal of Black Studies* 36, no. 3 (January 2006): 415–28.

Lemisch, Jesse L. "Who Won the Civil War, Anyway?" *Nation* 192, no. 14 (April 8, 1961): 300–302.

Levy, Peter B. *Civil War on Race Street: The Civil Rights Movement in Cambridge, Maryland*. Gainesville: University Press of Florida, 2003.

———. *The Great Uprising: Race Riots in Urban America during the 1960s*. Cambridge: Cambridge University Press, 2018.

Lewis, David Levering. *King: A Biography*. Champaign: University of Illinois Press, 2013.

Linenthal, Edward Tabor. *Sacred Ground: Americans and Their Battlefields*. Urbana: University of Illinois Press, 1991.

Lucks, Daniel S. *Selma to Saigon: The Civil Rights Movement and the Vietnam War*. Lexington: University Press of Kentucky, 2014.

MacLean, Nancy. *Freedom Is Not Enough: The Opening of the American Workplace*. Cambridge, MA: Harvard University Press, 2008.

McMahon, Robert J. *The Cold War: A Very Short Introduction*. New York: Oxford University Press, 2003.

Meyer, Stephen Grant. *As Long as They Don't Move Next Door: Segregation and Racial Conflict in American Neighborhoods*. Lanham, MD: Rowman & Littlefield, 2000.

Minchin, Timothy J. "Making Best Use of the New Laws: The NAACP and the Fight for Civil Rights in the South, 1965–1975." *Journal of Southern History* 74, no. 3 (August 2008): 669–702.

Minchin, Timothy J., and John A. Salmond. *After the Dream: Black and White Southerners since 1965*. Civil Rights and the Struggle for Black Equality in the Twentieth Century. Lexington: University Press of Kentucky, 2011.

Moore, John Hammond. "Running Up the Flag" *A Capital Blog*, University of South Carolina, University Libraries. July 10, 2015. https://digital.library.sc.edu/blogs/scpc/2015/07/10/running-up-the-flag-or-how-john-amasa-may-thumbed-his-nose-at-jfk/.

Mormino, Gary R. "Sunbelt Dreams and Altered States: A Social and Cultural History of Florida, 1950–2000." *Florida Historical Quarterly* 81, no. 1 (2002): 3–21.

Murray, Jennifer M. *On a Great Battlefield: The Making, Management, and Memory of Gettysburg National Military Park, 1933–2013*. Knoxville: University of Tennessee Press, 2014.

Neff, John R. *Honoring the Civil War Dead: Commemoration and the Problem of Reconciliation*. Modern War Studies. Lawrence: University Press of Kansas, 2005.

Neutra, Dion. *The Preservation Disaster of the 21st Century: The Life and Death of the Neutra Gettysburg Cyclorama*. Neutra Institute for Survival through Design, n.d.

Neutra, Richard Joseph. *Life and Shape*. New York: Appleton-Century-Crofts, 1962.

Nichols, David A. *A Matter of Justice: Eisenhower and the Beginning of the Civil Rights Revolution*. New York: Simon & Schuster, 2007.

Nora, Pierre. "Between Memory and History: Les Lieux de Mémoire." *Representations* 26, Special Issue: Memory and Counter-Memory (Spring 1989): 7–24.

Nossiter, Adam. *Of Long Memory: Mississippi and the Murder of Medgar Evers.* Cambridge, MA: Da Capo, 2002.

Oakes, Becky. "The Blue and Gray in Black and White: The Media's Portrayal of Veterans during the 75th Anniversary of the Battle of Gettysburg." *Civil Discourse* (blog). January 1, 2015. http://www.civildiscourse-historyblog.com/blog/2014/12 /30/the-blue-and-gray-in-black-and-white-the-medias-portrayal-of-veterans -during-the-75th-anniversary-of-the-battle-of-gettysburg-1.

Paradis, James M. *African Americans and the Gettysburg Campaign.* Lanham, MD: Scarecrow, 2005.

Pauley, Garth E. *LBJ's American Promise: The 1965 Voting Rights Address.* College Station: Texas A & M University Press, 2007.

———. *The Modern Presidency & Civil Rights: Rhetoric on Race from Roosevelt to Nixon.* College Station: Texas A & M University Press, 2001.

Peatman, Jared. *The Long Shadow of Lincoln's Gettysburg Address.* Carbondale: Southern Illinois University Press, 2013.

Phillips, Kimberley L. "'Did the Battlefield Kill Jim Crow?' The Cold War Military, Civil Rights, and Black Freedom Struggles." In *Fog of War: The Second World War and the Civil Rights Movement,* edited by Kevin M. Kruse and Stephen Tuck, 208–29. Oxford: Oxford University Press, 2012.

———. *War! What Is It Good for? Black Freedom Struggles and the U.S. Military from World War II to Iraq.* John Hope Franklin Series in African American History and Culture. Chapel Hill: University of North Carolina Press, 2012.

Platt, Barbara L. *This Is Holy Ground: A History of the Gettysburg Battlefield.* Harrisburg, PA: Huggins, 2001.

Plummer, Brenda Gayle, ed. *Window on Freedom: Race, Civil Rights, and Foreign Affairs, 1945–1988.* Chapel Hill: University of North Carolina Press, 2003.

Reardon, Carol. *Pickett's Charge in History and Memory.* Chapel Hill: University of North Carolina Press, 1997.

Richardson, Heather Cox. *To Make Men Free: A History of the Republican Party.* New York: Basic Books, 2014.

Richey, Iris, ed. *The Pennsylvania Manual, 1961–1962.* Harrisburg, PA: Commonwealth of Pennsylvania Department of Property and Supplies, 1962.

Risen, Clay. *The Bill of the Century: The Epic Battle for the Civil Rights Act.* New York: Bloomsbury, 2014.

Romano, Renee. "No Diplomatic Immunity: African Diplomats, the State Department, and Civil Rights, 1961–1964." *Journal of American History* 87, no. 2 (September 2000): 546–79.

Roosevelt, Franklin D. "Speech of the President, Gettysburg, July 3, 1938." Franklin D. Roosevelt Presidential Library and Museum. https://fdrlibrary.files .wordpress.com/2013/11/fdr-gettysburg-speech.pdf.

Rose, Chanelle N. *The Struggle for Black Freedom in Miami: Civil Rights and America's Tourist Paradise, 1896–1968.* Making the Modern South. Baton Rouge: Louisiana State University Press, 2015.

Rosenberg, Jonathan. *How Far the Promised Land? World Affairs and the American Civil Rights Movement from the First World War to Vietnam*. Princeton, NJ: Princeton University Press, 2005.

Rosiecki, Casimer. "Fighting Today for a Better Tomorrow." *From the Fields of Gettysburg* (blog), March 26, 2015. https://npsgnmp.wordpress.com/2015/03/26/fighting-today -for-a-better-tomorrow-the-civilian-conservation-corps-at-gettysburg/.

Rudy, John. "Interpreting Beyond the Battles: Could We Start with the Klan." *Civil War Connect* (blog). June 9, 2011. http://www.civilwarconnect.com/2011/06 /interpreting-beyond-battles-could-we.html.

Savage, Kirk. "The Politics of Memory: Black Emancipation and the Civil War Monument." In *Commemorations: The Politics of National Identity*, edited by John R. Gillis, 127–49. Princeton, NJ: Princeton University Press, 1994.

———. *Standing Soldiers, Kneeling Slaves: Race, War and Monument in Nineteenth-Century America*. Princeton, NJ: Princeton University Press, 1997.

Silber, Nina. "Reunion and Reconciliation, Reviewed and Reconsidered." *Journal of American History* 103, no. 1 (June 2016): 59–83.

———. *This War Ain't Over: Fighting the Civil War in New Deal America*. Chapel Hill: University of North Carolina Press, 2018.

Silver, James W. *Mississippi: The Closed Society*. New York: Harcourt, Brace & World, 1966.

Small, Melvin. *Antiwarriors: The Vietnam War and the Battle for America's Hearts and Minds*. Lanham, MD: Scholarly Resources, 2002.

Smith, Timothy B. *Altogether Fitting and Proper: Civil War Battlefield Preservation in History, Memory, and Policy, 1861–2015*. Knoxville: University of Tennessee Press, 2017.

Sokol, Jason. *All Eyes Are Upon Us: Race and Politics from Brooklyn to Boston*. New York: Basic Books, 2014.

———. *There Goes My Everything: White Southerners in the Age of Civil Rights, 1945–1975*. New York: Knopf, 2006.

Spencer, Robyn C. *The Revolution Has Come: Black Power, Gender, and the Black Panther Party in Oakland*. Durham, NC: Duke University Press, 2016.

"State of Mississippi Monument." Gettysburg Stone Sentinels. Accessed March 20, 2021. http://gettysburg.stonesentinels.com/confederate-monuments/confederate -state-monuments/mississippi/.

Stevens, Errol Wayne. *Radical L.A.: From Coxey's Army to the Watts Riots, 1894–1965*. Norman: University of Oklahoma Press, 2009.

Stine, Casey, ed. *The Pennsylvania Manual, 1963–1964*. Harrisburg, PA: Commonwealth of Pennsylvania Department of Property and Supplies, 1964.

Stoler, Mark A. "The Second World War in U.S. History and Memory." *Diplomatic History* 24, no. 3 (Summer 2001): 383–92.

Sugrue, Thomas J. "Hillburn, Hattiesburg, and Hitler: Wartime Activists Think Globally and Act Locally." In *Fog of War: The Second World War and the Civil Rights Movement*, edited by Kevin M. Kruse and Stephen Tuck, 87–102. New York: Oxford University Press, 2012.

———. *Sweet Land of Liberty: The Forgotten Struggle for Civil Rights in the North*. New York: Random House, 2008.

Sugrue, Thomas J., and Andrew P. Goodman. "Plainfield Burning: Black Rebellion in the Suburban North." *Journal of Urban History* 33, no. 4 (May 2007): 568–601.

Temple University Libraries. "Alexander, Raymond Pace." In *Civil Rights in a Northern City*. Accessed March 20, 2021. http://northerncity.library.temple.edu /exhibits/show/civil-rights-in-a-northern-cit/people-and-places/alexander --raymond-pace.

Theoharis, Jeanne. "'I'd Rather Go to School in the South': How Boston's School Desegregation Complicates the Civil Rights Paradigm." In *Freedom North: Black Freedom Struggles Outside the South, 1940–1980*, edited by Komozi Woodard and Jeanne Theoharis, 125–51. London: Palgrave Macmillan, 2003.

———. *A More Beautiful and Terrible History: The Uses and Misuses of Civil Rights History*. Boston: Beacon, 2018.

Theoharis, Jeanne, and Brian Purnell with Komozi Woodard, eds. *The Strange Careers of the Jim Crow North*. New York: New York University Press, 2019.

Trotter, Joe W., and Jared N. Day. *Race and Renaissance: African Americans in Pittsburgh since World War II*. Pittsburgh: University of Pittsburgh Press, 2010.

Tuck, Stephen. "'We Are Taking Up Where the Movement of the 1960s Left Off': The Proliferation and Power of African American Protest during the 1970s." *Journal of Contemporary History* 43, no. 4 (2008): 637–54.

Unrau, Harlan D. *Administrative History: Gettysburg National Military Park and Gettysburg National Cemetery, Pennsylvania*. Washington, DC: U.S. Department of the Interior, 1991.

U.S. Department of the Census. 1960 Census of Population, vol. 1.

Wakefield, Dan. "Civil War Centennial: Bull Run with Popcorn." *Nation* 190, no. 5 (January 30, 1960): 95–97.

Warren, Dan R. *If It Takes All Summer: Martin Luther King, the KKK, and States' Rights in St. Augustine 1964*. Tuscaloosa: University of Alabama Press, 2008.

Warren, Robert Penn. *The Legacy of the Civil War: Meditations on the Centennial*. New York: Random House, 1961. Reprint, Lincoln: University of Nebraska Press, 1998.

Warrick, Alyssa D. "Mississippi's Greatest Hour." *Southern Cultures* 19, no. 3 (Fall 2013): 95–112.

Weeks, James P. "A Different View of Gettysburg: Play, Memory, and Race at the Civil War's Greatest Shrine." *Civil War History* 50, no. 2 (2004): 175–91.

Weeks, Jim. *Gettysburg: Memory, Market, and an American Shrine*. Princeton, NJ: Princeton University Press, 2003.

Wefing, John B. *The Life and Times of Richard J. Hughes: The Politics of Civility*. New Brunswick, NJ: Rutgers University Press, 2009.

Weir, Robert E. "The Graying of Gettysburg National Military Park: Race, Erasure, Ideology, and Iconography." In *The Civil War in Popular Culture: Memory and Meaning*, edited by Lawrence A. Kreiser and Randall Allred, 61–81. Lexington: University Press of Kentucky, 2014.

Wesley, Charles H. "The Civil War and the Negro-American." *Journal of Negro History* 47, no. 2 (1962): 77–96.

Wiener, Jon. "Civil War, Cold War, Civil Rights: The Civil War Centennial in Context, 1960–1965." In *The Memory of the Civil War in American Culture*, edited by Alice Fahs and Joan Waugh, 237–57. Chapel Hill: University of North Carolina Press, 2004.

Winsboro, Irvin D. S., and Abel A. Bartley. "Race, Education, and Regionalism: The Long and Troubling History of School Desegregation in the Sunshine State." *Florida Historical Quarterly* 92, no. 4 (2014): 714–45.

Wolcott, Victoria W. *Race, Riots, and Roller Coasters: The Struggle over Segregated Recreation in America*. Philadelphia: University of Pennsylvania Press, 2012.

Woods, Randall B. *Prisoners of Hope: Lyndon B. Johnson, the Great Society, and the Limits of Liberalism*. New York: Basic Books, 2016.

Woodward, C. Vann. "Reflections on a Centennial: The American Civil War." *Yale Review* 50 (June 1961): 481–90.

Yale University Chaplain's Office. "John Vannorsdall." Accessed March 20, 2021. https://chaplain.yale.edu/john-vannorsdall.

Theses

Connelly, Margaret M. "In Dixie's Land I'll Take My Stand: The Confederate Flag in South Carolina's Politics from John May to Nikki Haley." BA thesis, Georgetown University, 2016. https://repository.library.georgetown.edu/handle/10822 /1041805/.

Conference Papers

Esenwein, Fred. "Modern Architecture and Preserving the Historical Milieu: Richard Neutra's Visitor Center and Cyclorama at Gettysburg." Conference paper, "A Century of Design in the Parks," June 21–23, 2016, Santa Fe, New Mexico, https://www.ncptt.nps.gov/events/century-of-design-in-the-parks/.

Index

Page numbers appearing in italics refer to illustrations.

Birmingham protests, 5–6, 77–78, 96, 116
Birth of a Nation, The, 15
Black American Legion, 68–69, 75, 79
Black Americans: CCC and, 17–18, 19;
    Civil War centennial and, 3, 42; as
    elected officials, 141, 161, 165;
    employment of, 9, 11, 17, 19–22,
    67–68, 72–73, 162; in Mississippi, 165;
    segregation and (*see* segregation); as
    tourists, 11–12; in town of Gettysburg
    (*see* Black Gettysburgians); Vietnam
    War and, 175. *See also specific Black
    Americans*
Black Gettysburgians: Battle of Gettys-
    burg and, 10; discrimination and
    segregation and, 6, 8–10, 21–26;
    employment and, 11, 19–20, 21,
    67–68; Klan and, 14–16; racial justice
    and, 67–72
Black Lives Matter movement, 179
Black Monday, 164
Blight, David, 3, 49
Blister, The, 14
Bloom, Robert, 35, 70, 90, 141, 157
Bohlinger, Neill, 162–63
Booth, Mabel, 102
Boston Globe, 95
Brady, Tom P., 164, 167, 168–69
Branch, Taylor, 79
Brandt, Willy, 132
Brevard County, Florida, 114–15
Brown, Thomas, 183n7
Brown v. Board of Education, 73, 143, 155,
    161, 162, 164, 196n21
Busby, Horace, 78
busing, school, 162, 165
bus tours, 32

Cambridge protests, 101–2
Campaign Gettysburg Sales Days, 81–82
campfire program, 81, 97, 152
canine corps, 73, 154
Canno, Betty, 132
Captive Nations Week, 96
Carter, Walter, 25

Carver, John, Jr., 106
Catton, Bruce, 28, 48–49
CCC (Civilian Conservation Corps),
    17–20
Chadwick, John E., 137, 140, 147
Chafee, John, 100
Chaney, James, 164, 166
Changing Times, 32
Charleston controversy, 42–43
Chicago Daily Defender, 102, 108, 143,
    154
Civilian Conservation Corps (CCC),
    17–20
civil rights: background and overview
    of, 5–6; Catton and, 48–49; Eisen-
    hower and, 102, 143–45; Florida and,
    115; Gettysburg Address and, 129;
    Gettysburg centennial and, 83, 96, 97,
    177, 178; Hughes and, 119; Johnson
    and, 65, 76–80, 108, 151; Kennedy
    and, 108–9, 116–17, 118; King and,
    108; Lawrence and, 47; Mississippi
    and, 164–66, 168–69; post-centennial,
    152–55, 162; press on, 95; protests
    for, 72–73, 77–78, 96, 101, 108–9, 154;
    South Carolina and, 111–13; Truman
    and, 112; Wallace and, 110–12; World
    War II and, 130–31
Civil Rights Bill: battle over, 72, 96, 97,
    108, 161; Gettysburg Address and,
    106; Kennedy and, 109; opposition to,
    111, 118; signing of, 151; support of,
    132, 139
Civil Rights Commission, 156
Civil War and Cold War connection. *See*
    Cold War and Civil War connection
Civil War centennial: background and
    overview of, 2, 7, 149; Cold War
    connection to, 2–3, 4, 7, 40, 41,
    188–89n31; commercialization and,
    28–29, 43; conclusions on, 157–58;
    criticism of, 42–43; CWCC and,
    40–44; Cyclorama Building and, 62; in
    Mississippi, 165; planning for, 36–40.
    See also Gettysburg Centennial

Soldiers Museum, 32

Soldiers' National Cemetery: Black internees at, 25; CCC and, 17; Cyclorama building and, 56; dedication of, 10–11, 128–29, 130, 137; Gettysburg Address ceremonies at, 129; Johnson's speech at, 5, 65, 76–80, 147; Memorial Day ceremonies at, 30–31, 173; protests at, 176, 180; rededication of, 91–93, 137, 142, 145–46; Vietnam War burial at, 171–72

Sons of Confederate Veterans (SCV), 50, 158, 159

Sons of Union Veterans (SUV), 45, 59, 122, 155, 159–60

Sons of Veterans Reserve, 45, 82

South Carolina, about, 111–12

South Carolina Confederate War Centennial Commission, 109

South Carolina monument at GNMP, 86–87, 97, 109–13

Southeast Georgia Brigade, 50

Southern Christian Leadership Conference (SCLC), 153, 175

Southern Manifesto, 161

Southworth, Edward, 69

Special Protocol Service Section (SPSS), 139

Spellman, Francis Cardinal, 101

Stackpole, Edward J., 128

stamp commemorating Gettysburg, 74, 81, 103

Star and Sentinel, 14–15

state monuments at GNMP: Alabama, 36, 86, 107; Arkansas, 158, 162–163; Florida, 97, 113–14, 115–16, 117–18, 202n46; Georgia, 50–52; Louisiana, 158, 162, 163–64, 167; Mississippi, 158, 161, 162, 166–69; New Jersey, 118, 119; North Carolina, 36, 118; South Carolina, 86–87, 97, 109–13; Tennessee, 103, 158; Virginia, 36, 118, 167

State of the Union address, 109

states' rights, 4–5, 107, 108, 110, 112–13, 127, 149–50

St. Augustine, Florida, 115

Stennis, John, 165

Stevens, Thaddeus, 105

St. Francis Xavier Catholic Church, 14, 24, 146

St. James Lutheran Church, 146

St. Joseph's Catholic Church, 146

St. Paul's AME Zion Church, 14–15, 24–25, 103

"Strength Through Unity" parade, 120, 122

Stuart, J. E. B., 45

Stuart raid pageant, 45

Student Nonviolent Coordinating Committee (SNCC), 108, 175

Sturdivant, Ed, 167

Summer Community Organization and Political Education (SCOPE), 153

Sun Yat-sen, 131

SUV (Sons of Union Veterans), 45, 59, 122, 155, 159–60

talking interpretive stations, 152

Tau Kappa Epsilon fraternity, 31, 153

technological diplomacy, 56

technology, 41, 55–56, 57

Teeter, Daniel, 45

Teeter Stone, Inc. ad, 98

Tennessee monument at GNMP, 103, 158

10th New York Cavalry, 45

Thant, U, 134

Third Ward of Gettysburg, 14, 19, 22, 154

Thomas, Richard, 15–16

Thurmond, Strom, 112, 139

Tilberg, Frederick, 35, 126, 160

Tilden, Freeman, 56

Till, Emmett, 164

Tobin, Daniel, 37, 38–39, 40, 54